Guide to Growing
Healthy
Houseplants

Meredith® Books
Des Moines, Iowa

Miracle-Gro Guide to Growing Healthy Houseplants

Project Editor: Kate Carter Frederick
Editor: Denny Schrock
Contributing Writers: Janna Beckerman, Kate Jerome, John Pohly,
    Ray Rothenberger, Curtis Smith, Jon Traunfeld
Contributing Technical Reviewer: Ashton Ritchie
Photo Researcher: Harijs Priekulis
Copy Chief: Terri Fredrickson
Editorial Operations Manager: Karen Schirm
Edit and Design Production Coordinator: Mary Lee Gavin
Editorial and Design Assistants: Kathleen Stevens, Kairee Windsor
Marketing Product Managers: Aparna Pande, Isaac Petersen,
    Gina Rickert, Stephen Rogers, Brent Wiersma, Tyler Woods
Book Production Managers: Pam Kvitne,
    Marjorie J. Schenkelberg, Rick von Holdt, Mark Weaver
Photographers: Marty Baldwin, Scott Little, Blaine Moats,
    Dean Schoeppner, Jay Wilde
Contributing Production Designer and Stylists: Brad Ruppert,
    Sundie Ruppert, Karen Weir Jimerson
Contributing Copy Editors: Barbara Feller-Roth, Fran Gardner
Contributing Technical Proofreaders: Deb Brown, B. Rosie Lerner,
    Mary H. Meyer, Bob Polomski, Ann Marie VanDer Zanden,
    Douglas F. Welsh
Contributing Proofreaders: Tom Blackett, Beth Havey,
    Mindy Kralicek
Contributing Map Illustrator: Jana Fothergill
Contributing Prop/Photo Stylist: Susan Strelecki
Indexer: Ellen Davenport

Additional Editorial Contributions from Shelton Design Studios
Director: Ernie Shelton

Additional Editorial Contributions from Art Rep Services
Director: Chip Nadeau
Illustrator: Dave Brandon

Meredith® Books
Executive Director, Editorial: Gregory H. Kayko
Executive Director, Design: Matt Strelecki
Executive Editor/Group Manager: Benjamin W. Allen
Senior Associate Design Director: Tom Wegner

Publisher and Editor in Chief: James D. Blume
Editorial Director: Linda Raglan Cunningham
Executive Director, Marketing: Jeffrey B. Myers
Executive Director, New Business Development: Todd M. Davis
Executive Director, Sales: Ken Zagor
Director, Operations: George A. Susral
Director, Production: Douglas M. Johnston
Business Director: Jim Leonard

Vice President and General Manager: Douglas J. Guendel

Meredith Publishing Group
President: Jack Griffin
Senior Vice President: Bob Mate

Meredith Corporation
Chairman and Chief Executive Officer: William T. Kerr
President and Chief Operating Officer: Stephen M. Lacy

In Memoriam: E.T. Meredith III (1933-2003)

All of us at Meredith® Books are dedicated to providing you with the information and ideas you need to enhance your home and garden. We welcome your comments and suggestions about this book. Write to us at:
    Meredith Gardening Books
    1716 Locust St.
    Des Moines, IA 50309-3023

If you would like to purchase any of our gardening, home improvement, cooking, crafts, or home decorating and design books, check wherever quality books are sold. Or visit us at: meredithbooks.com

Thanks to
Janet Anderson, Kathryn Anderson, Joyce DeWitt, Callie Dunbar, Don Harvey, Holubs Greenhouse, Rosemary Kautzky, Cathy Long, Mary Irene Swartz

Photographers
(Photographers credited may retain copyright © to the listed photographs.)
L = Left, R = Right, C = Center, B = Bottom, T = Top

Karen Bussolini/Positive Images: 94BL; **David Cavagnaro:** 32, 34BC, 35TC, 42B, 47BL, 51T, 58T, 79T, 101BL, 104T, 124T, 127BL, 130T, 133BL; **Alan & Linda Detrick:** 36B, 56BL; **Derek Fell:** 105T; **John Glover:** 37T, 66TC, 66TR, 92TR, 94B, 96BL, 101B, 103TR, 131T, 132BL, 133T; **John Glover/Positive Images:** 36T, 122T; **Harry Haralambou/Positive Images:** 61BL; **Jerry Howard/Positive Images:** 100B; **Jerry Harpur:** 50T, 68T; **Irene Jeruss/Positive Images:** 3BL, 43TC, 52BL, 87BL, 93BL; **Bill Johnson:** 41BC; **Rosemary Kautzky:** 7T, 38BL, 38B, 39TR, 41BL, 41BR, 43BC, 43TR, 44BL, 46T, 47BR, 55B, 56BR, 57TL, 57TR, 58TR, 62TR, 63TR, 65TR, 66BC, 66BR, 70BL, 70B, 73T, 74BL, 74CR, 74BR, 76T, 76TR, 77T, 77TR, 78TR, 78B, 79BL, 79BR, 80TR, 81T, 82BL, 83B, 84BL, 85T, 85TR, 86T, 86TR, 88B, 89BL, 89B, 92TC, 92B, 93T, 98T, 98TR, 98BL, 100BL, 103BL, 103BCL, 103BCR, 103BR, 108TR, 111BL, 111B, 112BL, 113B, 115B, 116B, 118B, 119T, 120BL, 120B, 121TR, 122TR, 126TL, 126TR, 128TR, 128B, 129B, 134T, 135BL, 135B, 136BL; **Andrew Lawson:** 68TC; **Lee Lockwood/Positive Images:** 76BL; **Thomas N. Munoz/Photographers Direct:** 51BL; **Jerry Pavia:** 3BR, 34TC, 35T, 40B, 44BR, 50BL, 52BR, 54BL, 63TL, 64T, 69T, 73B, 74T, 77BL, 78BL, 80T, 92T, 103T, 105BL, 106T, 111T, 114T, 116BL, 117B, 128T; **Helen Placanica/ Photographers Direct:** 51B; **Kenneth Rice:** 3T, 8T; **Susan A. Roth:** 50TR, 59T, 112T; **Scotts Training Institute:** 28BR, 28BL, 29TR, 29BR, 54BR, 60BR, 76B; **Michael S. Thompson:** 34T, 39T, 39B, 40BL, 43T, 47TC, 52T, 52TR, 52BC, 56BC, 59BL, 60BC, 64B, 66T, 66BL, 78T, 86BL, 88BL, 91T, 91B, 96T, 97B, 100T, 104BL, 108T, 111TR, 114BL, 118BL, 119B, 121TR, 123T, 126T, 129T, 129BL, 131TC, 135T; **Lee Anne White/Positive Images:** 96B

CONTENTS

Chapter 1

SELECTING & SITUATING PLANTS

You'll be at home with houseplants as soon as you determine where and how to purchase them. Once you choose plants that suit the growing conditions in your home, they'll add their color and texture to the place and complement the decor.

CHOOSING HOUSEPLANTS

Gardening indoors requires some careful thought initially. As long as you choose plants according to your home's conditions and the amount of care you're willing to give, you can grow them successfully. Many houseplants require little care. Try growing different ones and see which you like best.

In general, foliage plants should be lush and full and have good color. Stems and leaves should be firm, not wilted or distorted. Flowering plants in full bloom often fade quickly. Choose ones with lots of buds instead.

Healthy houseplants result in large part from selecting plants that are suited to your growing conditions, particularly the level of available light. If you have south-facing windows, houseplants that need a sunny location will do well. If you have only north-facing windows, success will come from choosing plants that thrive in shade. Plants sited in other than their preferred growing conditions will be stressed and thereby prone to diseases and insects. If you can prevent problems by proper siting, you will have better-looking plants and a happier caretaker—you!

If you decide on a particular plant with characteristics you like, make sure you can provide what it needs for optimal growth. Do some research to understand the ideal conditions for the plant, and make sure you have the right location at home. Or choose your site first, then select a suitable plant for it.

Most houseplants originate in tropical or desert climates and become favorites because they are adaptable enough to grow in a wide range of home conditions.

Tropical plants come from climates where temperatures rarely drop below freezing. Plants from temperate climates, where temperatures drop well below freezing, often need a cold period for survival. They also spend part of their life cycle in a dormant state, usually without leaves. For these reasons, plants from temperate climates seldom perform well as houseplants.

In addition to their needs for high to low light, houseplants vary in their preference for high to low humidity and moist to dry soil. As you map out the sites in your home for plants, keep in mind that the conditions may change from season to season. Home heating and cooling, drafts from open windows and doors, and the angle of the sun's rays through a window must all be considered. You may find that the perfect spot for a plant in winter is not appropriate for the same plant in summer.

SELECTING HEALTHY PLANTS

Once you've decided on the perfect species of plant, it's time to select one at the garden center. Although mail-order plants are acceptable, particularly for something unusual that your local garden center doesn't carry, mailed plants may be damaged during shipping, and weight limitations may mean that you must start with smaller plants than you might prefer. On the other hand, young plants acclimatize better than mature ones.

Whether you order by mail or visit the garden center, inspect the plant with a critical eye before introducing it into your houseplant display. Pests and diseases of any kind are not acceptable; if you see evidence of either, choose another plant.

Pull your new plant away from the other plants in the garden center and into the light to look at it carefully. Check the undersides of the leaves, the leaf axils, the base of the plant, and even the soil. Anything that isn't quite right, such as webbing, browning leaf tips, fertilizer buildup on the soil, or a sour smell, can indicate a problem. Find another plant or another garden center to ensure your investment.

Trust your instincts. If a store is clean and smells good and the plants appear healthy at first glance, chances are you've found a good supplier. Pick the healthiest plants you can find. Ask about the store's guarantee and return policies.

Check the backs of leaves carefully for pests before bringing the plant home. If a plant has pests, choose a healthy one instead.

BUYING HOUSEPLANTS

SHOP CAREFULLY

Houseplants are available almost everywhere. You'll find them in booths at flower and gardening shows, county fairs, and farmer's markets, in hardware and grocery stores, and even in cafes and drugstores. You will also find a wide selection is available from Internet and mail-order sources.

While you may see attractive plants at all of these places, you may not be able to obtain reliable information about caring for the ones you purchase. Plants sold by anyone other than a plant specialist might be mislabeled, mishandled, or unhealthy. Some sellers may not allow you to return or exchange unsatisfactory plants.

For the best selection and the best access to reliable information, go to plant specialists: a commercial greenhouse that specializes in houseplants, a garden center or nursery with a houseplant department, a home supply store with a greenhouse section, a florist's shop, or a botanic garden that sells plants.

Most of these sources employ knowledgeable people who can help you make good choices. And most are careful about the quality of their plants. Specimens with pest or disease problems are culled, and declining plants are removed from sale. That means the plants you buy from these sources are less likely to have pest or disease problems. Plant specialists also know how to pack plants properly for the trip home.

Specialty sources, such as orchid or bonsai suppliers, are an invaluable source of plants not available elsewhere. They're also a good place to look for tools and information. Look for rare plants in specialty stores or from mail-order nurseries, which usually offer a printed or online catalog. Some mail-order nurseries are specialist growers, dealing in only one or a few plant types, such as orchids, African violets, ferns, or cacti and succulents. Others have a wide range of both flowering plants and foliage plants. See the "Resources" listings on page 143 for information on some of these plant suppliers.

Ease a plant through its transition by moving it to interim locations with decreasing light intensity for two or three weeks at a time, before settling on its final site.

BRINGING THEM HOME

Take special care to control the temperature when transporting plants in a car in winter and summer.

If you are purchasing plants in summer, avoid leaving them in a hot car. Open the windows and provide plenty of air circulation. A few minutes at hot temperatures can literally cook a plant.

When transporting plants in winter, take care to avoid temperature stress. Some plants can be harmed by only a few minutes below 40°F. A plant sleeve helps, but it is intended for only a short distance. Warm your car before putting a plant in it; if possible, have the garden center put the plant and pot in a large plastic bag and tie the top securely, keeping a bubble of warm air around the plant. Even so, avoid leaving plants in the car for any length of time.

ACCLIMATING THEM

Once you bring a new plant home, it is wise to isolate it for a few days to make sure it has no insects or diseases you may have missed on initial inspection. Also, remember that the plant was most likely grown and displayed in the ideal conditions of a greenhouse—high light and high humidity—so give it a gradual adjustment to its permanent home. Watch it carefully over several weeks for any signs that the spot you've selected for it is not ideal.

Keep a new plant moderately moist during this period; avoid allowing it to dry out. Water it thoroughly and discard excess water from the drainage saucer.

SITING PLANTS

SUPPLEMENTAL LIGHT

Light exposure is the most critical element in siting a plant. When a plant has the light it requires for the best growth, it will look as good as it can.

The classifications of low, medium, and high light are general guidelines for siting plants. Low light comes from a north-, east-, or northeast-facing window, where plants get some light but nothing direct. Low light may keep a plant looking good but not be enough to make it bloom. High light generally means several hours of direct or indirect sun, usually a southern or western exposure. Medium light means several hours of bright but not necessarily direct light, such as an eastern or western exposure.

You can measure light intensity with a light meter, but a simpler method is to follow the light guidelines in this encyclopedia, place your plants, then observe them over several weeks. Remember that light intensity changes with the season. You can easily vary the amount of light a plant receives by changing its distance from the light source or by adding supplemental light.

The best supplemental light source for the average home is fluorescent lighting. Standard fluorescent bulbs come in warm white and cool white, each with different enhanced parts of the spectrum. Using a combination of the two types gives you a fairly wide spectrum in which plants will thrive. Another type of fluorescent bulb is the "grow light," which has almost 90 percent of the sun's spectrum. The drawback is that it is much more expensive than a standard fluorescent bulb.

The length of time that houseplants receive light is important because plants need a certain period of light for adequate photosynthesis. Most require 8 to 16 hours of light every day. Plants given too many hours of light each day tend to have elongated or curled leaves that may eventually drop off. Too few hours of light cause elongated shoots and thin, easily damaged leaves. You can control this ratio by adding supplemental light to lengthen the day or by turning off the lights to give more hours of darkness.

The sun's angle in summer makes the light intense.

Winter sun extends light far into the room but at less intense levels than in summer.

Many plants can thrive when grown under artificial lights, as a supplement for natural light or on a light cart where they receive only artificial light.

A gauze curtain reduces light in a bright window and keeps a plant from sunburning.

If there is enough sunlight in a room to read a newspaper or do needlepoint without turning on a light, the room is an appropriate place for plants that need low to medium light.

DESIGN BASICS

Houseplants can complement your decorating style with an almost endless array of choices. For example, if you have a Southwestern scheme in your home, complement it with cacti, succulents, and arid-climate plants. A Victorian parlor will look luscious filled with flowering plants, ferns, and a terrarium or two. An array of palms lends a tropical Caribbean flair.

If you have an open floor plan, large architectural plants will provide excellent focal points. For intimate spaces, small blooming plants and fine-textured specimens will enhance the coziness of the room.

Giving some consideration to the basics of design can make your collection of houseplants a lovely addition to your decor. As in an outdoor landscape, large plants form the "bones" of the display; use smaller plants to complement them. You will achieve the most effective presentation if you vary height, form, texture, and color.

An effective way to avoid dealing with the large pot and weight of an immense specimen is to "stage" a plant. This entails putting a smaller plant on a pedestal or an overturned pot to raise it in the display. Staging gives the appearance of a larger plant, yet allows the use of a smaller amount of space.

Texture—the appearance and feel of a plant—adds energy and movement to a room. Large, smooth leaves have a calming effect and make a room feel bigger. Fine-textured plants with small leaves generate excitement and activity, yet can also make a space feel intimate. An effective contrasting of textures makes a plant display interesting and diverse; combining similar textures gives a display simplicity and elegance.

Choosing color is perhaps the most fun aspect of designing a plant display. Bright colors such as scarlet and yellow are usually best used as focal points, surrounded by more subtle shades of green, white, and silver. Blues and pinks are easier to combine with other colors in the same palette but are beautifully set off with bits of silver- and white-variegated foliage or flowers.

A DECORATOR'S SECRET

Does your decor call for a houseplant where it is too dark for even low-light plants to thrive? Don't let that ruin your design ideas. Purchase two identical low-light-tolerant plants, and keep switching them back and forth. Place one in the desired spot for two weeks while the other basks in bright light and high humidity elsewhere in the house, then switch them around. Most foliage plants will thrive for years if they get enough light for just two weeks out of each month.

A shallow tray garden displays the cachepots as well as the artful arrangement of plants.

Silver and white containers provide a neutral background to show off your houseplants in their full beauty.

MOVING PLANTS OUTDOORS & IN

OUTSIDE FOR THE SUMMER

Houseplants benefit from being moved outdoors for the summer. Rain removes the dust from being indoors in winter, and natural predators can deter pests.

Allow plants to acclimate slowly to being outdoors so they can toughen and adapt to different conditions. Put them in a place where they are protected from wind, sun, and cold for the first couple of weeks. After this adjustment time, move them to where you can enjoy them as part of your patio or outdoor landscape.

Keep in mind that few plants grown as houseplants can tolerate direct outdoor sun, regardless of their usual light requirements. Tuck them under high-canopy trees where they might receive a couple of hours of morning sun. Place low-light plants under shrubs or eaves where they receive no direct light. Monitor moisture levels carefully. These plants may need daily watering.

Display houseplants outdoors in their pots, insert the pots into flower boxes, or plant the pots directly in the garden, sinking them just below ground level (provided the site has good drainage).

Put big, bold plants to work in your yard. These huge palms, purchased at a home center for less than $30 each, help turn an ordinary strip of grass into the boundary for a pretty and private dining area.

Potted citrus trees bring a tropical touch to a sunny room, especially in winter. If you start with a three- or four-year-old tree, you'll soon enjoy its fruit. Citrus plants need bright sunlight and added humidity to fare best indoors.

INSIDE FOR THE WINTER

Bring plants back indoors before temperatures begin to dip in autumn. That way the plants need adapt only to a decrease in light; the temperature and humidity remain much the same. A plant left outdoors during cool evenings will begin to slow down for winter and may react badly to the drier air of a heated interior. Some exceptions: You can keep plants that prefer cool weather, such as azaleas, Japanese aralia, and holiday cacti, outside late into fall, until frost threatens, even when evenings are chilly.

Set each plant on a bench or table outdoors where you can examine it carefully, and clip off every yellowed leaf, spent flower, and seedpod. If the plant has grown too large for its pot, reshape it with some careful pruning or repot it into a larger container. Clean both the plant and the outside of the pot with warm water. Examine the foliage carefully for pests and disease, and treat pest-infested plants with the appropriate control (see pages 28–29). Even if you don't see any pests, you may want to spray or wipe the entire plant with insecticidal soap. To get rid of insects hiding in the soil, soak the root ball in a vat of soapy water for 20 minutes or so, then drain.

Bring outdoor plants indoors as well. Many garden annuals, such as wax begonias and geraniums, have a history of use as houseplants. Try bringing in other plants that are tropical or subtropical perennials, such as calibrachoa or diascia, which are grown as annuals in cooler climates.

Chapter 2
PLANTING

Most plants are already in pots when you acquire them, but they'll outgrow their containers eventually. These pages tell you how to repot and when, as well as how to choose an ideal potting medium.

POTTING MEDIA

Growing houseplants is surprisingly easy to do with moderate care and basic supplies, such as good-quality potting mix and attractive containers. Garden soils are generally too heavy for use in containers and bring with them problems of disease and insects. Many potting mixes for indoor plants are actually soilless. Customize them according to individual plant needs if you want, but commercial mixes available at your local garden store are adequate for most plants.

Most commercial soilless mixes are composed of peat moss or decomposed bark and vermiculite or perlite. Free from pests, diseases, and weed seeds, they're also inexpensive, simple to use, and widely available.

If you find you need a potting mix with other ingredients, mix your own or purchase a ready-made specialty mix. Commercial potting blends for flowering plants contain more organic materials that retain moisture, such as shredded bark or compost, because flower buds are sensitive to water loss. Cacti and other succulents need a mix that has sand or calcined clay for extremely good drainage. Bromeliads and orchids need a coarse mix of bark chips, which provide plenty of air for the roots.

When choosing a growing mix, look for one that is of medium weight. Those that are too light, such as straight peat moss, can't adequately anchor a plant. Too heavy a mix, such as sterilized topsoil, causes drainage problems. If you are potting a very large plant that will not be repotted often or has the potential to become top-heavy, mix one part commercial sterilized topsoil to three parts standard potting mix.

Create your own potting mix by combining ingredients, such as bark chips, perlite, and sphagnum moss.

When transplanting, place fresh potting mix in the bottom of the new pot before nestling the plant's root ball into it.

African violets need a rich potting mix that drains well. Premium specialty potting mixes ensure an appropriate balance of ingredients for optimum blooms.

SPECIALTY MIX INGREDIENTS

■ African violets, flowering plants: Equal parts sand, peat moss, sterilized topsoil, and leaf mold.

■ Epiphytes, orchids, bromeliads: Equal parts sphagnum moss, coarse bark, and coarse perlite. Add 1 tablespoon dolomitic lime and 1 cup horticultural charcoal to 3 quarts mix.

■ Cacti and succulents: Two parts sterilized soil, 1 part coarse sand, 1 part calcined clay. Add 2 tablespoons dolomitic lime and ⅓ cup charcoal to 4 quarts mix.

■ Ferns: Three parts peat moss-based potting mix, 2 parts perlite, 3 parts leaf mold. Add 1 cup charcoal to 2 quarts mix.

■ Soil-based mix: One part sterilized soil; 1 part peat moss, bark, or leaf mold; 1 part coarse sand or perlite.

INDIVIDUAL INGREDIENTS

■ Topsoil: Packaged all-purpose potting mixes may contain some topsoil that has been sterilized to kill fungi and weed seeds. By itself, topsoil is too heavy and drains too poorly for use as a potting soil.

■ Peat moss: Partially decayed plant material mined from the middle and bottom of peat bogs. It has an acidic pH and is highly moisture retentive but adds no nutritive value.

■ Sphagnum moss: Plant matter harvested from the top of peat bogs with fibers longer than those of peat moss. Decomposes slowly. Use it to line baskets and in orchid mixes. It is rarely used in regular potting mixes.

■ Perlite: Expanded volcanic rock that is moisture and nutrient retentive and lightweight, and improves drainage and aeration.

■ Vermiculite: Mica expanded by heating to become moisture retentive.

■ Sand: Adds drainage and weight. Lime-free, coarse river sand is best. Beach sand may contain harmful salts.

■ Shredded bark: Finely shredded or ground hardwood or pine bark. Equivalent in use to peat moss. It has no nutritive value.

■ Charcoal: Absorbs salts and byproducts of plant decay, keeps the soil sweet, and removes acidity. Use only horticultural grade.

■ Leaf mold: Decayed leaves of all types. An excellent organic additive for moisture retention and some nutrition.

■ Calcined clay: Clay pulverized by heating, most commonly available as unscented cat litter. Adds weight, drainage, and aeration.

■ Plant food: A balanced formula, sometimes in a continuous-feed form, is added to some potting mixes.

PLANTING IN CONTAINERS

TYPES OF CONTAINERS & MEDIA

Suitable containers run the gamut from elegant galvanized flower buckets and glazed terra-cotta to recycled wooden vegetable crates. Inexpensive plastic troughs may not add a lot of beauty to your balcony, but they are durable, inexpensive, and produce excellent results. An array of sizes, shapes, and materials can be selected or constructed to fit any unique space and aesthetic look. When choosing a pot, consider how it drains and what the shape and size are in relation to the size of the plant and its root system. Beyond that, selection is a matter of personal preference.

Large, heavy containers become weightier still when filled with potting soil, water, and plants, and can be difficult to move. Conversely, lightweight containers with large plants may tip over easily.

Potting mixes work well in all types of containers. The selection of potting medium and container depends on the plant you intend to grow.

IS IT TIME TO REPOT?

To determine whether a plant needs repotting, lift up the pot and check the drainage holes to see if roots have begun to grow out of the pot. Tap the plant out of the pot and look at the root system. If the roots are spread out with few (or none) growing through the pot's drainage holes, repotting may not be necessary. However, if the root ball is a tight mass of roots with virtually no loose soil left among them, the time has come.

When a plant appears as if it needs feeding but doesn't respond to plant food, replace all or part of the soil. For partial replacement, remove the plant from its pot and knock off some of the old soil; tease out the roots a bit to encourage them to grow into the new soil. Repot the plant.

Another option is to top-dress the plant, or scrape off the top inch or so of soil and add new soil. Topdressing is the easiest way to replace soil for plants that prefer to be somewhat pot-bound (rooted snugly in its pot), such as cyclamen, jasmine, and spider plant.

If the soil is completely depleted of nutrients or infested with insects, remove as much of the soil from around the roots as possible. Tap off loose soil, then rinse the roots with warm water. Examine the roots for any problems, prune diseased or damaged areas, and repot.

PREVENT WATER DAMAGE

Protect the surfaces of your furniture and countertops from potential water damage: Always use a waterproof tray or saucer underneath a pot—even under a pot without drainage holes—to catch moisture that eventually seeps out. To do a good job, the saucer must be at least as wide as the pot's upper diameter to hold excess water that may flow through the potting mix during watering.

REPOTTING STEP-BY-STEP

1 Grasp a pot-bound plant gently by the crown and tap it out of its pot.

2 Gently tease the roots apart and remove some of the existing soil.

3 Set the plant in its new pot at the same level and fill with soil, tamping gently.

Repotting is not a necessity for all plants. In fact, some plants perform better if their roots are bound tightly in a pot. A plant needs repotting if it is outgrowing its container, if the soil is depleted, or if there are pests in the soil. Repotting is best done in spring just before active growth begins.

Resist the urge to step up into a much bigger pot. One or two inches bigger in diameter is best. Or you can prune the roots and put the plant back in the same pot to keep the plant at a particular size.

Take these steps to complete the process of repotting:
■ Thoroughly water the plant a day or two before you plan to repot it.
■ Gather needed supplies, such as a pot, a screen to cover drainage holes, newspaper to cover your work surface, and potting mix.
■ Moisten the potting mix by adding warm water and mixing it in with a spoon to make it easier to handle. Potting soil is hard to wet once it's in the pot.
■ Loosen the plant by running a knife around the inside edge of the pot or tapping the pot on a table. Slip the plant out of the pot. Hold the top of a small plant between your fingers, supporting the root ball in your palm. Remove a larger plant by laying the pot on its side and sliding out the plant.
■ Unwind circling roots and cut off any that look rotted. If the plant is pot-bound, make shallow cuts from the top

to the bottom of the root ball with a sharp knife. Cut off an inch or so of the root ball if you intend to put the plant back into the same pot.
■ Pour some potting mix into the new pot and center the plant at the depth to which it was planted before. Then fill in more mix around the roots.
■ Tamp the soil lightly with your fingers as you work; pressing too hard will compact the growing mix. Water the plant well.
■ If the roots were pruned substantially, cut back the top of the plant accordingly.

For extremely heavy plants, remove an inch or so of the old soil on top and add new soil without removing the plant from its pot.

Plant roots need adequate air and moisture. For this reason the potting mix must be loose enough to allow air in but contain enough organic materials to retain moisture and plant nutrients. Commercial potting mixes are readily available and fairly inexpensive.

Choose a pot with a drainage hole. Filling the bottom of a nondraining pot with gravel does not create good drainage and can be detrimental to the plant.

Make sure the pot is large enough to accommodate the roots without too much extra soil, and be sure there will be at least an inch from the top of the soil to the top of the pot for ease of watering.

DIVIDING

You can divide overgrown plants that have multiple stems or crowns and repot them as multiple new plants. Doing so rejuvenates plants that have overgrown their pots and provides you with free new plants.

Remove the plant from the pot and place it on a solid surface. Boston fern, spider plant, and a few others produce foliage from underground stems that are not visible on the surface. Using a large, sharp knife, cut down through the plant and soil. Depending on the size of transplants desired, cut the parent plant in half, quarters, or smaller divisions. You may need to saw some plants apart, but others gently break apart by hand. Make sure each division includes some of the main root and stem system.

When planting divisions into new containers, you may need to remove the bottom few inches of soil and roots for a proper fit. Divisions usually suffer some transplant shock; new growth may not appear for several weeks. Once new roots start growing, new top growth soon follows.

Plant the divisions immediately in permanent containers with potting soil and water thoroughly. Keep them in bright light but out of direct sun, watering frequently until they root. You also can put the potted divisions inside clear plastic bags to reduce moisture loss. When they appear upright and healthy, place them in a permanent location and care for them as you would mature plants.

Chapter 3

GROWING

Successful gardening indoors depends on meeting plants' needs for water and nourishment as well as occasional grooming. You'll soon be ready to expand your plant collection.

WATERING

A plant's water requirements vary as the seasons change. Watering according to a set schedule—for example, once a week—doesn't take into account these variations. Instead, check your houseplants every four or five days, and keep in mind all the factors that affect their watering needs.

Plants absorb more water when humidity is low. If your skin is dry, your plants are probably dry too. However, plants grow more slowly in the cooler, shorter days of winter, a sign that they're using less water. So if you compensate for dry air by watering on a schedule suited to the warm days of summer, you'll end up overwatering.

High humidity slows transpiration, which reduces moisture uptake by roots. Unless the plant is in a breezy area where wind moves moisture away from the leaves, you'll need to water less often.

Light affects water uptake too. Overcast skies in spring and fall slow plant growth and reduce water requirements. Plants exposed to bright light use more water than those in low light, depending on humidity.

A plant too large for its pot may be dry only a few days after a thorough watering. The type of plant also affects water needs. A cactus or succulent might need watering only once a month or so during winter, for example.

WHEN TO WATER

How do you know when to water? It's simple: Give plants water when they need it. The secret lies in learning to recognize the individual signals each plant gives.

Look at your plant. A well-watered plant appears healthy. Its tissues are firm because all the cells are filled with water and its leaves are glossy. Many plants show signs of decline before wilting entirely. Their leaves have lost their sheen and are slightly limp and pale.

To know when plants are ready for water, check the moisture level of the soil by touching it. Insert a finger (down to the second knuckle in the case of plants in large pots; first knuckle in smaller pots) into the potting mix. If a plant needs moist soil, the surface should be damp. If a plant should dry somewhat between waterings, the top inch or two of soil will feel dry to the touch, but if it's dry below that point, water the plant. Letting a plant dry out completely may damage the roots, sometimes beyond help.

THE BEST WAY TO WATER

For most plants, the best and easiest watering method is to pour water on the soil surface. Pour until water runs out the pot's drainage hole, an action that also leaches excess salts from the soil. The goal is to moisten the growing mix thoroughly.

If dry soil has pulled away from the sides of the pot so that water runs down the sides without wetting the soil, immerse the entire pot in a bucket of tepid water. Let it sit for about 30 minutes, then drain. This technique, called submerging, is also useful for plants that need massive amounts of water, such as blooming plants or florist's hydrangea and other gift plants that dry out quickly.

A few plants, such as African violets, benefit from bottom watering because cold water droplets mark their leaves. Simply set the pot in a saucer of tepid water and allow capillary action to draw water into the soil. This method takes longer than top watering, but it keeps water off the leaves. Wick watering systems and self-watering pots are other ways to bottom-water.

Watering from the bottom keeps droplets off plants with sensitive leaves, such as this African violet.

Water most plants from the top, making sure the soil is evenly moist and adding water until it runs out the bottom of the pot.

A half-inch layer of pea gravel covering the soil surface of a potted plant helps preserve the soil's moisture level.

WATER QUALITY

USING MOISTURE METERS

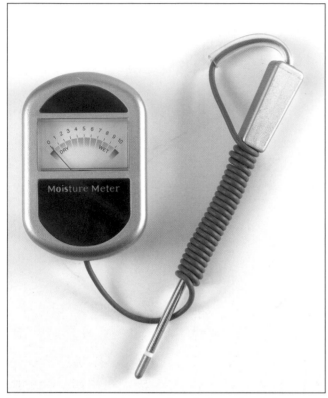

Moisture meters help determine when plants need watering.

Small pots—those less than 8 inches in diameter—are easy enough to water: When the soil at the top is dry, the rest of the root ball is probably fairly dry as well. In big pots, especially 12-inch standard pots and larger, the same may not hold true. The mix may be dry on the top yet still soaking wet at the bottom. That bottom layer needs to dry out before you water again, or stagnation, a precursor to rot, can set in. For such pots, use an inexpensive water meter. Insert the meter's long metal probe deep into the root mass, and water when it reads "dry." Replace the meter once a year, because meters tend to give false readings after extended use.

Another type of water meter sings when plants need water. Shaped like a bird, cow, frog, or other figure with a corresponding voice, this type of meter is designed to be left inserted in a pot rather than moved from plant to plant as with traditional meters. When the soil dries out too much, its vocal warning reminds you that it's time to water. Most models also have a photoelectric eye so they won't sound off in the middle of the night. Although these meters may seem like a gimmick, many gardeners find them helpful. Use one per room in the plant that always seems to dry out first. When the meter sings, it's time to water that plant and check the others as well.

WHEN YOU'RE AWAY

If you're going to be away for a week to 10 days and can't find someone to care for your plants, you easily can set up a self-watering system. Simply line a sink or bathtub with old towels, newspapers, or any thick, absorbent material. Set pots with drainage holes directly on the matting. Soak the matting well, leaving an inch of water in the sink or tub. The plants will draw up moisture as needed.

Another temporary self-watering method: Make a wick out of nylon stocking, and put one end into the drainage hole of the plant you want to water, making sure it is in contact with the potting mix. Run the other end into a bowl of water. Water will move slowly from bowl to plant. Cover the bowl with a plate if you have pets that might drink the water. Several plants can share the same water source this way, but make sure there is enough water in the bowl to last throughout your absence.

As an option, you can clean up your plants, removing dead and fading leaves and flowers, water them well, and cover them with large, transparent plastic bags. Place them away from full sun or they will cook! Inside the plastic bags air still circulates yet little water escapes, so your plants can go for weeks without a drop of added water.

Set up a self-watering system by pouring an inch or two of water into the bottom of a cachepot (without a drainage hole) and placing a potted plant in it to gradually wick up the water through its drainage hole.

WHAT KIND OF WATER?

To avoid shock and possible root damage from extreme temperatures, use tepid water when watering. Many gardeners let water stand overnight to reach room temperature, but standing water actually can be considerably colder than room temperature.

Tap water is fine for houseplants unless the species you are growing is known to be sensitive to hard or softened water. Unless your municipal water supplier issues a treatment warning, there is no need to let tap water stand for 24 hours before using it. The small amount of chlorine it normally contains is not dangerous to most plants.

If your tap water is hard (alkaline) and you're growing plants that require an acid soil, such as azaleas and hydrangeas, you'll need to amend the soil. For example, regularly repotting in a growing mix with added acid soil amendments, such as peat moss, will provide the acidity needed to release nutrients. You also can use plant foods designed specifically to retain soil acidity while nourishing the plant.

Alkaline conditions make it difficult for plants to absorb iron and other trace elements. Regular applications of iron chelate, included in some fertilizers, help keep foliage green. When the new foliage on acid-loving plants is yellow, it's a sign that the plant may need extra iron chelate in addition to acidic plant food.

Softened water contains sodium that may accumulate in the soil and harm plants. If your home has a water softener, use an outdoor tap for plant water or install a bypass tap in the water line before it enters the softener so you'll have a source of hard water for plants. If this is not possible, draw water just before the softener cycle, when sodium is at the lowest level.

REDUCING WATERING NEEDS

If watering every four or five days is too frequent for your schedule, there are a few ways you can keep plants moist a bit longer.

Double pots: An easy method of reducing watering needs for plants in clay pots is to double pot. Simply place the pot inside a larger cachepot, adding peat moss, sphagnum moss, Spanish moss, or perlite to fill the void around the inner pot. When you water, moisten the filler material as well as the soil. Water will slowly filter through the porous clay walls into the potting mix. Double potting also lowers the soil temperature, thus further reducing watering needs and humidifying the air. Mulching similarly keeps soil moister and cooler while increasing air humidity.

Self-watering pots: These special containers have a water reservoir that needs attention only when it gets low, usually every couple of weeks. Because fertilizer is typically added to the water at the same time, feeding and watering become something you do twice a month instead of every few days. Meanwhile, the pot automatically delivers water at the rate the plant uses it, adjusting to changes in light, humidity, or temperature. Plants in self-watering pots are usually more evenly watered than plants in conventional pots, but because the soil is kept constantly moist, plants that need to dry out between waterings don't perform well in them.

Self-watering pots operate on the principle of capillary action. In the same way water moves upward to moisten an entire towel when just one corner dips into the sink, water moves from the reservoir into the potting mix above. All that's needed is a link—a wick of some sort—between the water and the growing medium.

Many types of self-watering containers are available. Some have built-in reservoirs. Others are actually two pots: a grow pot and an outer pot or cachepot that fits around the grow pot like a reservoir.

Self-watering pots have different ways of indicating when the reservoir is empty. Some pots show the water level with a float, often colored red for maximum visibility.

Others have a clear plastic gauge along one side of the reservoir. In still others, the entire reservoir is made of a transparent material so you can see the water level even from a distance. The disadvantage of the latter is that the water is exposed to light, which encourages the growth of unsightly algae.

Most containers have an opening in the side or on the top into which you can pour the water. Always wait until the reservoir is empty before watering again.

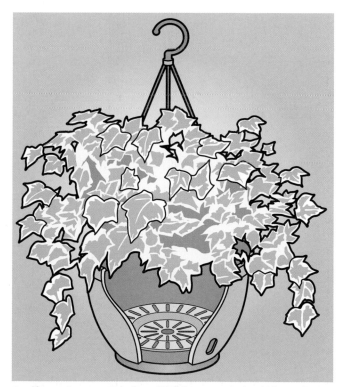

A self-watering container has a built-in reservoir that helps reduce watering frequency.

INDOOR ENVIRONMENTS

TEMPERATURE

Most homes maintain a year-round temperature between 60°F and 75°F, to which the average houseplant is perfectly suited. However, keeping temperatures cooler at night than during the day helps plants do best. If you can, lower the temperature in your home at least 5°F at night. A 10°F drop triggers blooms in orchids, flowering maples, and other plants.

Even though indoor temperatures are stable compared with outdoor ones, they do vary somewhat from season to season, from room to room, and even within a single room. Although most houseplants do well in average indoor temperatures, there are exceptions, and these are the plants that profit from special temperature levels within your home.

For example, if you have plants that require cool temperatures, such as cyclamens, azaleas, and some orchids, a sunny, unheated porch or place close to a window in winter provides a cool microclimate.

Because cool air sinks, the air near the floor is cooler than the rest of the room. This is a great place to put plants that don't tolerate natural summer heat or home heating in winter. If you close the shades to keep the house cool in summer, you may need to supply bright-light plants with some additional lighting.

Hot air rises, so the top shelf of a bookcase or the top of a kitchen cabinet provides an extra bit of warmth for a plant that doesn't tolerate cold. These out-of-the-way locations ensure that the plant won't suffer from too much air movement. Because they are out of the way, however, you'll need to be extra careful not to neglect them.

In your home's hottest areas, such as around fireplaces, heat vents, incandescent lights, and windows in the summer, use plants that thrive on heat, such as cacti and euphorbias. In areas that are both hot and humid—such as near a dishwasher, clothes dryer, or humidifier—try tropical flora, such as prayer plants and bougainvilleas.

Great variations within a single room can be used to your advantage once you are aware of them. They can also spell disaster if you're not. For example, cold drafts near windows and entrances in winter can make plants cold and cause their leaves to droop. When the temperature drops below 50°F, chilling drafts can injure plants. The injury shows up on the leaves, which appear water-soaked or blackened. In these places, use plants, such as Norfolk Island pine, that tolerate the chilly microclimate.

Drafty doors, bright windows, heat registers, and humid spaces all create specific microclimates in your home.

AIR CIRCULATION

A certain amount of air movement is vital to good plant growth. Air movement removes moisture from the leaves and therefore prevents disease. It also benefits plants in other ways. Regular movement of the leaves produces sturdier, denser plants. In addition, good air movement may keep some insect populations in check.

You can increase air movement by opening a window in warm weather (when it's not raining, of course). A ceiling fan or a small fan placed near plants also keeps air moving and is preferable to setting plants near vents and registers for heat or air-conditioning.

HUMIDITY

A plant that comes from a naturally humid climate will need a source of extra humidity that isn't present in the home.

The most efficient (but most expensive) way to raise humidity is with a humidifier installed directly on the furnace. This will raise the humidity throughout the house. Or you can use a room humidifier placed near plants that need extra humidity.

A simple way to increase humidity is to group plants. This reduces some of the air circulation around them and keeps the ambient humidity higher than if each plant were on its own.

Another simple yet effective way to increase humidity is to place the plant pot on a tray of pebbles or shells that are kept moist. Avoid sinking the pot into the pebbles, which would keep the soil soggy.

An alternative is the pot-in-pot or double-potting method. Simply place the potted plant in another decorative pot a couple of inches larger in diameter, and fill the cavity between them with sphagnum or Spanish moss that you keep damp. Be sure to elevate the interior pot so it does not sit in water.

Misting plants by hand is no longer considered efficient in raising humidity, because its results are so temporary.

To increase humidity, place one pot inside another with moist sphagnum moss tucked between the pots.

Grouping plants closely raises the ambient humidity for the entire collection and reduces moisture loss overall.

FEEDING

DETERMINING PLANT FOOD NEEDS

Many people believe that fertilizer feeds plants because we call it "plant food." Actually it feeds the soil in which they're planted. Photosynthesis provides plants with the sugar and other carbohydrates they need for energy. Plant foods amend the soil with minerals needed to sustain plants' healthy growth. Because houseplant potting mixes are typically highly fertile with plenty of organic matter, houseplants can survive for months without additional plant food.

Over time, however, watering leaches nutrients from potting mixes. Plants that lack nutrients grow slowly and may exhibit pale or dropped leaves, weak stems, and small or nonexistent flowers. Under most circumstances, you'll need to give plants supplemental food on a regular basis, but forgetting or skipping a feeding does not have the same disastrous results as forgetting to water.

READ THE LABEL

Plant foods come in many different formulations to suit various types of plants. Their labels list three numbers that represent the percentages of nitrogen, phosphorus, and potassium in the plant food. A plant food labeled 12-6-6 is 12 percent nitrogen, 6 percent phosphate (phosporus), and 6 percent potash (potassium). These three elements are the nutrients plants need most.

Nitrogen primarily enriches the greenness of the foliage and promotes stem growth. Phosphorus encourages flowering and root growth. Potassium contributes to stem strength and disease resistance. Plant foods formulated for flowering plants usually contain less nitrogen and more phosphorus and potassium. Those designed for foliage plants tend to have higher nitrogen content and less phosphorus and potassium. You also can find specialized plant foods made for some plant groups, such as orchids. If you grow many different types of plants, it's simpler to apply a good all-purpose plant food or to alternate between food for a flowering plant and one for foliage.

In addition to the three major nutrients, plants need three secondary nutrients—sulfur, calcium, and magnesium —and minute quantities of iron, manganese, zinc, copper, chlorine, boron, and molybdenum. The latter are called micronutrients, or trace elements. A lack of trace elements causes hard-to-diagnose symptoms, such as stunted growth and yellowing or reddening of leaves. If you suspect such a problem in your

Feed flowering plants with a formula high in phosphorus, which is made to stimulate root growth and enhance flowering.

plants, apply a soluble plant food rich in trace elements as you water to alleviate the symptoms of deficiency.

Fill the inch of space between the soil and the top of the pot with water containing plant food and let it soak into the soil.

TYPES OF PLANT FOOD

Plant foods are available in many forms: water-soluble pellets, time-release pellets, powders, liquids, and dry tablets or sticks that you insert in the soil. Their value and strength vary widely; if you have questions, consult a houseplant specialist or extension agent.

When applying plant food, always read the label first and follow the directions carefully. Remember that more is not better: Excess plant food can burn roots and leaves.

Most plant foods on the market are soluble or liquid concentrates designed to be diluted in water. (Ready-to-use liquid fertilizers contain mostly water.) These plant foods usually have been formulated for use once a month. If that's how you prefer to use them, simply follow the instructions on the label, remembering that it's okay to use less plant food but not more.

Many gardeners find it easier to add small doses of plant food each time they water. That way, it becomes part of their regular watering routine, and they are less likely to forget. If that's your choice, reduce the suggested dose of plant food to one-quarter of the monthly amount if you

water weekly, or one-eighth of the amount if you water on demand, and apply with each watering.

Apply soluble and liquid plant foods whenever plants are in active growth, usually spring through summer. Reduce or dilute applications in fall and stop entirely during the winter. Plants maintained in constant growth under artificial lights require plant food throughout the year.

Slow-release plant foods are generally designed for a single yearly application and last for six to nine months under normal growing conditions. Many indoor gardeners find them practical. Apply time-release plant foods according to instructions on the label. Some are tablets or sticks you insert into the soil.

Foliar feeding entails nourishing plants by spraying or misting diluted plant food onto their leaves. Use only plant foods recommended for foliar application and follow the label directions. Foliar feeding acts quickly but lasts a relatively short time. It is best used as a supplement to plant food applied directly to the potting mix.

IF YOU OVERFEED

Before deciding that a plant needs extra plant food, review its other care requirements to determine whether they are being met. The worst time to feed is when a plant is ailing or lacking in light. Sickly plants decline even more rapidly and may die if heavily fed.

Overfeeding is a common mistake that people make, particularly with plants growing in low light. Such plants do best with little or no plant food. Dormant plants also do not require plant food. Too much plant food causes leaf burn, poorly shaped leaves, and a white crust on the pot and the surface of the growing medium.

If you accidentally overfeed a plant, leach it thoroughly several times with tepid water and discard the drainage water. In mild weather, you can do this outdoors using a garden hose.

Leaching also helps wash out accumulated mineral salts, which can build up and harm the plant. Salt buildup shows up as a whitish deposit on pot surfaces or as salt burn on the edges of leaves. You may have to leach weekly for several weeks to alleviate it.

Another way to control salt buildup is to gently wash the old soil from the roots, then repot the plant in fresh growing mix.

Apply premixed liquid plant food straight from the container onto the soil of houseplants and other potted plants.

Use a balanced plant food that's specially formulated to nourish the plants in your home, such as an acid-rich food made for gardenias, azaleas, and others.

Apply a foliar food early in the morning on a warm or cool day with the plant sitting in shade or partial shade—not in hot sun—to prevent damaging the leaves.

HOUSEKEEPING

Houseplants need regular grooming to look their best. It takes little time and makes the difference between plants that look healthy and attractive and ones that look neglected. More important, regular grooming keeps you literally in touch with your plants, providing a chance to detect and control disease and insect problems early, when they can be easily controlled.

The amount of time you spend grooming will vary according to the type of plant. Some plants naturally shed and require more time than others to have their dead leaves, stems, and flowers removed. A little housekeeping performed each time you water, however, reduces the need to do major work often.

GROOMING

1 Dust a large-leaf plant to control pests and improve it's appearance.

2 Pinch off stem tips to encourage lush, branching growth.

3 Pin vining plants to a stake using wire pins to hold them in place until they root in.

Plants look much better and are healthier in the long run when they are groomed and pruned.

The largest grooming task is removing faded leaves. If a leaf has begun to yellow, remove it; it will not turn green again unless there is a fertility problem that you can correct. Assess whether yellowing leaves are part of the plant's natural leaf shed or whether there is a cultural problem you need to address.

Another easy step of grooming is to give a plant a quarter turn every time you water it. This will keep the plant symmetrical.

Every couple of weeks, dust plant leaves to remove particles that can clog the pores and prevent light from reaching the leaf surface. Wipe large-leaved plants with a soft, dry cloth (a wet cloth will make mud and more work).

Once every month or two, give the plant a shower. In summer do this outdoors; in winter you can use a tub or deep sink. Use tepid water to avoid shocking the plant.

Many plants look better if pinched back or pruned regularly. This helps keep them shrubby and full, can help correct structural problems, and for some varieties can rejuvenate the plant and produce new flowering wood.

STAKING

A stake used to hold up a plant that has been poorly grown doesn't accent the plant but rather accentuates the fact that the plant is lopsided or uneven. In these cases, it's probably better to start over by drastically pruning the plant or tossing it altogether.

Sometimes a stake is necessary only temporarily to correct a problem; once the plant starts growing well, the stake can be removed. In other cases, the stake is an integral part of the plant/pot combination, a permanent addition to the overall look of the plant.

Staking and training usually work best if you start with young plants. Whereas older plants have stems that don't bend as easily, young plants are pliable and can be pruned

as they grow to cover their support. Training plants onto a form may require a couple of years.

Choose stakes or trellises that are at least as thick as the stem you are supporting. Tie the plant loosely to the stake in a figure-eight form with a natural-color material, such as twine, raffia, grape tendrils, or green twist ties.

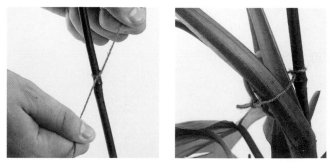

Use natural materials to tie plants to stakes. Make a snug loop around the stake and then a loose loop around the plant, creating a figure eight. This allows the plant stem some movement. Tie the plant in several places instead of one. With just one tie, the stem becomes vulnerable to breakage.

DO PICK THE FLOWERS

Unless the plant develops attractive fruits, such as citrus, Jerusalem cherry, or ornamental pepper, simply cut or pinch off faded flowers. The process of seed formation continues and drains the plant's energy if faded flowers are left on the plant.

PROPAGATING

STEM CUTTINGS

Growing houseplants from cuttings is the most popular method of vegetative propagation. It is an easy way to duplicate the attractive features of the original plant—the new plant is a clone of the original.

Cuttings taken several inches down a stem of a plant, below the tip or terminal, are called stem cuttings. Remove the lower leaves from stem cuttings, dip the cuttings in rooting hormone, and place them in soilless rooting mix. Place the cut end of the cutting into the rooting mix.

When taking cuttings from vining plants, such as pothos and philodendron, place the stem cuttings on the surface of the medium. Make cuttings at least 6 inches long. Exert

slight pressure to press the stem into contact with the soilless mix. Rooting hormone speeds root development on most species. It is unnecessary to remove leaves unless they prevent the stem from touching the rooting mix. Roots form at nodes, areas where leaves attach to the stem.

New roots are fragile and easily damaged. When checking cuttings to see whether roots have formed, gently tug on the cutting. If the cutting resists being pulled from the rooting mix, roots have probably formed. Use fingers or a pencil to gently dig under the cutting and lift it from the rooting mix to avoid damaging the new roots. Transplant the new plant into its own pot.

Rooting hormone promotes rooting on most cuttings.

Coleus cuttings root easily in water or rooting mix. One plant produces many cuttings.

Make an English ivy cutting just below a leaf. New roots develop best at the node (point of leaf attachment).

LEAF CUTTINGS

Most plants cannot be started from leaf cuttings, but a few can, including African violet, peperomia, Rex begonia, and gloxinia. African violet and peperomia leaves, with their petiole (stemlike structure that attaches the leaf to the crown of the plant), root easily to start new plants. Cut or snap the petiole and attached leaf from the crown of the plant. Dip the base of the petiole in rooting hormone and insert the lower 1 to 2 inches in soilless rooting mix. Place the soilless mix and cutting in a bright location but out of direct sunlight. Within a few months, the petiole will form roots and new leaves at its base. A short time later, the new leaves will push up through the medium.

An alternative method is to place the petiole in a container of water, with the attached leaf above the water. In a clear container, the formation of roots and leaves can

1 Nick the veins on the underside of the leaf.

2 Place the begonia leaf on moist soilless mix with the cut veins contacting the soil mix.

be easily observed. To keep the leaf above the water, place a piece of waxed paper over the top of the container and partway down the sides. Use a rubber band around the container to hold the waxed paper in place. Cut an X in the middle of the paper and insert the petiole through the cut and into the water.

Leaf cuttings are used to start new plants of gloxinia and Rex begonia. Remove a leaf from the plant and turn it over, exposing the veins on the underside of the leaf. Use a knife or sharp blade to slice through major veins, then apply rooting hormone to each cut. Place the leaf flat on the propagation soil mix with the sliced veins facing down and in contact with the soil mix. New plantlets form at the sliced veins as well as at the end of the petiole. Once the plantlets are an inch tall, separate them from the leaf and pot them individually.

Cut an African violet leaf from the parent plant to start a new plant.

Dip the leaf petiole of jade in rooting hormone to stimulate development of new roots.

LAYERING

In many cases where cuttings will not work, air layering is used to produce new plants.

When houseplants such as rubber tree, croton, or split-leaf philodendron grow too tall, it is time for air layering. Air layering produces a new plant and reduces the height of the existing plant.

Select a place on the stem where you will prompt the plant to develop new roots. At that point, remove a 1-inch length of bark around the stem. An alternate method is to make a 1½-inch slanting cut upward, extending halfway through the stem. Use a toothpick or sliver of wood to wedge in the cut so it will not close and grow back together. Apply rooting hormone to the wounded area.

Moisten long-fibered sphagnum moss and form it into a ball (about the size of a baseball) around the wound. Wrap clear plastic over the moss and fasten it with twist ties, tape, or string above and below the moss. Check every few weeks to make sure the moss is still moist. When you see roots within the clear plastic, remove it. Use pruners to cut the stem below the root mass, and pot the new plant. The old plant will produce new shoots below the cut, resulting in a shorter, bushier parent plant.

1 Make a slanting cut upward, halfway into the stem.

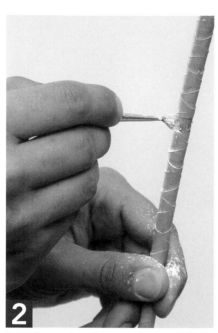

2 Dust the notch with rooting hormone, then loosely wrap plastic around the stem. Hold it at the base with tape or a twist tie.

3 Fill the plastic with dampened sphagnum moss.

4 Close the top of the plastic with tape or twist ties. Check weekly for moistness, opening slightly to add water if needed.

5 After roots develop, cut the stem of the plant below the plastic. Remove the plastic and the moss.

6 Plant in fresh potting soil. New stems will probably sprout below the cut on the parent plant.

DIVIDING PLANTLETS & OFFSETS

Houseplants such as Boston fern, peace lily, snake plant, cast-iron plant, prayer plant, and spider plant are easily divided. Make divisions when the plant gets too large for its pot or location and repotting to a larger container is not feasible. You may also divide plants when new plants are desired.

Plantlets

Several common houseplants reproduce by sending out miniature new plants on runners or shoots. These include the spider plant *(Chlorophytum)*, flame violet *(Episcia)*, and many varieties of Boston fern *(Nephrolepis exaltata)*. Some even produce plantlets on leaves, such as piggyback plant *(Tolmiea menziesii)* and several kalanchoes. The plantlets can be cut away from the parent plant and repotted.

Offsets

Small new plants that form at the base of an old plant and remain attached to it are known as offsets. You can break them off and plant them just as you would divisions. Detach offsets only when they are mature enough to survive on their own—usually when

1 Gently separate an offset from the parent, using a knife if needed. It may be necessary to remove the parent plant from its pot for easier access.

2 Plant the offset in growing mix at the depth at which it grew in the original pot. Tamp the soil lightly, then water. Give the offset the same care as the parent plant.

they have taken on the look of the mature plant. You can propagate the screw pine *(Pandanus veitchii)* and many bromeliads using this method. Plant the divisions immediately in

individual pots of fresh potting soil and water thoroughly. Keep them in bright light but out of direct sun until they resume growing.

1 You may need to tease apart the roots in order to remove the offsets of some plants.

2 Offsets will propagate easily if they are well developed and have healthy roots.

SEEDS

Most houseplants can be grown from seed, but usually they are easier to propagate vegetatively. A number of excellent houseplants, however, can be propagated only from seed. Single-trunk palms, cyclamen, and many annuals used in hanging baskets fall into this category. As an experiment, try starting citrus plants from seeds that you've washed and allowed to dry. Lemon, lime, orange,

and citron all make lovely houseplants, although they may not produce fruit.

Houseplant seeds are available from garden centers and mail-order nurseries. Sow them the same way you would sow seeds for outdoor plants, in warm temperatures (70°F to 75°F) with consistent moisture. Bottom heat from heating cables expedites germination.

Chapter 4
PROBLEM SOLVING

Plant health care is a holistic, preventive approach to plant maintenance. Focus on providing a plant with the proper care so it will thrive. Prevent conditions that encourage insects or pathogens.

PREVENTING PROBLEMS FROM THE START

The greatest impediment to plant health is usually the home gardener. When confronted with a plant problem, most gardeners assume an insect or disease is involved, then wonder what pesticide to spray. However, most plant problems are due not to disease-causing agents (pathogens) or insects but to environmental conditions and stresses. And more often than not, these problems are due to actions taken by gardeners.

In a perfect world, you could bring new plants home, find a spot where the environmental conditions are exactly right, and maintain them with basic care. But sometimes environmental conditions aren't perfect, and people forget to water and fertilize. When plants seem healthy, it's easy to forget about them, but stressed or neglected plants are susceptible to insect infestations and diseases that can cause serious damage.

Because you can correct a problem much more easily when you catch it early, make it a habit to examine and touch your plants every time you water them. Check for signs of insects or disease, and if you notice any, move the plant away from others while you take steps to control the problem. Check nearby plants to make sure any infection or infestation has not already spread. Then use the information in this chapter to diagnose and fix the problem.

With just a little know-how, you can easily keep your houseplants in top shape. An integrated pest management system is a practical and responsible method for trouble-shooting problems and improving plant health. Start with clean, healthy plants. Next, make sure your plants receive proper culture. Understand your plants' needs and give them what they require to reduce stress and prevent problems. Be especially attentive to changes in the way they look. When

you discover a problem, isolate the plant. Then correctly identify the pest or disease.

After determining what the problem is, decide on a method of control. These steps will take you through a logical progression of methods to use:

■ Correct cultural problems that may be stressing the plant.
■ Prune out the infested parts if this can be done without harming the plant or destroying its pleasing form.
■ Wash the foliage with a strong spray of water to dislodge insects.
■ If weather permits, move the plant outdoors to let natural predators handle the pests.
■ Remove pests physically with a fingernail, tweezers, or cotton balls or swabs dipped in alcohol or horticultural oil. Wipe the leaves with a soft, clean cloth.
■ Wash all parts of the plant with warm, soapy water.
■ Apply horticultural oil or insecticidal soap.
■ Repot if you have root pests or disease.
■ Treat with an appropriate pesticide.
■ Discard the plant.

Isolate new plants initially to make sure there are no pests or diseases you might have missed at the garden center.

Before you take steps to remedy a pest or disease, identify it correctly. A magnifying glass can be a big help. Here, the problem appears to be mealybug, an insect that feeds on plant sap.

SENSIBLE PRECAUTIONS

Begin practicing prevention at the garden center. Examine any plant you want to buy, checking carefully for signs of insects and diseases. In the case of whiteflies, for instance, inspection is easy: Brush against an infested plant, and the insects rise in a dusty cloud of white. Other pests, such as scale insects and aphids, sometimes require a more diligent search. That includes inspecting the undersides of leaves for insects and egg casings.

More harmful and more difficult to control than insects, diseases typically develop in the greenhouse or at home as a result of poor care. Before you buy a plant, look for the telltale signs of problems, especially viruses, which kill the plant they attack and spread easily to other plants.

Prevention extends to bringing the plants home: Isolate any new purchases for one to two weeks to make sure they are free of insects and disease.

INSECTS

The most common insect problems that occur with houseplants include scale insects, aphids, mealybugs, spider mites, fungus gnats, and whiteflies.

Scale insects are some of the hardest pests to control. The damage shows as leaf yellowing and eventual leaf drop. Sticky residue may coat the leaves. Control scale with horticultural oil, which smothers the adult insect.

Aphids are soft-bodied, slow-moving insects that are easily controlled with a strong spray of water, hand-picking, insecticidal soap, or horticultural oil. Aphid damage shows as distorted new leaves, stem tips, and buds. Aphids also excrete sticky residue.

Mealybugs appear as cottony masses in the leaf axils. They secrete a waxy coating, making themselves impervious to insecticides. Control them by dipping a cotton swab in alcohol or horticultural oil and rubbing it on the insects.

Spider mites are troublesome pests that thrive in heat and low humidity. Correcting these cultural problems will often take care of many of the mites. Spider mite damage shows as yellow stippling of the leaves; once the populations are high, you will see webbing on the undersides of leaves. Washing off the leaves regularly takes care of most mites; the remaining populations can be controlled with horticultural oil.

Small, dark fungus gnats fly around plants and run across soil and leaves. They may also be found on windows. They lay their eggs in organic-rich soil. Larvae hatch and, in large enough numbers, may feed on roots of plants, killing seedlings. Hang yellow sticky traps among plants to kill adults. Let soil mix dry out between waterings (larvae cannot survive in dry soil). Apply Bti (*Bacillus thuringiensis israelensis*) according to label directions.

Whiteflies feed mainly on the undersides of leaves, fluttering around when you touch the plant. The tiny winged insects excrete a sticky substance, which coats leaves. Use sticky traps to catch adult whiteflies; wipe off larvae using a cloth soaked in alcohol. Spray severe infestations weekly with insecticidal soap as long as you continue to see any insects.

Scale insects will leave sticky residue on houseplants and can usually be controlled with horticultural oil.

Mealybugs tend to congregate in the leaf axils and cover themselves with a waxy coating.

Whiteflies feed mainly on the undersides of leaves. Isolate infested plants until the problem is resolved.

Fungus gnats feed on fungi that grow on decaying organic matter. Control them by using yellow sticky traps and keeping plants dry.

DISEASES

The most common disease problems are fungal leaf spots. Typically, the disease appears on leaves as circular reddish brown spots surrounded by a yellow margin. In most cases, spotting is unsightly but not harmful. On susceptible plants, the leaves may weaken and die. Clip off badly affected leaves. Water carefully to avoid splashing leaves and prevent spreading the disease. Changing the cultural conditions may help prevent the return of the spots.

Other leaf problems include viral and bacterial diseases, none of which are easily controlled. It is often more cost effective to discard the plant.

Plants that sit in soggy soil or standing water often develop root or crown rots, which are fungal in nature. They can often be cured by drying out the plant. It also may help to repot the plant, pruning off damaged and diseased roots at the same time.

Botrytis appears as light brown patches on leaves, stems, or flowers and gradually darkens, turning into a soft, grayish mold. Infected plant parts curl up and fall off. This common airborne fungal disease affects a wide range of plants and spreads quickly, especially in humid conditions and inside closed containers, such as terrariums. Remove affected plant parts and treat the rest of the plant with a fungicide or a fungicidal soap. Improve air circulation around plants to keep humidity low.

Powdery mildew, caused by fungi, appears as white or grayish powdery patches on leaves, stems, and flowers. The disease flourishes in dim light and warm days with cool nights. Plants in dry soil are more susceptible than those in moist soil. Remove affected leaves and spray plants with a fungicidal soap. Move plants to a location with more light and adequate air circulation.

When a virus infects a plant, there is no cure. Plants grow slowly and without vigor; their growth appears stunted. Leaves are mottled and distorted, and are often streaked with yellow or have ringed yellow spots. Viruses are carried from plant to plant by insects or infected tools. Destroy infected plants. To prevent viruses, keep insects at bay through preventive treatment. When pruning, dip tools into a disinfectant (bleach or rubbing alcohol) between each cut.

Botrytis is an airborne fungal disease that is especially common in humid conditions.

Most leaf spots are caused by fungal diseases and can be controlled by simply removing the leaf.

No cure exists for bacterial leaf blight. Prevent it by using fresh, well-draining potting mix and keeping leaves dry.

CULTURAL PROBLEMS

The most common cultural problem affecting plants is over- or underwatering. Both practices produce the same symptoms. If a plant is overwatered repeatedly, the saturated soil kills the root hairs, which take up water. The plant loses color, wilts, and eventually dies if the soil is not dried out somewhat to allow new root hairs to grow. Underwatering is easily corrected by providing water. However, if a plant wilts completely from lack of water, it may not recover; if it does, it may never look the same.

Another common symptom, brown leaf tips or edges, is most often caused by a lack of humidity. But the same symptom can occur when a plant does not receive enough moisture or is sensitive to chemicals found in water. Plants that are pot-bound and have little soil with which to hold water are susceptible.

Plants drop leaves for many reasons. In most cases, it is natural leaf shed. However, if a plant's leaves turn brittle and fall, or if a substantial number of leaves yellow and fall, you need to check the plant's cultural conditions.

Placing a plant in direct sun may cause leaf bleaching or actual sunburn, in which the leaf tissue bleaches to white and then shrivels.

Leaf spots not attributable to disease can be caused by splashing when watering.

There are many reasons why a plant may fail to flower during its blooming season, when it seems in perfect health otherwise. Typically, the problem is attributable to a lack of

When watering African violets, feed them with a water-soluble plant food balanced especially for them. If you feed weekly, do so at half the rate called for on the label. Always water and feed the plants from the bottom. This keeps water spots from marring the hairy leaves.

light, insufficient humidity, or improper temperature. Or the plant may be too immature to flower. Try moving the plant to a somewhat brighter spot, placing it on a humidity tray, or addressing its temperature requirements. Give it a food formulated for flowering plants, in case a lack of minerals or an excess of nitrogen is a cause of the problem.

Plants generally fail to grow well when there is a lack of light. The leaves may be lighter green and smaller than normal; they may turn yellow and drop. Although foliage plants typically need less light than those grown for their flowers or fruit, plants with colorful foliage have a relatively high need for light. Gradually move a plant to a brighter situation and see if it responds. If the available lighting is not adequate, provide supplemental lighting.

When humidity is too low, plant growth is slow and leaves tend to curl downward. Plants wilt rapidly and tips may brown and turn up, which is a major problem, especially during the heating season, when indoor air is naturally drier. Place plants on a humidity tray or keep them in a room with a humidifier. Use the whole-house humidifier on your furnace, if it has one. Group plants together; the vapor given off by each one in transpiration increases the air humidity around them all.

If plants fail to grow, wilt, lose their glossiness, or appear light green or yellow, check their roots. If the root ball has become mushy and brown, the plant may be receiving too much water. If the soil in the bottom of the

You will soon recognize the difference between a healthy plant, such as this strawberry begonia, and one that needs help.

pot is soggy and has a foul odor, it likely isn't draining well. Do not water the plant again until the soil is almost dry. Prevent the problem by using a light soil with good drainage; ensure the pot has a drainage hole. Discard the plant if it doesn't improve.

Yellowing of leaves can be an indication of several conditions, including high temperature or a nutrient deficiency. When temperatures are too warm, leaves turn yellow, then brown, and plants stop forming flower buds or cease to grow well. In this case, move plants to a cooler environment or put them near a window at night. Keep plants adequately watered and fed.

If their newest leaves turn yellow at the margins and the yellowing progresses inward until the entire leaf loses its green color, there may be an iron deficiency. It's a common problem for acid-loving plants, such as gardenias and azaleas, which grow best in soil with a pH between 5.5 and 6.5. Correct the situation by applying a plant food containing chelated iron.

Foliage plants need more nitrogen than do flowering plants. Nitrogen is easily leached from the soil during regular watering. Of all the plant nutrients, it is the one the soil is most likely to lack. Older leaves, usually the lower ones, turn yellow and may drop. Yellowing starts at the leaf margins and progresses inward without producing a distinct pattern. Growth is slow and new growth may be small. When plants begin to show signs of nitrogen deficiency, amend or replace the potting soil. For a quick but temporary fix, spray leaves with a foliar plant food. Feed at regular intervals as recommended on the plant food label.

Once or twice a week, run tepid water through the pot; drain the pot in the sink, then return to the display. Never leave an orchid standing in water.

GALLERY OF
HOUSEPLANT CARE

Gardening indoors removes plants from their natural environments. You control the amount of light, moisture, and warmth they receive through the care that you provide. The rewards of lush foliage and blooms in your living space are well worth the effort.

COMMON NAME	BOTANIC NAME	SEE PAGE
African mask	Alocasia ×amazonica	40
African milk tree	Euphorbia trigona	78
African tree grape	Cissus antarctica	57
African violet	Saintpaulia ionantha	123
Agave	Agave americana	39
Airplane plant	Chlorophytum comosum	56
Air plant	Kalanchoe daigremontiana	95
Algerian ivy	Hedera canariensis	88
Alii fig	Ficus maclellandii	82
Aloe	Aloe vera	41
Aluminum plant	Pilea cadierei	114
Amaryllis	Hippeastrum spp.	90
Angel wing begonia	Begonia coccinea	48
Anthurium	Anthurium andraeanum	42
Arboricola	Schefflera arboricola	125
Areca palm	Chrysalidocarpus lutescens	56
Arrowhead vine	Syngonium podophyllum	131
Artillery plant	Pilea microphylla	115
Asparagus fern	Asparagus densiflorus	45
Azalea	Rhododendron spp.	122
Baby rubber plant	Peperomia obtusifolia	110
Baby's tears	Soleirolia soleirolii	129
Balfour aralia	Polyscias scutellaria	119
Bamboo palm	Chamaedorea erumpens	55
Banana leaf fig	Ficus maclellandii	82
Barroom plant	Aspidistra elatior	46
Bay tree	Laurus nobilis	96
Beautiful hoya	Hoya lanceolata ssp. bella	93
Bird's nest fern	Asplenium nidus	46
Bishop's cap cactus	Astrophytum spp.	47
Bishop's hat cactus	Astrophytum spp.	47
Bloodleaf	Iresine herbstii	94
Blushing bromeliad	Neoregelia carolinae	101
Boat lily	Tradescantia spathacea	134
Boston fern	Nephrolepis exaltata	102
Bottle palm	Beaucarnea recurvata	48
Brake fern	Pteris cretica	120
Buddhist pine	Podocarpus macrophyllus	118
Bunny ear cactus	Opuntia microdasys	102
Burn plant	Aloe vera	41
Burro's tail	Sedum morganianum	127
Butterfly palm	Chrysalidocarpus lutescens	56
Button fern	Pellaea rotundifolia	107
Calamondin orange	×Citrofortunella microcarpa	58
Calla lily	Zantedeschia aethiopica	136
Candelabra plant	Euphorbia trigona	78
Cape primrose	Streptocarpus ×hybridus	131
Cast-iron plant	Aspidistra elatior	46

COMMON NAME	BOTANIC NAME	SEE PAGE
Cathedral windows	Calathea picturata	51
Cattleya orchid	Cattleya hybrids	52
Century plant	Agave americana	39
Ceylon creeper	Epipremnum aureum	75
Chenille plant	Acalypha hispida	36
Chicken gizzard	Iresine herbstii	94
China doll	Radermachera sinica	121
Chinese evergreen	Aglaonema commutatum	40
Chinese fan palm	Livistona chinensis	97
Chinese lantern	Abutilon ×hybridum	36
Chinese rose	Hibiscus rosa-sinensis	90
Chirita	Chirita sinensis	55
Christmas cactus	Schlumbergera ×buckleyi	126
Cineraria	Senecio ×hybridus	128
Clivia	Clivia miniata	60
Coffee	Coffea arabica	61
Coleus	Solenostemon scutellarioides	130
Compact wax plant	Hoya compacta	92
Copperleaf	Acalypha wilkesiana	37
Coralberry	Ardisia crenata	44
Corn plant	Dracaena fragrans	71
Cow tongue	Gasteria spp.	86
Creeping fig	Ficus pumila	84
Cretan brake	Pteris cretica	120
Croton	Codiaeum variegatum var. pictum	60
Crown-of-thorns	Euphorbia milii	77
Crystal anthurium	Anthurium crystallinum	42
Cuban oregano	Plectranthus amboinicus	116
Cut-leaf philodendron	Philodendron bipinnatifidum	111
Cyclamen	Cyclamen persicum	65
Cymbidium orchid	Cymbidium spp.	66
Dendrobium orchid	Dendrobium hybrids	68
Devil's backbone	Pedilanthus tithymaloides	105
Devil's ivy	Epipremnum aureum	75
Donkey's tail	Sedum morganianum	127
Drop tongue	Homalomena rubescens	91
Dumb cane	Dieffenbachia amoena	68
Dumb cane	Dieffenbachia picta	69
Dumb cane	Dieffenbachia seguine	70
Dwarf papyrus	Cyperus alternifolius	66
Earth star	Cryptanthus bivittatus	63
Easter cactus	Rhipsalidopsis spp.	122
Elephant ear	Alocasia ×amazonica	40
Elephant foot	Beaucarnea recurvata	48
Emerald feather	Asparagus setaceus	45
Emerald ripple peperomia	Peperomia caperata	109
English ivy	Hedera helix	89

**Boston fern,
Nephrolepis
exaltata**

**Cyclamen,
Cyclamen persicum**

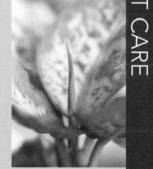

Dieffenbachia picta

**English ivy, Hedera
helix**

CHAPTER

5

GALLERY OF HOUSEPLANT CARE

Flame violet, *Episcia reptans*

Mosiac plant, *Fittonia verschaffeltii*

Polka dot plant, *Hypoestes phyllostachya*

Regier begonia, *Begonia*

COMMON NAME	BOTANIC NAME	SEE PAGE
Painted leaf begonia	*Begonia Rex Cultorum hybrids*	49
Panama hat palm	*Carludovica palmata*	51
Panda plant	*Kalanchoe tomentosa*	96
Parlor maple	*Abutilon ×hybridum*	36
Parlor palm	*Chamaedorea elegans*	54
Peace lily	*Spathiphyllum wallisii*	130
Peacock plant	*Calathea makoyana*	50
Peanut cactus	*Chamaecereus sylvestri*	54
Peppermint-scented geranium	*Pelargonium tomentosum*	107
Persian violet	*Exacum affine*	79
Piggyback plant	*Tolmiea menziesii*	132
Pineapple dyckia	*Dyckia brevifolia*	74
Pink quill	*Tillandsia cyanea*	132
Pleomele	*Dracaena reflexa*	72
Plumose fern	*Asparagus setaceus*	45
Poinsettia	*Euphorbia pulcherrima*	78
Polka dot plant	*Hypoestes phyllostachya*	93
Ponytail palm	*Beaucarnea recurvata*	48
Pothos	*Epipremnum aureum*	75
Prayer plant	*Maranta leuconeura*	99
Primrose	*Primula spp.*	120
Princess Astrid peperomia	*Peperomia orba*	110
Purple heart	*Tradescantia pallida*	133
Purple-leaved Swedish ivy	*Plectranthus purpuratus*	118
Purple passion	*Gynura aurantiaca*	87
Purple shamrock	*Oxalis regnellii*	104
Purple velvet plant	*Gynura aurantiaca*	87
Pussy ears	*Kalanchoe tomentosa*	96
Pygmy date palm	*Phoenix roebelenii*	113
Queen Victoria century plant	*Agave victoria-reginae*	39
Rabbit's foot fern	*Davallia fejeensis*	67
Rattail cactus	*Aporocactus flagelliformis*	43
Red dracaena	*Cordyline fruticosa*	62
Red flame ivy	*Hemigraphis alternata*	89
Red-leaf philodendron	*Philodendron erubescens*	112
Reed palm	*Chamaedorea erumpens*	55
Rex begonia	*Begonia Rex Cultorum hybrids*	49
Ribbon plant	*Chlorophytum comosum*	56
Ribbon plant	*Dracaena sanderiana*	73
Roman laurel	*Laurus nobilis*	96
Rosary vine	*Ceropegia linearis ssp. woodii*	53
Rose mallow	*Hibiscus rosa-sinensis*	90
Rose-scented geranium	*Pelargonium graveolens*	106
Rubber tree	*Ficus elastica*	81
Sago palm	*Cycas revoluta*	65
Satin pothos	*Epipremnum pictum*	76
Schefflera	*Schefflera actinophylla*	125
Schefflera	*Schefflera arboricola*	125
Screw pine	*Pandanus veitchii*	105

COMMON NAME	BOTANIC NAME	SEE PAGE
Sensitive plant	*Mimosa pudica*	99
Silverleaf peperomia	*Peperomia griseoargentea*	109
Silver vase plant	*Aechmea fasciata*	38
Snake plant	*Sansevieria trifasciata*	124
Snowball cactus	*Mammillaria bocasana*	98
Song of India	*Dracaena reflexa*	72
Spider plant	*Chlorophytum comosum*	56
Spineless yucca	*Yucca elephantipes*	135
Split-leaf philodendron	*Monstera deliciosa*	100
Spotted dumb cane	*Dieffenbachia maculata*	69
Sprengeri fern	*Asparagus densiflorus*	45
Spurflower	*Plectranthus forsteri*	117
Staghorn fern	*Platycerium bifurcatum*	116
Strawberry begonia	*Saxifraga stolonifera*	124
Strawberry geranium	*Saxifraga stolonifera*	124
String-of-beads	*Senecio rowleyanus*	128
String of hearts	*Ceropegia linearis spp. woodii*	53
Striped inch plant	*Tradescantia fluminensis*	133
Swedish ivy	*Plectranthus australis*	117
Sweet bay	*Laurus nobilis*	96
Sweetheart plant	*Philodendron scandens*	113
Sweet myrtle	*Myrtus communis*	100
Sweet olive	*Osmanthus fragrans*	103
Swiss-cheese plant	*Monstera deliciosa*	100
Sword fern	*Nephrolepis exaltata*	102
Table fern	*Pteris cretica*	120
Tahitian bridal veil	*Gibasis geniculata*	86
Tail flower	*Anthurium andraeanum*	42
Teddy bear vine	*Cyanotis kewensis*	64
Thanksgiving cactus	*Schlumbergera truncata*	127
Touch-me-not	*Mimosa pudica*	99
Trailing velvet plant	*Ruellia makoyana*	123
Tree ivy	*×Fatshedera lizei*	79
Tree philodendron	*Philodendron bipinnatifidum*	111
Umbrella plant	*Cyperus alternifolius*	66
Umbrella tree	*Schefflera actinophylla*	125
Urn plant	*Aechmea fasciata*	38
Velvet-leaf philodendron	*Philodendron scandens f. micans*	112
Velvet plant	*Gynura aurantiaca*	87
Venus flytrap	*Dionaea muscipula*	70
Wandering Jew	*Tradescantia zebrina*	134
Watermelon begonia	*Peperomia argyreia*	108
Watermelon pellionia	*Pellionia repens*	108
Watermelon peperomia	*Peperomia argyreia*	108
Wax plant	*Hoya carnosa*	92
Weeping fig	*Ficus benjamina*	80
Yucca	*Yucca elephantipes*	135
Zebra haworthia	*Haworthia fasciata*	88
Zebra plant	*Aphelandra squarrosa*	43
Zeezee plant	*Zamioculcas zamiifolia*	136

**Sago palm,
*Cycas revoluta***

**Hawaiian ti plant,
*Cordyline terminalis***

**Weeping fig,
*Ficus benjamina***

**Silverleaf
peperomia,
*Peperomia
griseoargentea***

FLOWERING MAPLE

Abutilon ×hybridum *a-BEW-tih-lahn HY-brih-dum*

Flowering maple is also know as Chinese lantern or parlor maple.

SIZE: 5'h × 3'w
TYPE: Woody shrub
FORM: Treelike or weeping
TEXTURE: Medium
GROWTH: Fast
LIGHT: Medium

MOISTURE: Moist
SOIL: Potting soil mix
FEATURES: Maple-shaped green or variegated leaves
USES: Focal point
FLOWERS: ■ ■ ■ ■ □

SITING: Flowering maple performs well in medium light but also tolerates full sun. Provide temperatures of 60–75°F while it blooms, but move it into a cooler situation in winter. Flowering maple performs well with 30 percent or greater humidity.
CARE: Water to keep the soil moist while it is blooming, but in winter allow the top 2" of soil to dry between waterings. The plant may drop leaves when it receives too little water. Feed weekly with a dilute solution of plant food for flowering plants or once monthly with a full-strength solution during the blooming season. Feed every 2 months with acid food. Flowering maple blooms best when pot-bound, but if growth is active, it may need repotting annually. Give plants a shower once a month to remove dust. Deadhead the spent flowers regularly. As the plant begins spring growth, pinch out branch tips to encourage bloom. Cut the entire plant back by half after blooming to make it shrubby and full.
PROPAGATION: Root semihardwood stem cuttings from the annual pruning in fall. Take softwood tip cuttings at any time, or start plants from seed immediately after the pods have dried on the plant. Use bottom heat for germination.
PESTS AND DISEASES: Treat mealybugs and aphids with horticultural oil.

1 Training a plant to grow as a standard will take initial pruning and shaping and occasional pruning.

2 Begin by pruning off the lower branches and heading back some of the upper shoots to side buds.

3 A finished plant grown as a standard gives an indoor landscape a formal touch.

CHENILLE PLANT

Acalypha hispida *ak-uh-LIE-fuh HISS-pih-duh*

Chenille plant offers not only attractive flowers, but also striking foliage even when it is not blooming.

SIZE: 3–6'h × 3'w
TYPE: Woody shrub
FORM: Upright
TEXTURE: Coarse
GROWTH: Fast
LIGHT: High

MOISTURE: Evenly moist
SOIL: Potting soil
FEATURES: Large, fuzzy leaves
USES: Focal point
FLOWERS: ■ ■ ■

SITING: Chenille plant blooms best when given full sun in winter and bright, indirect light in summer. Direct sun in summer will cause the leaves to fade and will reduce flowering. The plant tolerates lower light but won't bloom well. Provide warm temperatures (70–75°F) and higher than average humidity. The pot-in-pot method works well to increase humidity.
CARE: Keep the soil evenly moist but not soggy during active growth in spring and summer. Allow the soil to dry slightly between waterings in winter. Feed only three times in summer during active growth with a formula for blooming plants. Repot annually when the plant is small; when it gets too large to repot, remove the top couple inches of soil and replace with fresh potting mix. Cut the plant back by about one-third in early spring to keep it shrubby and attractive when blooming.
PROPAGATION: Chenille plant tends to get leggy, so take semihardwood stem cuttings every 2 years or so to start new plants. Dust cuttings with rooting hormone and provide bottom heat for root development.
PESTS AND DISEASES: Deter spider mites by raising the humidity and giving the plant a shower once a month.
RELATED SPECIES: *Acalypha hispida* var. *alba* has creamy white flowers. *Acalypha repens* is a trailing form with the same flowers as *A. hispida*.

***Acalypha hispida*, Chenille plant, is a favorite with children because of its soft pink and red "tails."**

COPPERLEAF

Acalypha wilkesiana ak-uh-LIE-fuh wilk-see-AY-nuh

Copperleaf, also known as Jacob's coat or Fiji fire plant, has uniquely variegated leaves to use as a colorful focal point.

SIZE: 4'h × 3'w
TYPE: Woody shrub
FORM: Upright
TEXTURE: Coarse
GROWTH: Fast
LIGHT: High
MOISTURE: Evenly moist

SOIL: Potting soil mix
FEATURES: Variegated bronze-green leaves
USES: Foliage display, focal point

SITING: Provide copperleaf with bright light but keep it out of direct sun. The plant will tolerate lower light, but the bright crimson, purple, lime, green, gold, pink, or cream variegation of the leaves will fade somewhat. Warm temperatures (70–75°F) are essential. The plant performs best when the nighttime temperature doesn't drop much, so avoid leaving it near a window where the temperature drops considerably at night. Provide high humidity or the plant will drop leaves. Place on a saucer of moist pebbles or near a humidifier.

CARE: Keep the soil evenly moist but not soggy during the growing season. Let it dry out slightly between waterings in winter. Feed only three times in summer during active growth with a formula for foliage plants. Repot annually when the plant is small. When it gets too large to repot, remove the top 2" of soil and replace with fresh potting mix. Cut back plants in spring to keep them shrubby. Pull off faded leaves regularly, and give the plant a monthly shower.

PROPAGATION: Plants tend to become leggy, so propagate new plants every couple of years. Take semihardwood stem cuttings in midsummer to early fall. Dust cuttings with rooting hormone and provide bottom heat for root development.

PESTS AND DISEASES: Copperleaf may have spider mites and drop leaves when the humidity is low.

RELATED SPECIES: Cultivars are available with all types of variegation, including curled leaves and miniatures that are popular for bonsai.

MAIDENHAIR FERN

Adiantum pedatum ah-de-AN-tum peh-DATE-um

Maidenhair fern, also known as Northern maidenhair fern, offers soft, arching fronds that lend a touch of elegance to any room.

SIZE: 18"h × 18"w
TYPE: Fern
FORM: Arching, mounded
TEXTURE: Fine
GROWTH: Slow
LIGHT: Medium to high, filtered

MOISTURE: Moist
SOIL: Potting soil
FEATURES: Bright green leaflets on shiny stems
USES: Terrarium, textural accent

SITING: Maidenhair fern, with its shiny black or maroon stems and bright chartreuse to deep green fronds arranged in a half-circle, performs best in medium to bright, indirect light. It is quite tolerant of lower light but will tend to be more open and airy. This fern thrives in average to warm temperatures (60–80°F) and needs high humidity. A pebble tray is an excellent method to keep the humidity high around the plant.

CARE: Keep moist but not soggy in spring, summer, and fall; let soil dry out only slightly during the winter. Feed every month during active growth with general houseplant food and every 2 months during its resting phase in winter. Remove the occasional faded frond or fronds browned from lack of humidity.

PROPAGATION: Maidenhair fern is difficult for the novice to propagate. The most successful methods are spreading spores on soil mix with bottom heat and constant moisture, or carefully dividing the root clump.

PESTS AND DISEASES: Treat scale with horticultural oil.

RELATED SPECIES: There are no readily available cultivars of maidenhair fern. There are many related species (all similar to *Adiantium pedatum* in appearance), among them *A. formosum, A. aleuticum, A. raddianum,* and *A. pubescens.*

Setting a pot on a tray of wet pebbles will raise the humidity surrounding the fern.

SILVER VASE PLANT

Aechmea fasciata AYK-mee-a fas-see-AH-tah

Silver vase plant, also known as urn plant, is a unique, trouble-free plant that provides a room with long-lasting color.

SIZE: 12–18"h × 18–24"w
TYPE: Bromeliad
FORM: Vase-shaped
TEXTURE: Coarse
GROWTH: Slow
LIGHT: High

MOISTURE: Dry between waterings
SOIL: Epiphyte mix
FEATURES: Blue-gray leaves streaked with white
USES: Focal point
FLOWERS: ■■ ■■

SITING: Vase plants require high light to bloom, but they don't do well in direct sun. The plants thrive at 60–85°F and 10–60 percent humidity.

CARE: Let the soil dry out almost completely between waterings, but keep the "vase" full of water. Every couple of months, empty and refill the vase to keep the water fresh. Feed by applying blooming plant formula to the potting soil three times in summer or by adding half-strength formula to the vase every month. Repot only when the potting mix begins to break down and no longer has recognizable chunks of bark. When the main flower spike has faded, the plant begins to develop side shoots. When these

Silver vase plant's leaves form a cup at their bases, which should be kept filled with water.

are about 6" tall, remove the main vase and leave the side shoots to grow.

PROPAGATION: Propagate by removing the offsets or side shoots when they are about one-third the size of the parent plant. Pot up the offsets and keep them in a warm, bright spot until they establish themselves.

PESTS AND DISEASES: Treat scale with horticultural oil.

RELATED SPECIES: The cultivar 'Morgana' has dusty gray-green leaves with silvery cross bands. Its flower spike is bright fuchsia with small lavender-blue flowers.

Induce a silver vase plant to flower by putting it in a plastic bag with an apple for a couple of weeks.

LIPSTICK PLANT

Aeschynanthus radicans (lobbianus) ess-cuh-NAN-thus RAD-ih-kanz (lob-ee-AY-nus)

Lipstick plant blooms with bright tubular flowers nestled into rich green foliage on softly vining stems.

SIZE: 1'h × 3'w
TYPE: Gesneriad
FORM: Mounded, vining
TEXTURE: Medium
GROWTH: Medium
LIGHT: High
MOISTURE: Medium

SOIL: Epiphyte mix
FEATURES: Glossy green foliage on vines
USES: Hanging basket
FLOWERS: ■

SITING: Provide lipstick plant with bright light but not direct sun. It prefers average to warm temperatures (60–80°F) and high humidity (65 percent or higher). The pot-in-pot method is the most practical for

raising humidity when this plant is grown in a hanging basket.

CARE: Allow the soil to dry slightly between waterings, but let it dry considerably during the winter rest. Feed every 2 weeks when blooming with a formula for blooming plants, and every 2 months in fall and winter. Lipstick plant blooms best when pot-bound, so repot only when watering becomes difficult

Cut back the vines to rejuvenate the plant and keep it blossoming.

because of a large root mass. Plants must be mature to bloom well. The blossoms look like tubes of lipstick (hence its common name) and fall cleanly from the plant. Although lipstick plant usually has draping vines that can reach 2–3' long, it becomes scraggly if not rejuvenated occasionally. Pinch back the tips to make it look better while blooming; after it has finished flowering, cut the plant stems back to 6". Lipstick plant may shed leaves when it's too cold; the leaves may brown and dry when the humidity is too low.

PROPAGATION: Propagate by taking softwood stem or tip cuttings in spring before blooming.

PESTS AND DISEASES: Spider mites may take hold in low humidity. The plant may also develop botrytis, a fungal disease that shows as black leaf spots. Pull off the affected leaves or cut back the stems and let the potting soil dry out somewhat.

RELATED SPECIES: 'Black Pagoda' has mottled red and green foliage and brown-specked yellow and green flowers. *A. micranthus* is smaller than *A. radicans; A. speciosus* has orange-yellow flowers.

CENTURY PLANT

Agave americana *uh-GAH-vee a-mer-ih-CAHN-a*

Century plant, also known as agave, gives a room a dramatic southwestern flair with its architectural form.

SIZE: 3'h × 3'w
TYPE: Succulent
FORM: Upright rosette
TEXTURE: Coarse
GROWTH: Slow
LIGHT: High
MOISTURE: Dry between waterings

SOIL: Cactus mix
FEATURES: Blue-white leaves with sharp spines
USES: Architectural accent
FLOWERS: ☐

SITING: Provide the brightest, most direct sun possible. Agaves do well in any common indoor temperature or humidity, although they benefit from a 10-degree temperature drop at night. Be sure to locate plants away from traffic. The sharp spines can injure animals and people.
CARE: Allow the soil to dry out substantially between waterings. Water only once a month in winter while the plant is resting. Overwatering rots the roots. Root rot is indicated by a sour smell, and the plant eventually will fall over. Feed once every 3–4 months during active

Place agaves out of traffic areas because they have very sharp spines on each leaf that can inflict injury.

growth with a general plant food. Repot only when the bottom leaves make it difficult to reach the soil with a watering spout. A small pot restricts the plant's size. Agaves can reach up to 6' tall if not pot-bound. Remove damaged leaves and give the plant a shower occasionally to remove dust.
PROPAGATION: If your plant blooms indoors, which can take up to 10 years, quickly start new plants from the offsets; as soon as the flower spike fades, the parent plant dies. Simply cut away the offsets, including a few roots, and pot them.
PESTS AND DISEASES: Agaves have few pests or diseases.
RELATED SPECIES: The cultivar 'Marginata' has a yellow leaf margin. 'Mediopicta' has a yellow center stripe. Threadleaf agave (*A. filifera*) has broad leaves with white margins and threads peeling off them. Little princess agave (*A. parviflora*) has the same leaves as *A. filifera,* only in miniature.

QUEEN VICTORIA CENTURY PLANT

Agave victoria-reginae *uh-GAH-vee vick-TOR-ee-uh reh-GEEN-aye*

Queen Victoria century plant has elegant, striking foliage for an extraordinary flair. It is also known as painted century plant.

SIZE: 6"h × 12"w
TYPE: Succulent
FORM: Upright rosette
TEXTURE: Coarse
GROWTH: Slow
LIGHT: High

MOISTURE: Dry between waterings
SOIL: Cactus mix
FEATURES: Triangular leaves edged in white
USES: Focal point

SITING: Provide the brightest, most direct sun possible. These are perfect plants for a sunny, Southwestern-style decor. Agaves do well in any common indoor temperature or humidity, although they benefit from a 10-degree temperature drop at night.
CARE: Allow the soil to dry out substantially between waterings, and water only once a month in winter while the plant is resting. Feed every 3–4 months during active growth with a general plant food. Feeding more often will cause the plant to outgrow its pot and may contribute to root rot. Repot only when the bottom leaves make it hard to reach the soil with a watering spout. A small pot restricts the plant's size, keeps the plant looking its best, and prevents it from rotting. As it gets bigger, it loses the attractive attributes for which it is grown. Keeping the plant pot-bound also makes it produce offsets. Remove damaged leaves and shower off the plant occasionally to remove dust.
PROPAGATION: If your plant blooms indoors, which can take many years, quickly start new plants from the offsets; as soon as the flower spike fades, the parent plant dies. Simply cut away the offsets, including a few roots, and pot them. Agaves can also be started from seed (available from suppliers), and the plants take a long time to mature.
PESTS AND DISEASES: Agaves have few pests or diseases.
RELATED SPECIES: *A. victoria-reginae variegata* is a spectacular cultivar with delicately dipped edges of cream.

CHINESE EVERGREEN
Aglaonema commutatum *ag-lay-oh-NEE-ma kom-yew-TAH-tum*

Chinese evergreen is a carefree charming foliage plant that is especially nice in low light areas.

SIZE: 3'h × 2'w
TYPE: Herbaceous
FORM: Vase-shaped
TEXTURE: Medium
GROWTH: Medium to fast
LIGHT: Low to medium

MOISTURE: Dry between waterings
SOIL: Potting soil
FEATURES: Lance-shape, variegated leaves
USES: Low light
FLOWERS: □

SITING: Chinese evergreen is best suited to medium light to show off its leaf variegations, but the plant also performs well in low light. Provide average temperature (60–75°F) and high humidity.

Leaf tips may brown if the humidity is too low. These plants do not tolerate drying winds or cold drafts, so put them in a spot that is sheltered from doors, windows, and heat registers.

CARE: Allow the soil to dry slightly between waterings. Avoid letting the plant stand in water or it will rot. If growing in low light, feed only a couple of times a year with a general plant food. In higher light, feed three times in summer and not at all in winter. In higher light, repot every 3 years or so. Shower the plants

1 Rejuvenate Chinese evergreen by division.

2 Cut the root ball in half and pot up the two divisions.

occasionally to keep the glossy leaves clean. Remove spent flowers and damaged or faded leaves.

PROPAGATION: Propagate by dividing the root ball, by removing basal shoots when the plant is young, or by taking stem cuttings anytime. Stem and tip cuttings can be rooted in water, but they get a faster, sturdier start if rooted directly in potting soil. As plants mature and form woody stems, they can also be air layered.

PESTS AND DISEASES: Control mealybugs and spider mites with horticultural oil.

RELATED SPECIES: Cultivars with differing leaf variegation include 'Silver Queen', which is probably the most well known with its beautiful silvery striping and flecking, 'Emerald Beauty', with its dark green leaves splashed with chartreuse patches, and 'Silver King', with almost completely white leaves and green flecks. *A. crispum*, *A. modestum*, and *A. costatum* are close cousins to Chinese evergreen but are not as readily available.

AFRICAN MASK
Alocasia ×*amazonica* *al-oh-CAY-see-uh am-uh-ZONE-ih-cuh*

African mask will bring comments of awe with its rich tropical appearance. It is also known as elephant ear.

SIZE: 2'h × 3'w
TYPE: Herbaceous
FORM: Shrubby
TEXTURE: Coarse
GROWTH: Fast
LIGHT: Medium
MOISTURE: Moist

SOIL: Potting soil
FEATURES: Variegated dark green and white leaves
USES: Focal point, texture

SITING: African mask looks best when given bright to medium light in winter and indirect, medium light in summer. It should not receive direct sun at any time. It thrives in average home temperatures of 60–75°F but requires

high humidity (above 65 percent). A pebble tray is effective in raising the humidity around the plant. If the plant is chilled or dries out, it immediately drops its leaves and goes dormant. If you correct the problem, it will send out new leaves.

CARE: Keep the soil moist at all times during the active growing season; allow it to dry somewhat in winter. The top 2" of soil should dry out before watering again. Feed once a month during the growing

The substantial velvety leaves of African mask are quite unlike any other houseplant.

season with standard foliage plant food; do not feed in winter. Repot annually; divide at this time if needed. Wipe the velvety dark green leaves occasionally to clear them of dust and keep them looking pristine.

PROPAGATION: Propagate by carefully dividing the root ball, making sure to have several pieces of the fleshy rhizome on each division. You can also propagate by removing suckers from the sides of the shoot with roots attached, or by lifting the plant from the pot, removing a rhizome, and cutting it into pieces for rooting.

PESTS AND DISEASES: African mask is generally pest free, but you may see spider mites and scale on plants that are stressed. Treat infestations with horticultural oil.

RELATED SPECIES: The cultivar 'Polly' has bright silvery-white veins on almost black leaves with purple undersides, and 'Hilo Beauty' has ivory mottling on bright green leaves. Dwarf elephant ear (*A. corozon*) has pewtery leaves with a waxy surface. Hooded dwarf elephant plant (*A. cucullata*) has heart-shaped dark green leaves with a twisted tip and upturned margins.

MEDICINE PLANT
Aloe vera (barbadensis) AH-low VEH-rah (bar-bub-DEN-sis)

The sap from medicine plant leaves has long been used to soothe burns and insect bites. It is also called burn plant or aloe.

SIZE: 3'h × 3'w
TYPE: Succulent
FORM: Vase-shaped
TEXTURE: Medium
GROWTH: Fast
LIGHT: High
MOISTURE: Dry between waterings

SOIL: Cactus mix
FEATURES: Spiky leaves with white marks
USES: Dish garden, Southwestern theme
FLOWERS: ☐

SITING: Provide aloe with bright light. In lower light it becomes leggy. A bright kitchen window where the soothing sap in its leaves is handy for burns is perfect. Aloe thrives in average to hot temperatures (60–85°F) and low humidity (below 30 percent).

CARE: Allow the soil to dry out fairly well between waterings, then thoroughly soak. Make sure the pot drains well; the plant will quickly rot if it sits in water. Repot only if the plant becomes top-heavy. It performs best in a terra-cotta pot, which allows the soil to dry out easily. Feed three times in summer with a foliage formula. Remove damaged leaves.

PROPAGATION: Divide when the plant has a substantial root system or separate the offsets that form around the base.
PESTS AND DISEASES: Treat the occasional mealybug infestation with horticultural oil.
RELATED SPECIES: Tree aloe (*A. arborescens*) has a stalk and bears its leaves at the top. *A. zanzibarica* has stubby, thick leaves and remains small. Spider aloe (*A. humilis*) looks like a spider with incurved blue-green leaves.

1 Aloe plants produce small plantlets at the base that can be easily separated from the mother plant.

2 Once potted into well-drained potting mix, small plants will grow quickly into sturdy plants.

LACE-FLOWER VINE
Alsobia dianthiflora al-SO-bee-a dye-an-thi-FLOR-a

Lace-flower vine makes a handsome display as a ground cover beneath a larger plant.

SIZE: 6"h × 12"w
TYPE: Gesneriad
FORM: Semitrailing
TEXTURE: Fine
GROWTH: Fast
LIGHT: High, indirect
MOISTURE: Evenly moist

SOIL: African violet mix
FEATURES: Dark green leaves, drooping stems
USES: Hanging basket, floral display
FLOWERS: ☐

SITING: Lace-flower vine shows the best color on its velvety leaves in bright, indirect light. The graceful hanging stems will be covered with lacy-edge flowers in optimum growing conditions. Provide average temperatures (60–75°F) but avoid cold drafts. *Alsobia* needs medium to high humidity (30–65 percent).

CARE: Keep the soil evenly moist but not soggy. Feed with African violet food at half strength at every watering. Once a month, water with clear water to flush out salt buildup. Like other gesneriads, *Alsobia* blooms best when pot-bound, so repotting is seldom necessary. Prune back the long stems occasionally to keep the plant fresh; if training on a topiary frame, simply tuck the stems in around the frame.

PROPAGATION: Propagate by dividing the crown when the plant is mature or taking stem cuttings, which are easy and fast rooting.
PESTS AND DISEASES: Spot-treat mealybugs with horticultural oil. Avoid spraying the entire plant with oil; it will cause severe leaf spotting.
RELATED SPECIES: The cultivar 'Cygnet' has larger flowers and is more floriferous than the species. 'San Miguel' has large blooms with maroon dots. 'Costa Rica' has scalloped leaves.

The fringed edges of its white flowers with purple spots give lace-flower vine its common name.

Lace-flower vine has tiny leaves and wiry stems that are easily trained and pruned into a topiary.

FLAMINGO FLOWER

Anthurium andraeanum an–THUR–ee–um an–dree–AN–um

Flamingo flower makes a room feel like a tropical paradise with its striking foliage and bold flowers.

SIZE: 3'h x 2'w
TYPE: Herbaceous, blooming
FORM: Rounded
TEXTURE: Medium
GROWTH: Medium
LIGHT: Low to medium
MOISTURE: Dry between waterings

SOIL: Half average, half epiphyte mix
FEATURES: Heart-shape leaves on slender petioles
USES: Focal point, blooming plant
FLOWERS: ■▨☐

SITING: Provide low to medium light and no direct sun to keep the striking, long-lasting flowers coming. Anthurium does well in average to high temperatures (60–80°F) and high humidity (up to 65 percent). If stressed by low humidity, it stops blooming. If given the right conditions, the plant will produce enough flowers for cutting.

CARE: Allow the soil to dry out only slightly between waterings. Feed every other month with blooming plant food; repot only when stems crowd the pot and watering is difficult. Pinch out faded leaves and flowers. Staking is generally not necessary, although you may need to support the flowers on some large cultivars. Thin bamboo skewers are excellent for this. Simply insert the skewer into the soil and gently tie the flower stem to it with soft thread.

PROPAGATION: Divide the root ball or separate side shoots when they form roots. Growing from seed is difficult.

PESTS AND DISEASES: Spider mites can be a problem. Give the plant an occasional shower to keep spider mites from developing high populations. Use insecticidal soap, horticultural oil, or a miticide if necessary. You may see physical damage to leaves and flowers if the plant is placed in a high-traffic area. Flamingo flower is not an easy plant to keep in the average home, so be prepared to give it extra care.

RELATED SPECIES: Pigtail flower (*A. scherzerianum*) has large, leathery leaves, a curved spadix, and large, bright red flowers.

Anthurium flowers may be red or pink. They are sometimes known as tail flower.

Remove faded blossoms regularly to keep flamingo flower in constant bloom and looking its best.

Flamingo flower blossoms are long-lasting and thus make superb cut flowers.

CRYSTAL ANTHURIUM

Anthurium crystallinum an–THUR–ee–um cris-tahl-INE-um

Crystal anthurium makes a shining statement with its velvety green foliage striped in silver.

SIZE: 3'h x 2'w
TYPE: Herbaceous, blooming
FORM: Rounded
TEXTURE: Medium
GROWTH: Medium
LIGHT: High
MOISTURE: Moist

SOIL: Half average, half epiphyte mix
FEATURES: Vertical deep green leaves with silver marks
USES: Foliage, focal point
FLOWERS: ☐

SITING: Crystal anthurium needs bright, indirect light. Full sun will fade and eventually kill the bronze-purple leaves, which turn velvety deep green with silver markings. Provide warm temperatures (above 60°F) to keep this plant healthy and attractive. Cold drafts will harm the leaves. Humidity above 65 percent is a must. Provide it by grouping plants, setting pots on pebble trays, or using the pot-in-pot method. It would help to use more than one method. Yellowing leaves that eventually drop are indicators of dry soil and humidity that is too low.

CARE: Keep the soil moist but not soaking wet. Drying out at any time may mean loss of leaves. Feed monthly with a general foliage food. Repot only when the plant becomes leggy. Place the root ball high in the pot; as the plant grows, it will develop new roots above the soil line. Pack sphagnum moss around the plant;

the new roots will penetrate it. Once new roots have formed in the sphagnum moss, cut off the plant below the new roots and repot it. Wipe the leaves gently once a month to keep clean and reduce spider mite populations.

PROPAGATION: Propagate by dividing the root ball in spring or by growing from seed.

PESTS AND DISEASES: Watch the leaves for mites, scale, and mealybugs. Give the plant an occasional shower to keep spider mites at bay. Use horticultural oil to manage outbreaks of scale or mealybugs.

RELATED SPECIES: Queen anthurium (*A. warocqueanum*) has large, tapered dark leaves with blond veins, and king anthurium (*A. veitscheii*) has puckered emerald green leaves.

ZEBRA PLANT

Aphelandra squarrosa a-fub-LAN-dra square-OH-sa

A warm humid room is the perfect place to display the striking zebra plant.

SIZE: 3'h × 2'w
TYPE: Herbaceous
FORM: Upright stems, horizontal leaves
TEXTURE: Medium to coarse
GROWTH: Medium
LIGHT: High to medium

MOISTURE: Evenly moist
SOIL: Potting soil
FEATURES: Large dark leaves with silver veins
USES: Focal point, blooming
FLOWERS: ■

SITING: Zebra plant grows best in medium light; it tolerates low light but won't bloom. Give the plant direct sun in winter. Constant warmth is necessary to keep the leaves looking their best; any exposure to cold will cause the plant to drop its leaves. High humidity (65 percent or more) is essential.

CARE: Keep the soil moist but not soggy. Reduce the watering during winter dormancy. The leaves will likely drop from dry soil, so cut the plant back hard to rejuvenate it for spring growth. Feed three times in summer or at half the rate at each watering during its active growth period. Zebra plant seldom needs repotting and blossoms best when pot-bound. Remove the flower spike after the plant blooms to force it to develop side shoots.

PROPAGATION: Remove side shoots complete with roots and pot them up. Stem cuttings are also successful.

PESTS AND DISEASES: Few pests bother zebra plant.

RELATED SPECIES: 'Dania' has silvery veins and yellow-orange flowers and is more compact than the species. *A. squarrosa louisae* has creamy white veins and red-tip bracts. *A. aurantica* has orange-scarlet blooms and gray-veined leaves.

The unique blossom of zebra plant emerges from the leaves like a glowing flame.

Even a very brief exposure to cold will cause a zebra plant to quickly drop its leaves.

RATTAIL CACTUS

Aporocactus flagelliformis a-POUR-o-cac-tuss fla-jel-li-FOUR-miss

Rattail cactus is a unique hanging cactus with magnificent blossoms, just right in a hanging basket.

SIZE: 6' long × 1'w
TYPE: Cactus
FORM: Trailing
TEXTURE: Medium
GROWTH: Fast
LIGHT: High
MOISTURE: Dry between waterings

SOIL: Cactus mix
FEATURES: Long stems covered with spines
USES: Hanging basket, focal point
FLOWERS: ■

SITING: Full sun will make rattail cactus produce exquisite 3" fuschia-pink blossoms along the 6' stems in spring. The flowers will last up to 2 months. Rattail cactus needs 60–80°F in summer and 55°F in winter. If given the same temperatures year-round, it will not flower. Low humidity prevents stem scarring and leaf spots.

CARE: Keep soil well watered in summer but allow it to dry slightly between waterings. Provide little water in winter. Feed only once in spring. This plant seldom needs repotting. Clip out any browning stems to keep the plant looking pristine.

PROPAGATION: Propagate by stem cuttings. The long stems will form roots along the entire length, so small pieces are all that are needed for a cutting. Allow the cuttings to dry a few days to form a callus before potting them.

PESTS AND DISEASES: Watch for mites and mealybugs. Wash mites off the plant with a forceful spray of water. Swab rubbing alcohol on mealybugs to control them.

RELATED SPECIES: *A. martianus* has thicker stems and larger flowers than rattail cactus. *A. flagriformis* has fewer spines, more slender stems, and carmine-pink flowers.

The growing tips of rattail cactus have an attractive pink cast to them.

Remove shriveled brown shoots regularly to keep the rattail cactus looking its best.

NORFOLK ISLAND PINE

Araucaria heterophylla *ar-aw-CARE-ee-uh het-er-oh-PHIL-luh*

Norfolk Island pine lends stature and an architectural statement to any room.

SIZE: 5'h x 4'w
TYPE: Woody, evergreen
FORM: Upright, pyramidal
TEXTURE: Fine
GROWTH: Slow
LIGHT: Medium to high

MOISTURE: Moist in summer, dry in winter
SOIL: Average
FEATURES: Bright green needles, drooping branches
USES: Architectural accent

SITING: Provide indirect, bright light to keep this tree, with its gracefully drooping branches, healthy. It tolerates temperatures of 50–80°F in summer but should be kept around 55°F in winter. It needs average to high humidity (50–75 percent) and often suffers in dry, warm homes. Low humidity causes branch loss and tip browning.
CARE: Keep the soil evenly moist in summer; allow it to dry between waterings in winter. Feed only once a year to restrict growth; use a food for acid-loving plants. Lower branches periodically die; remove them with a clean cut. Turn the plant frequently to keep it symmetrical. Move outdoors to a protected spot in summer.

PROPAGATION: This plant requires greenhouse conditions to propagate successfully. Try air-layering the top if the plant becomes too spindly.
PESTS AND DISEASES: Pests include spider mites and mealybugs. Use rubbing alcohol or horticultural oil to control mealybugs, and insecticidal soap or horticultural oil for spider mite outbreaks.
RELATED SPECIES: New Caledonian pine (*A. columnaris*) is similar in appearance but seldom available as a houseplant.

When using as a Christmas tree, use only lightweight ornaments and avoid Christmas lights that can injure the plant.

Because Norfolk Island pines naturally lose their lower branches, group small plants at the base for an attractive display.

CORALBERRY

Ardisia crenata (A. crispa) *ar-DEE-zee-uh kreh-NAY-tuh (KRISP-uh)*

Coralberry thrives in a cool spot and will produce attractive blossoms and fruit almost year-round.

SIZE: 24"h x 18"w
TYPE: Woody shrub
FORM: Single stem, rounded crown
TEXTURE: Medium
GROWTH: Slow
LIGHT: High, indirect
MOISTURE: Evenly moist, dry in winter

SOIL: Potting soil
FEATURES: Glossy green leaves, bright red berries
USES: Focal point, holiday decor
FLOWERS: ☐

SITING: Provide bright, indirect light year-round to keep the plant producing glossy red berries. They remain for several months. Ripe and green berries often occur simultaneously, making a more attractive display. The plant performs well in cool to average temperatures (55–70°F) and requires high humidity (above 65 percent).
CARE: Keep the soil moist but not soggy. Allow to dry out between waterings in winter. Feed with a blooming plant food three times in summer. Repot only when the roots fill the container. Lightly prune back after the berries drop and put it outside for the summer. This will cause the plant to produce berries for the following winter holiday season.
PROPAGATION: Propagate by semihardwood stem cuttings in summer or by seed when the berries shrivel.
PESTS AND DISEASES: Spider mites can be a problem if the plant is grown in low humidity. Treat the plant with a forceful water spray to dislodge them, or use insecticidal soap, horticultural oil, or a commercial miticide to control large populations of mites.
RELATED SPECIES: Japanese marlberry (*A. japonica*) is smaller and has leathery leaves. Some cultivars develop yellow to cream markings on the foliage.

Coralberry fruits make a striking display, especially because there are often green and red fruits on the plant at the same time.

ASPARAGUS FERN

Asparagus densiflorus uh-SPARE-uh-guss den-sih-FLOR-us

Asparagus fern, also known as Sprengeri fern, is a longtime favorite for hanging baskets and as a foil for other blooming plants.

SIZE: 1'h × 2'w
TYPE: Herbaceous
FORM: Arching, mounding
TEXTURE: Fine
GROWTH: Medium
LIGHT: High to medium

MOISTURE: Moist in summer, dry in winter
SOIL: Potting soil
FEATURES: Needlelike leaves on arching stems
USES: Hanging basket, filler
FLOWERS: ☐

SITING: Asparagus fern thrives in bright to medium light and tolerates lower light, although it will be less full. Provide average temperatures (60–75°F) and average humidity (30–65 percent).
CARE: Keep evenly moist in summer; allow the soil to dry slightly during the winter. Feed with a dilute solution of foliage plant food every time the plant is watered. Repot annually; otherwise, the thick tuberous roots will push out of the soil and break the pot. It is time to repot when the plant must be watered daily. Prune only when needed for aesthetics; be mindful of small thorns at the leaf nodes. Too much sun or dry soil will yellow the foliage, and the plant may drop its leaves when the light is too low. This is common when plants come in from a summer outdoors. Plants often receive enough light outdoors to produce small red berries. Be aware when bringing in the plants that these berries may drop and are poisonous to animals and children.

PROPAGATION: Propagate by seed if your plant produces fruits. Otherwise, divide the root ball. Slip the plant from its pot and use a sharp knife to cut the root ball into two or more pieces. It may be necessary to remove some of the potatolike tubers to fit the plants into new pots. This will not harm the plant.
PESTS AND DISEASES: Asparagus fern often has spider mites when the humidity is low; aphids may be attracted to the shoots, which resemble asparagus, as they emerge from the soil.
RELATED SPECIES: The foxtail fern *A.d.* 'Meyersii' has compact, upright fronds that resemble cattails.

1 Asparagus fern fills its pot quickly with fleshy roots and will need division every year.

2 Slip the plant out of its pot and slice cleanly through the root ball with a sharp knife.

3 Repot the pieces in clean potting soil, making sure they are at the same soil level as before.

PLUMOSE FERN

Asparagus setaceus (plumosus) uh-SPARE-uh-guss seh-TAY-see-us (ploo-MOH-sus)

Plumose ferns are also known as emerald feather and lace fern. They give an airy feel to terrariums and tabletop groupings.

SIZE: 3'h × 1'w
TYPE: Herbaceous
FORM: Upright, horizontal fronds
TEXTURE: Extremely fine
GROWTH: Medium
LIGHT: High

MOISTURE: Moist
SOIL: Average
FEATURES: Spreading branches, fernlike leaves
USES: Terrarium, foliage
FLOWERS: ☐

SITING: Provide bright, indirect light to keep the plant full. Average temperatures (60–75°F) and average humidity (30–60 percent) will keep the plant producing healthy fronds, which make beautiful additions to cut bouquets. As a young plant, it works well in a hanging basket. The ferny foliage is held at right angles to the upright stems but arches gracefully out of a pot. With age, the plant becomes more erect, with nearly a climbing growth habit. The long fronds may be trained up a trellis, or you can trim them back to keep the plant more compact. At intermediate stages, the foliage of layered needles resembles an aged pine tree, providing an appearance of bonsai.
CARE: Plumose fern will drop its leaves if it dries out. Feed with a dilute solution of foliage plant food every time the plant is watered. Repot only when roots fill the pot. This plant can become spindly with age, so prune old stems to allow new growth to appear. Plants can be cut back completely to the soil and will resprout with vigorous new growth.
PROPAGATION: Propagate by dividing the root ball into several pieces, or by seed if your plant produces blue-black berries. This usually happens only when the plant is taken outdoors for the summer.
PESTS AND DISEASES: Watch for spider mites in low humidity. Keep them at bay by giving the plant an occasional shower of water.
RELATED SPECIES: The cultivar 'Nanus' is 3–6" tall. 'Pyramidalis' is up to 2' tall with erect instead of horizontal fronds. Asparagus fern (*A. densiflorus*) is a coarser plant but requires similar care. 'Sprengeri' is the most widely available cultivar. Foxtail fern (*A. d.* 'Meyersii') has compact, cattail-like fronds that are upright.

CAST-IRON PLANT
Aspidistra elatior *as-pih-DIS-tra ee-LAY-tee-or*

Cast-iron or barroom plant is aptly named because it tolerates any light conditions as well as the occasional missed watering.

SIZE: 2'h × 2'w
TYPE: Herbaceous
FORM: Upright, vase-shaped
TEXTURE: Medium
GROWTH: Slow
LIGHT: Low to medium

MOISTURE: Dry between waterings
SOIL: Average
FEATURES: Lance-shape, dark green leaves
USES: Very low light

SITING: Cast-iron plant is best situated in medium light; direct sun causes the leaves to fade. This plant does well in all house temperatures and amounts of humidity, making it one of the most tolerant houseplants. It grows and looks good in very low light, and its attractive dark green leaves are striking in any situation.

CARE: Allow the soil to dry somewhat between waterings. Cast-iron plant is tolerant of the occasional missed watering, but it will not tolerate overwatering. Feed every 3–4 months when growing in low light with half-strength plant food for foliage plants. If growing in higher light, feed monthly with a full-strength solution. Repot only every couple of years, when the plant begins to push out of its container. Wash the leaves occasionally to remove dust.

PROPAGATION: Divide the root ball every couple of years if needed, or simply pull a leaf with a crown portion attached off the root ball and pot it up.

PESTS AND DISEASES: Control spider mites with horticultural oil. The plant also gets fungal leaf spots. Prune out damaged leaves and cut back on watering.

RELATED SPECIES: 'Milky Way' has white spots; 'Variegata' has yellow stripes. *A. caespitosa, A. linearifolia, A. longiloba, A. lurida,* and *A. saxicola* are available as outdoor plants for southern climates.

1 Black plastic nursery pots are usually unattractive in a display, so use your imagination to find an attractive container.

2 Remove the plant from its pot, settle it into the decorative container, and fill in around the edges with clean potting soil.

3 Water the plant in well after potting to settle out any air pockets in the soil and give the roots a boost.

BIRD'S NEST FERN
Asplenium nidus *as-PLEE-nee-um NYE-duss*

Bird's nest fern unfurls its unique wavy light green fronds toward the ceiling as if presenting them to the viewer.

SIZE: 15"h × 12"w
TYPE: Fern
FORM: Upright, vase-shaped
TEXTURE: Medium
GROWTH: Slow
LIGHT: Medium to high

MOISTURE: Moist
SOIL: Epiphyte mix or potting soil
FEATURES: Wavy, glossy green fronds
USES: Foliage, focal point

SITING: Bright to medium, indirect light is best for bird's nest fern. In high light the glossy fronds bleach out. Provide average to warm temperatures (60–80°F) with no drafts. High humidity (65 percent or more) is essential. This is an excellent plant for use in a terrarium or a tropical grouping.

CARE: Keep the soil moist at all times. Water somewhat less in winter but don't

Bird's nest fern must have a well-drained potting mix and seldom needs repotting because of a very small root system.

allow it to dry out. Keep moisture out of the cup that is formed by the fronds—the "bird's nest." Feed only twice a year, once in spring and once in summer, with a foliage plant food. It seldom needs repotting because it has a minuscule root system; it can even be grown on a slab as long as you provide extremely high humidity. Remove older leaves as they fade. The most common leaf problems are frond-tip dieback, from lack of humidity; frond death, from the potting mix drying out; and severely curled leaf tips, from being too cold.

PROPAGATION: Propagate by dividing the root ball or by starting from spores.

PESTS AND DISEASES: Bird's nest fern can have fungal leaf spots, scale, aphids, and mealybugs. Learn what the fern spores look like (they will be in regular lines) to distinguish them from scales (irregularly scattered).

RELATED SPECIES: The cultivar 'Fimbriatum' has notched leaves. *A. crispifolium* is similar to *A. nidus* except it has crinkled edges on its fronds.

BISHOP'S CAP CACTUS
Astrophytum spp. *a-stro-PHY-tum*

Bishop's cap or bishop's hat cactus get their names from their unique shapes, quite unlike any other cactus or houseplant.

SIZE: 24–48"h × 6"w
TYPE: Cactus
FORM: Ball-shape
TEXTURE: Medium to coarse
GROWTH: Slow
LIGHT: High

MOISTURE: Dry
SOIL: Cactus mix
FEATURES: Spiraling ribs, grooves
USES: Dish garden, focal point
FLOWERS: ☐

SITING: Being a true cactus, *Astrophytum* needs full sun to keep its striking, unique look. Keep the plants warm (65–85°F) when in active growth; allow them cooler temperatures (55–60°F) during the winter dormant period. Low humidity (20–30 percent) keeps them looking their best.

CARE: Let the soil dry out considerably between waterings. Overwatering causes root rot. Feed with half-strength plant food only after flower buds form. A small root system makes repotting seldom necessary.

PROPAGATION: Propagate by seed, or graft to speed growth.

Monk's hood, another type of *Astrophytum*, is covered with spines and may be adorned with delicate yellow flowers.

PESTS AND DISEASES: Mealybugs and scale can mimic the plant's natural flecks and spots. Examine plants closely for presence of these insect pests.

RELATED SPECIES: Available species include sea urchin cactus (*A. asterias*), monk's hood (*A. ornatum*), and bishop's cap (*A. myriostigma*).

The true Bishop's cap looks quite like a mitre and may also be topped with soft golden flowers.

JAPANESE AUCUBA
Aucuba japonica *AW-cube-a juh-PAN-nih-kuh*

Japanese aucuba lends itself to most any conditions and provides deep green foliage, often with yellow flecks.

SIZE: 4'h × 4'w
TYPE: Woody shrub
FORM: Rounded
TEXTURE: Medium
GROWTH: Fast
LIGHT: Medium to low

MOISTURE: Moist to dry
SOIL: Potting soil
FEATURES: Small green leaves, may be spotted with yellow
USES: Foliage

SITING: Medium light is best for Japanese aucuba, although it tolerates high and low light. Avoid full sun in summer; it will bleach the leaves. This plant tolerates cool temperatures (to 50°F), although it does best in medium temperatures (60–75°F). Provide high humidity (65 percent or higher) to keep the plant looking its best.

CARE: Keep moist at all times in high light; let it dry out between waterings in medium and low light. Feed three times in summer only, or it will quickly outgrow its pot. Repot annually to keep up with growth. Pruning keeps it within bounds and looking shrubby and full. It can be pruned into a hedge shape as an attractive backdrop to focal-point houseplants. Put it outdoors for the summer. In ideal conditions, cultivars that have a male shoot grafted onto a female plant will produce attractive red berries.

PROPAGATION: Propagate by semihardwood stem cuttings taken in late summer.

PESTS AND DISEASES: Mealybugs and spider mites may be pests in dry situations.

RELATED SPECIES: The cultivar 'Variegata' has gold flecks, 'Crotonifolia' has gold and white variegation, and 'Rozannie' is self-fruitful. *A. chinensis* has narrower leaves but is the same in all other aspects. *A. japonica* f. *longifolia* leaves are much longer than wide.

Japanese aucuba will reach four feet high and wide but can be easily pruned to keep it smaller. It can even be pruned in a hedge shape.

PONYTAIL PALM
Beaucarnea recurvata (Nolina) *boh-CAR-nee-uh ree-cur-VAH-tuh (no-LEE-nuh)*

Ponytail palms are also known as bottle palm and elephant foot. They are carefree plants that provide elegant architectural drama to any room.

SIZE: 3'h × 2'w
TYPE: Succulent
FORM: Treelike
TEXTURE: Medium
GROWTH: Medium
LIGHT: High to low
MOISTURE: Dry between waterings

SOIL: Half average, half cactus mix
FEATURES: Curved leaves, large-footed base
USES: Architectural accent
FLOWERS: □

SITING: Bright light with some direct sun keeps this plant looking its best, although it tolerates medium and even low light. Ponytail palm performs best in average to high temperatures (60–80°F) when it is actively growing, and cool temperatures (50–55°F) when in winter dormancy. Low humidity keeps the plant healthy.

CARE: Ponytail palm generally needs dry conditions because it is susceptible to root rots. It stores water in its large base; water the potting mix thoroughly, then let it dry between waterings. You may need to water only once a month. Hold back water in winter; if in doubt, don't water. You have overwatered if the new growth is a light color. Underwatering is indicated by shriveling of the stem. Feed only once a year, in spring, with general foliage plant food. Ponytail palm rarely needs repotting. Wash the leaves occasionally and remove dead leaves. The plant will naturally shed its long, curly, straplike leaves as it grows.

PROPAGATION: Ponytail palm is usually propagated commercially by seed. Because the plants rarely flower in the home, you will have to rely on purchasing new plants rather than trying to grow your own.

PESTS AND DISEASES: Overwatering causes stem rots and bacterial soft rot. Control mealybugs, spider mites, and scale with horticultural oil.

RELATED SPECIES: Oaxacan ponytail palm (*B. longifolia*) has straplike leaves up to 7' long.

The "foot" of the Ponytail palm is a water-storage organ, indicating that the plant needs infrequent watering.

ANGEL WING BEGONIA
Begonia coccinea *beh-GON-yuh cahk-SIN-ee-uh*

Angle wing begonias have graceful wing-shaped speckled and spotted leaves on long canes.

SIZE: 3'h × 4'w
TYPE: Herbaceous
FORM: Upright
TEXTURE: Medium to coarse
GROWTH: Fast
LIGHT: High, indirect
MOISTURE: Moist

SOIL: Average
FEATURES: Elongated leaves, long canes
USES: Foliage, blooming
FLOWERS: ■ ▨

SITING: Bright, indirect light provides the most attractive plants, although they tolerate medium light as well. Provide average to warm temperatures (60–80°F) and high humidity.

CARE: If growing angel wing begonia in high light, keep the soil somewhat moist. In medium light, allow it to dry slightly between waterings. Feed the plant monthly with a foliage plant food when active, then every 2 months when resting. This begonia can be repotted every spring, but because it declines quickly, you will have more attractive plants if you start new ones annually. The canes on angel wing begonia will get large quickly and can outgrow the pot. Clip out any leaves that show tattering or browning. Trim faded flowers and flower stems. Prune back long canes to the base to encourage new growth from the bottom of the plant.

PROPAGATION: Propagate by tip, stem, or leaf cuttings or by seed. Leaf cuttings are particularly successful.

PESTS AND DISEASES: Angel wing begonia can have leaf spots, root and stem rots, and powdery mildew if grown in stressful conditions.

RELATED SPECIES: *B. ×corallina* 'Lucerna' has silver-dotted leaves with salmon-rose flowers; *B. radicans* is a trailing variety with red flowers.

1 Cut a stem tip about 3–5" long and remove all but one or a partial leaf.

2 Dip the stem in rooting hormone, and insert it into the potting soil mix.

3 Cover the cuttings with a plastic bag to keep the humidity high.

IRON CROSS BEGONIA
Begonia masoniana beb-GON-yuh may-soh-nee-AH-nuh

Iron cross begonias are unique with their crinkled leaves and distinct black to brown markings.

SIZE: 18"h × 12"w
TYPE: Herbaceous
FORM: Mounded
TEXTURE: Medium
GROWTH: Medium
LIGHT: High to medium
MOISTURE: Dry between waterings

SOIL: Potting soil
FEATURES: Black pattern on hairy leaves
USES: Hanging basket, blooming
FLOWERS: ☐ ▦

SITING: Iron cross begonia keeps its attractive color best in bright, indirect light. It tolerates medium light and benefits from some direct sun in winter. Average temperatures (60–75°F) are fine, but avoid windows where it might become chilled. It requires high humidity. A pebble tray works well.

CARE: If growing iron cross begonia in high light, keep the soil somewhat moist. In medium light, allow it to dry slightly between waterings. Feed monthly with a foliage plant food when active, then every 2 months when resting. This begonia can be repotted every spring (pot-bound plants lose their leaf color), but because begonias notoriously decline quickly, you will have more attractive plants if you start new ones annually. Clip out any leaves that show tattering or browning. Iron cross begonia may randomly go dormant and shed its leaves, but the surface rhizomes will soon produce new ones.

PROPAGATION: Propagate by dividing the rhizomes or taking leaf cuttings.

PESTS AND DISEASES: These plants may occasionally have mealybugs, but a more prominent problem is powdery mildew. To avoid, keep leaves dry. A plant with mildew can be treated, but you might have better luck starting a new plant from shoots or leaves without any mildew.

RELATED SPECIES: There are hundreds of begonia species available, with all shapes of leaves and sizes and colors of flowers.

Iron cross begonias can be easily propagated by dividing the creeping rhizomes that meander across the soil.

REX BEGONIA
Begonia Rex Cultorum hybrids beb-GON-yuh

Rex begonias are fairly easy to grow and come in a phenomenal variety of leaf colors. It is also known as painted leaf begonia.

SIZE: 1'h × 2'w
TYPE: Herbaceous
FORM: Mounding
TEXTURE: Medium
GROWTH: Medium
LIGHT: Medium to indirect

MOISTURE: Moist
SOIL: Potting soil
FEATURES: Variegated leaves
USES: Foliage
FLOWERS: ☐

SITING: Bright light makes the cream, pink, and chartreuse leaf variegations brighter on some varieties; lower light enhances the metallic sheen on others. Provide high humidity and temperatures of 60–80°F.

CARE: If growing rex begonia in high light, keep the soil somewhat moist. In medium light, allow it to dry slightly between waterings. Feed monthly with a foliage plant food when active, then every 2 months when resting. Repot every spring; because begonias decline quickly, you will have more attractive plants if you start new ones annually. Clip any leaves that show tattering or browning. Because the flowers are not attractive and can detract from the foliage display, remove them unless you want the seed.

PROPAGATION: Propagate by tip, stem, or leaf cuttings or by seed. Sprinkle the seeds on top of the soil and press in lightly.

PESTS AND DISEASES: Rex begonia can have numerous problems, including leaf spots, root and stem rots, and powdery mildew, if grown in stressful conditions.

RELATED SPECIES: Rex begonia comes in three basic classes: brilliant leaves, spiral (wavy) leaves, or miniature (less than 8"). Beyond these classifications hundreds of cultivars are available, each with different characteristics.

1 To propagate begonias by leaf cuttings, simply remove a leaf with part of the petiole attached.

2 Lay the leaf on sterile potting soil and pin it to the soil with a hairpin. Make slits across the veins to induce plantlets to form.

LADY OF THE NIGHT ORCHID

Brassavola nodosa *bra-SAH-voh-luh no-DOSE-uh*

The mysterious lady of the night orchid has a magnificent blossom that sends out an intoxicating fragrance at night.

SIZE: 15"h × 6"w
TYPE: Orchid
FORM: Upright
TEXTURE: Medium
GROWTH: Medium
LIGHT: Medium to high

MOISTURE: Moist
SOIL: Orchid, slab
FEATURES: Fragrant flowers
USES: Focal point
FLOWERS: ☐ ▪

SITING: Medium light is best, but this orchid can tolerate higher light if kept moist. This may mean watering every 2–3 days, but the extra care is worth it when you experience the spidery white to pale yellow blossoms with red or purple specks in the throat. *Brassavola* thrives in temperatures of 75–90°F during active growth and 65–75°F during winter rest. If it is cooler than this during rest, reduce watering even more. Provide with 80 percent humidity if possible.

CARE: Keep the soil moist throughout the growing season, watering every few days if needed. *Brassavola* needs at least a 2-week rest period in winter to produce flowers.

Lady of the night orchid is a parent of hybrids such as this hybrid of Brassavola × Laelia 'Richard Mueller' × Brassavola × Cattleya 'Walanae Leopard'.

During this time, allow it to dry out somewhat, and water only once every 2–3 weeks. Feed with a balanced plant food at half-strength weekly while it is actively growing. A plant food with high phosphate (the middle number in the analysis) in fall will improve blooming for the next season. Leach the pot once a month. Do this by watering with plain water until excess water flows out the bottom of the pot. Repot as soon as new growth begins or immediately after flowering. Plants grown on a tree-fern slab should be watered daily.

PROPAGATION: Propagate by seed or dividing the rhizome. Be sure to have at least three healthy pseudobulbs in old and new plants for survival and faster blooming.

PESTS AND DISEASES: Control scale with horticultural oil.

RELATED SPECIES: *B. digbyana (Rhyncholaelia)* has green flowers with ruffled edges. It is used in hybridization.

PEACOCK PLANT

Calathea makoyana *cub-LAY-thee-uh mak-o-YAH-na*

Peacock plants offer a wide array of beautifully variegated foliage with all shades of purples, greens, pinks, and silvers.

SIZE: 12–15"h × 12–15"w
TYPE: Herbaceous
FORM: Mounded
TEXTURE: Medium
GROWTH: Medium
LIGHT: Medium to low

MOISTURE: Moist
SOIL: Potting soil
FEATURES: Variegated foliage
USES: Foliage, architectural accent

SITING: Provide medium to low light, keeping in mind that the beautiful purples and silvers of this plant develop better in medium light. Provide average to warm temperatures (71–85°F) and high humidity (60 percent or more). This is an ideal terrarium plant.

CARE: Keep constantly moist through spring, summer, and fall. In winter the plant usually goes into a resting state and needs much less water. Feed only three times in summer with a foliage plant food. Repot before plants become pot-bound— usually every 2 years. Plant growth slows down as winter approaches. Plants begin to look ragged—a good time to tuck the plant out of the way for a while. Reduce watering. When new sprouts appear, prune old leaves and water the plant well.

PROPAGATION: Propagate by dividing the root ball.

PESTS AND DISEASES: Watch for mealybugs and spider mites.

RELATED SPECIES: *C. warscewiczii* has leaves in many hues of green with purple undersides; *C. vittata* has bright yellow stripes on rich green leaves.

1 Peacock plants will need dividing every 2 years. Lift the rootball out of the pot and cleanly slice it in half.

2 Set the divided plants into pots with clean potting soil, fill with more soil, tamp gently, and water in well.

CATHEDRAL WINDOWS

Calathea picturata cuh-LAY-thee-uh pik-chur-AH-tuh

Cathedral windows gets its name from the beautifully picturesque veining and striping on the leaves that resembles stained glass.

SIZE: 12–15"h × 12–15"w
TYPE: Herbaceous
FORM: Mounded
TEXTURE: Medium
GROWTH: Medium
LIGHT: Medium to low

MOISTURE: Average
SOIL: Moist
FEATURES: Variegated foliage
USES: Foliage, architectural accent

SITING: Cathedral windows may need a little extra care in siting, but the beautiful foliage is worth the effort. Provide medium to low light, keeping in mind that the purples and silvers of the foliage develop better in higher light. Provide average to warm temperatures (71–85°F) and high humidity (60 percent or more). This is an excellent terrarium plant.

CARE: Keep the soil constantly moist through spring, summer, and fall. It needs much less water during the winter. Feed only three times in summer with a foliage plant food. Repot before it becomes so pot-bound that it no longer takes up water—usually every 2 years. The plant begins to look ragged, indicating that it's time to tuck it out of the way for a while. Continue to keep the humidity high. As soon as new sprouts appear, prune out the old leaves and water the plant well.

PROPAGATION: Propagate by dividing the root ball.

PESTS AND DISEASES: Pests include mealybugs and spider mites.

RELATED SPECIES: 'Argentea' has a central silver stripe with a green border and wine undersides. 'Vandenheckei' has elliptical dark green leaves with feathery white central and marginal bands.

To keep the plant looking its best, trim out any damaged or shriveled leaves, especially if watering has been neglected.

PANAMA HAT PALM

Carludovica palmata kar-loo-DOH-vih-kuh pal-MATE-uh

Panama hat palm adds a classic tropical appearance anywhere. Give it plenty of space.

SIZE: 5–8'h × 4–5'w
TYPE: Palmlike
FORM: Tree
TEXTURE: Coarse
GROWTH: Medium
LIGHT: Medium
MOISTURE: Dry between waterings

SOIL: Potting soil
FEATURES: Fan-shape leaves
USES: Architectural accent

SITING: Panama hat palm is not a true palm. It thrives in average home conditions. Provide medium light; the leaves bleach out in high light. It tolerates minimal direct sun. It prefers average home temperatures (60–75°F) but will tolerate 85–90°F. It performs best in high humidity (above 65 percent), although it tolerates 30–65 percent. Frond tips may become brown in low humidity. Keep out of drying winds to prevent damaging the wide fronds.

CARE: Allow to dry only slightly between waterings, then soak the soil (it should be well drained). Keep it fairly dry during its winter rest. Feed only three times in summer with a foliage plant food. Feeding more often will cause it to outgrow its site quickly. Repot annually in March. For large plants that are hard to maneuver, remove the top inch of soil and replace it with fresh soil. Wash the leaves monthly to remove dust. Prune only to remove damaged leaves.

PROPAGATION: Propagate by dividing the rhizome in spring.

PESTS AND DISEASES: Control spider mites and mealybugs with monthly washing of the leaves.

RELATED SPECIES: This is the only species used in the home, although there are several used in landscaping in southern climates.

The immense stiff fronds add an architectural flair not easily obtained with plants of lesser stature.

FISHTAIL PALM

Caryota mitis *kar-ee-OH-tuh MITE-is*

SIZE: 6–8'h × 3'w
TYPE: Palm
FORM: Upright
TEXTURE: Coarse
GROWTH: Medium
LIGHT: High to medium
MOISTURE: Moist
SOIL: Potting soil
FEATURES: Leaflets like fish tails
USES: Architectural accent

A fishtail palm will brighten a dull corner with its crinkled gray-green leaves on upright stiff stalks.

SITING: Fishtail palm thrives in bright, filtered light but performs well in medium light. It prefers average to warm temperatures (65–85°F) and average to high humidity (30 percent or above).

CARE: Keep evenly moist except during its winter rest, when it should be a bit drier. Stem rot results from too much water. Feed once a month in the growing season with foliage plant food. Repot in spring if the plant is outgrowing its pot, but keep in mind that it does best when pot-bound. Remove damaged fronds. Shower off the plant once a month to keep dust down and control mites.

PROPAGATION: Although it can be grown from seed, it rarely blooms in the home, so you must acquire seed from a supplier. Or separate the plantlets found at the base of the parent plant, pot them, and keep them warm until roots are established.

PESTS AND DISEASES: Spider mites can become bothersome in low humidity.

RELATED SPECIES: *C. urens* and *C. obtusa* are both called giant fishtail palm and may be available through specialty suppliers. Both grow to 12' or more.

Asymmetrical leaflets called pinnae have an almost whimsical appearance with ragged edges that make them look like a fish tail.

CATTLEYA ORCHID

Cattleya hybrids *kat-LAY-uh*

Cattleya orchids are some of the easiest of all the orchids to grow, as long as they receive bright indirect light.

SIZE: Varies
TYPE: Orchid
FORM: Upright
TEXTURE: Medium
GROWTH: Slow
LIGHT: High
MOISTURE: Dry between waterings

SOIL: Orchid mix
FEATURES: Exquisite blossoms
USES: Blooming accent
FLOWERS:

SITING: Cattleya orchid needs bright light, but avoid direct sun in the middle of the day. It prefers 75–80°F but will tolerate higher temperatures if the light is decreased and the humidity is increased. It needs humidity levels of 50–80 percent, which can be provided with a pebble tray or a pot-in-pot system.

CARE: Mature cattleya orchid should dry out fairly well between waterings, but younger plants and seedlings must be kept moist. Use unsoftened water above 50°F. Because cattleyas are grown for their flowers, feed with a blossom-boosting food every 4–6 weeks. Feed with foliage food every 2 weeks or at half strength at every watering. When the plant is resting, feed only once a month. Flush out fertilizer salts once a month. Repot when the rhizomes creep over the edge of the pot or when the potting mix breaks down and doesn't drain thoroughly. Repot before new roots appear—after blooming or in spring. When the flower stem appears, place an orchid stake close to the center of the plant, making sure not to pierce the pseudobulbs when doing so. Gently tie the flower spike to the stake.

PROPAGATION: Propagate by dividing the root ball. The plant must be mature enough to provide 3 to 5 pseudobulbs for each division. After dividing the plant, cut off any damaged or diseased roots, and spread the remaining roots on a small mound of soil in the bottom of the new pot. Fill with orchid mix, pack down firmly, and place a stake in the pot if necessary. Keep in a cool spot with lower light and dry roots until established.

PESTS AND DISEASES: Cattleya orchid is prone to leaf spots when the air is still and cool. Provide air circulation and keep the plants warm.

RELATED SPECIES: There are hundreds of cattleya orchids available as well as many crosses with other species.

'Nacouchee' has delicate lavender flowers.

'Landate' features variegated petals surrounding a pink center.

OLD MAN CACTUS

Cephalocereus senilis seh-ful-oh-SEER-ee-us seh-NILL-us

SIZE: 1'h × 4"w
TYPE: Cactus
FORM: Upright
TEXTURE: Coarse
GROWTH: Slow
LIGHT: High
MOISTURE: Dry
SOIL: Cactus mix
FEATURES: Wavy white hairs
USES: Dry garden, accent

Old man cactus is aptly named with its tall stature and covering of whitish hairs over spines.

SITING: Old man cactus needs full sun to keep its unique form. Keep the plant warm (65–85°F) when in active growth and provide cooler temperatures (55–60°F) during the dormant period in winter. Low humidity levels (20–30 percent) will keep it looking its best.

CARE: Let the soil dry out between waterings during active growth, and even more during the dormant stage. Feed with half-strength plant food only after flower buds form. Old man cactus has a small root system, so repotting is seldom necessary. Root rot is caused by overwatering. Occasionally a plant will die from overwatering yet remain standing until someone knocks it over and finds it is hollow.

PROPAGATION: Because of the form of this cactus, the only way to propagate is by seed. It seldom flowers in the home, so you will need to acquire seed from a supplier.

PESTS AND DISEASES: Pests include mealybugs and scale, which may be hidden under the long, wavy white hairs.

RELATED SPECIES: Several species are appropriate for growing only outdoors.

The hairs of old man cactus look soft, but actually cover spines that can inflict a painful wound.

ROSARY VINE

Ceropegia linearis ssp. *woodii* seer-oh-PEE-jee-a lin-ee-AIR-is WOOD-ee-eye

Rosary vine is also known as hearts entangled, hearts-on-a-vine, and string of hearts.

SIZE: 2–4' long
TYPE: Herbaceous
FORM: Vining
TEXTURE: Fine
GROWTH: Fast
LIGHT: High to medium
MOISTURE: Dry between waterings
SOIL: Potting soil
FEATURES: Heart-shape leaves on long vines
USES: Hanging basket, focal point
FLOWERS: ☐

SITING: Give rosary vine bright light for the best form. It will tolerate medium light but will not be as full. It performs best in warm temperatures (70–75°F) during the summer and cooler temperatures (60–65°F) in winter. This plant tolerates low to average humidity. If you see signs of stress such as browning leaves, provide more moisture by placing it on a tray of moist pebbles.

CARE: Allow to dry considerably between waterings, then soak the soil well. When it is resting in winter, water sparingly. Feed monthly with half-strength foliage plant food during active growth; do not fertilize in winter. It performs best when pot-bound. If necessary repot in April before new growth begins. A summer outdoors in dappled light will benefit the plant.

PROPAGATION: Propagate with stem cuttings, by seed, or by planting the small tubers that form at the leaf bases. Press a tuber into potting soil while it is attached to the parent plant; keep moist, then sever it from the parent plant when rooted.

PESTS AND DISEASES: Occasional pests are mealybugs and spider mites, but generally the plant is tolerant of neglect.

RELATED SPECIES: *C. ampliata* has white flowers and twining stems. *C. gemmifera* has succulent stems and leaves.

"Beads" form along the stem and can be used to propagate new plants by resting them on soil and keeping them moist.

PEANUT CACTUS

Chamaecereus sylvestri (Echinopsis chamaecereus) *kam-eh-SEER-ee-us sil-VEST-rye*

Peanut cactus is a diminutive cactus in gray-green covered with white hairs. It is tolerant of neglect.

SIZE: 6"h × 2"w
TYPE: Cactus
FORM: Upright
TEXTURE: Medium
GROWTH: Slow
LIGHT: High

MOISTURE: Dry
SOIL: Cactus mix
FEATURES: Peanutlike knobs on main stem
USES: Dish garden

SITING: Peanut cactus needs full sun to thrive. Keep the plant warm (65–85°F) when in active growth; provide cooler temperatures (55–60°F) during the dormant period in winter. Low humidity levels (20–30 percent) will keep it looking its best.

CARE: Let the soil dry out considerably between waterings during active growth, and even more during the dormant stage. Feed with half-strength plant food only after flower buds form. Peanut cactus has a small root system, like other cactus, so repotting is seldom necessary.
PROPAGATION: Propagate peanut cactus by separating the peanuts from the parent plant. They root easily when they are in contact with moist soil.
PESTS AND DISEASES: Root rot results from overwatering.
RELATED SPECIES: There are hundreds of other species, few of which are suitable for home culture. Some cultivars are available, but they are mostly for outdoor use.

1 Propagate by removing the offsets that form at the base of the plant.

2 Set offsets at the same soil level and keep the soil moist until they take root.

PARLOR PALM

Chamaedorea elegans (Neanthe bella) *cam-ee-DOH-ree-ah EL-e-ganz (nee-AN-thuh BELL-uh)*

Parlor palms have graced homes for centuries because of their ability to adapt to almost any cultural situation.

SIZE: 3–6'h × 1–2'w
TYPE: Palm
FORM: Upright
TEXTURE: Medium
GROWTH: Fast
LIGHT: High to low
MOISTURE: Dry between waterings

SOIL: Potting soil
FEATURES: Elegant fronds
USES: Architectural accent, foliage
FLOWERS: ☐

SITING: A worthy feature of the parlor palm is its adaptability. Although it performs best in bright light, it will adapt to medium and even low light. The fronds will be somewhat lighter in bright light and dark green in low light. Parlor palm does well in warm temperatures (75°F and above) but adapts to average temperatures. It is adaptable to low humidity; very low humidity causes the frond tips to turn brown. Keep the plant out of drafts, which may also brown the tips. Plants suffering from under- or overwatering have yellowing fronds and dropping leaves.
CARE: Allow the soil to dry slightly between waterings while in active growth; let dry more during winter rest. Feed monthly with a foliage plant food during spring and summer only. Repotting is seldom necessary; parlor palm does well when pot-bound. Shower off the plant monthly to keep it looking pristine and to deter spider mites. Remove faded fronds occasionally. When you remove a frond, wait to remove the leaf sheath until it is brown and dry and pulls away easily.

PROPAGATION: Propagate by seeds, which take 1–6 months to germinate.
PESTS AND DISEASES: Spider mites, mealybugs, and scale can be problems in dry conditions.
RELATED SPECIES: The cultivar 'Bella' is a compact form.

Keep a close eye out for mites and scale insects. If you find them, treat the plant with horticultural oil or a good shower.

BAMBOO PALM
Chamaedorea erumpens cam-ee-DOH-ree-ah ee-RUM-penz

Bamboo palm, also known as reed palm, offers an attractive architectural statement because of its size.

SIZE: 7–12'h × 3–4'w
TYPE: Palm
FORM: Upright, open
TEXTURE: Medium
GROWTH: Medium
LIGHT: High, medium
MOISTURE: Dry between waterings
SOIL: Average
FEATURES: Clustered stems, bamboolike
USES: Foliage, architectural accent

SITING: Bamboo palm is used extensively in indoor culture because it is extremely adaptable. It prefers bright, indirect light, although it adapts to medium and even low light. Direct sun will bleach the fronds. Bamboo palm prefers warm temperatures (75°F and above) but adapts to the average temperatures of most homes and offices. It tolerates lower temperatures better than parlor palm. High humidity (65 percent or more) is best; low humidity causes the frond tips to turn brown. Keep the plant out of drafts, which may brown the tips.
CARE: Allow the soil to dry slightly between waterings while in active growth; let dry out more during winter rest. Under- or overwatering causes browning leaf tips, yellowing fronds, and dropping leaves. Feed monthly with a foliage plant food during spring and summer only. Repotting is seldom necessary; bamboo palm does well when pot-bound. Shower the plant monthly to keep it looking pristine and deter spider mites. Remove faded fronds. Trimming brown tips off the leaves often makes the leaf brown farther down, so removing the entire frond is preferable (but do not remove the leaf sheath until it is brown and dry and pulls away easily). Rotate the pot every time you water to keep the plant growing in a symmetrical shape.
PROPAGATION: Seeds take 1–6 months to germinate but then grow fairly quickly. Bamboo palm is easily propagated by dividing the root ball.
PESTS AND DISEASES: Spider mites, mealybugs, and scale can be problems, especially in dry conditions.
RELATED SPECIES: *C. glaucifolia* has bluish-green foliage with glaucous stems and frond ribs. *C. microspadix* has wide blue-green leaflets.

To divide bamboo palm you may first need to saw through its tough roots.

Bamboo palm benefits from monthly showers to remove dust and mites.

CHIRITA
Chirita sinensis kee-REE-tuh sih-NEN-sis

Chirita is grown for its striking quilted leaves with silver patterns. In the right light conditions the plants will produce clusters of lavender tubular blossoms.

SIZE: 6–10"h × 6–10"w
TYPE: Gesneriad
FORM: Mounded
TEXTURE: Medium
GROWTH: Medium
LIGHT: High
MOISTURE: Evenly moist
SOIL: Organic
FEATURES: Thick quilted leaves in rosette with silver pattern
USES: Blooming accent
FLOWERS: ■

SITING: Chirita thrives in the same conditions as African violets, with bright, indirect light or even artificial light if desired. Full sun bleaches or scorches the attractively quilted and patterned leaves, so early-morning and late-afternoon sun is appropriate but not midday sun. Chiritas do well in temperatures of 65–85°F and average to high humidity (greater than 30 percent).
CARE: Keep chirita evenly moist, but the soil must be porous and free-draining to prevent rotting. It can be bottom-watered, although it loses some of its compact shape. Chirita goes semidormant during the winter, so reduce watering and let it rest. Feed chirita by using half-strength blooming plant food at every other watering. Pruning is not necessary, and the only grooming needed is occasionally removing a faded leaf or spent flowers.
PROPAGATION: Propagate chirita from leaf cuttings. Simply remove a leaf with the petiole attached, dip it in rooting hormone, and stick in sterile potting soil. Soon a cluster of tiny plants will form at the soil level and can be lifted, separated, and potted as individual plants.
PESTS AND DISEASES: Cyclamen mites may be a problem and are quite difficult to get rid of. It may be necessary to discard the plant if an infestation persists. Otherwise chirita has few problems. Bronzed leaves indicate too much light or possible overfertilization.
RELATED SPECIES: 'Hisako', with bright silvery markings on the leaves and lavender flowers, is one of the most popular cultivars. *C. s. angustifolia* has lavender flowers with yellow throats and thin dark leaves veined with silver.

SPIDER PLANT
Chlorophytum comosum *clor-oh-FIE-tum co-MOE-sum*

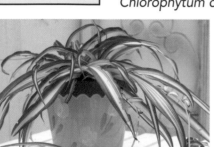

Spider plant is also known as airplane plant or ribbon plant. This cultivar is 'Vittatum'.

SIZE: 1'h × 2'w
TYPE: Herbaceous
FORM: Mounded
TEXTURE: Medium
GROWTH: Medium
LIGHT: Medium
MOISTURE: Evenly moist

SOIL: Average
FEATURES: Variegated or solid green leaves
USES: Hanging basket
FLOWERS: ☐

SITING: Spider plant prefers bright, indirect light; it will sunburn or fade in direct sunlight. In lower light it will not produce plantlets unless you supplement the light to mimic outside light in fall. Spider plant thrives in a cool home (55°F) but tolerates average temperatures. It is superb at cleaning toxins from the air.

CARE: Keep the soil moist but not soggy. Allow to dry slightly in winter. Feed once a month with a foliage plant food. Spider plant fills the pot with water-storing thickened roots, so it needs to be repotted regularly—as soon as watering becomes difficult. Wash off the plant regularly to keep it healthy and mite-free. Spider plant almost always gets brown tips, so trim them regularly. Eventually the leaf will become ragged looking and should be removed. When brown tips become

To start new spider plants, place plantlets into a pot of soil mix. They root quickly.

rampant—a sign of water stress—repot or divide the plant. Brown tips may also indicate excess salts in the soil.

PROPAGATION: Propagate by dividing the root ball or planting offsets. To propagate by offsets, place a small pot next to the parent plant, set the plantlet (still attached to the parent plant) on moist soil, and pin it down with a hairpin. When the plant has extended its roots in the soil, sever it from the parent plant. You can also root the plantlet in the same pot as the parent plant. When it has rooted, dig it up carefully and move it to its own pot.

Water stress causes brown tips which are easily trimmed from the leaves.

PESTS AND DISEASES: Spider plant may develop scale and spider mites when it is water stressed.

RELATED SPECIES: 'Picturatum' has a central creamy stripe. 'Variegatum' has a creamy white margin. 'Vittatum' has a central white stripe on each leaf.

ARECA PALM
Chrysalidocarpus lutescens (Dypsis lutescens) *kris-al-ih-doh-CAR-puss loo-TES-ens*

Areca palm, also known as butterfly palm, has majestic long fronds that extend upward and then arch gracefully.

SIZE: 10–12'h × 4–5'w
TYPE: Palm
FORM: Upright, vase-shaped
TEXTURE: Coarse
GROWTH: Slow
LIGHT: Medium, indirect

MOISTURE: Evenly moist
SOIL: Average
FEATURES: Long tropical fronds
USES: Architectural accent

SITING: Areca palm maintains its attractive, upright shape in bright, indirect light. It will not tolerate full sun. Give it average temperatures (60–75°F) and high humidity (65 percent or more) to prevent browning tips. It will not tolerate cool temperatures or drying winds.

CARE: Areca palm takes a good bit of care to keep it looking good in the home. Water with distilled water or rainwater to keep the plant from getting spots on the leaves. Keep the soil evenly moist. Do not let the plant sit in water or it will rot. Feed with foliage plant food only once or twice a year. Overfertilization causes tip burn. Repot only when it becomes difficult to water; it prefers being pot-bound. Remove fronds as they yellow and trim off brown tips. Give plants a shower at least once a month to deter spider mites.

PROPAGATION: Propagate by dividing the root ball or by seed.

PESTS AND DISEASES: The only pests are spider mites.

RELATED SPECIES: *C. lastelliana* has a red trunk. Triangle palm *(C. decaryi)* is another unusual specimen houseplant.

Areca palms are a lovely architectural feature in a site with bright, indirect light.

These palms benefit greatly from monthly showers to keep them clean and mite-free.

KANGAROO VINE

Cissus antarctica SIS-us ant-AHR-ti-kuh

Kangaroo vine, also known as African tree grape, is an adaptable plant that can hang elegantly or be trained to climb.

SIZE: 4' long
TYPE: Climbing vine
FORM: Mounded, ground cover
TEXTURE: Medium
GROWTH: Fast
LIGHT: High to low

MOISTURE: Dry between waterings
SOIL: Potting soil
FEATURES: Long vines
USES: Foliage, ground cover

SITING: Kangaroo vine is adaptable to most home situations. It grows best in bright to medium light but will tolerate lower light if the soil is kept somewhat dry. It prefers 60°F or below and moderate to high humidity (30–70 percent), although it tolerates drier air.

CARE: Keep the soil slightly moist in active growth; allow it to dry somewhat during resting phase. Feed with a foliage plant food three times in summer only. It seldom needs repotting. Pinch back the tips to keep it shrubby. The plant climbs by tendrils and will cover a frame to make a delightful room divider or living curtain.

PROPAGATION: Propagate by stem cuttings. Take cuttings anywhere along the stem, remove all but one leaf at the tip of the cutting, dip the base into rooting hormone, and insert it in sterile potting mix. The plants can also be propagated by layering. Simply bend a vine so a leaf node comes in contact with moist soil. Hold in place with a hairpin. When roots have formed in the soil, sever the vine from the parent plant and pot it.

PESTS AND DISEASES: Spider mites are usually the only pest. Wash off in the shower occasionally and treat with horticultural oil if necessary.

RELATED SPECIES: The cultivar 'Minima' is a small-leaved, spreading type that works well in a hanging basket.

To train a kangaroo vine to climb, start by wrapping the vines around a frame. The plant will eventually climb on its own.

GRAPE IVY

Cissus rhombifolia SIS-us rom-bib-FOLE-ee-uh

Grape ivy, also known as oakleaf ivy, tolerates bright to low light, making it one of the most versatile houseplants.

SIZE: 4' long
TYPE: Climbing vine
FORM: Mounded, ground cover
TEXTURE: Medium
GROWTH: Medium
LIGHT: High to low

MOISTURE: Dry between waterings
SOIL: Potting soil
FEATURES: Bronze leaves, tendrils
USES: Hanging basket, foliage

SITING: Grow grape ivy in high to low light but not full sun. In lower light, pinch it frequently to keep it shrubby. It prefers 60–80°F but tolerates lower temperatures. Average humidity is best. Ensure good air circulation to prevent powdery mildew.

CARE: Keep it somewhat dry between waterings, because it is prone to root rot. Feed with half-strength foliage plant food. More fertilizer can cause leaf burn. Grape ivy seldom needs repotting. Pinch back the tips to keep it shrubby. To rejuvenate a lanky plant, cut back about one-third of the vines in early spring to about 6" long. As new growth appears, cut back the other vines, never removing more than one-third of the plant at a time. To encourage grape

Grape ivy makes an excellent soft ground cover when planted in a pot with a larger plant.

ivy to climb, insert a stake or bamboo frame into the root ball. Tie the vines to the stake with soft twine and let the ends gently drape.

PROPAGATION: Propagate by stem cuttings. Take cuttings anywhere along the stem. Remove all but one leaf at the tip of the cutting, dip the base into rooting hormone, and insert in sterile potting mix. The plant can also be propagated by layering. Simply bend a vine so a leaf node comes in contact with moist soil. Hold it in place with a hairpin. When roots have formed in the soil, sever the vine from the parent plant and pot it.

PESTS AND DISEASES: Occasional bouts with spider mites are inevitable. Shower off the plant periodically and use horticultural oil to control them. Control powdery mildew by pruning out the affected parts.

RELATED SPECIES: 'Ellen Danica' was the first improved cultivar on the market. 'Manda Supreme' has larger, more succulent leaves. Miniature grape ivy (*C. striata*) has bronze-green leaves. Rex begonia vine (*C. discolor*) has dark green and silver leaves with maroon undersides.

CALAMONDIN ORANGE
×*Citrofortunella microcarpa* *sih-troh-for-toon-ELL-uh my-kroh-KAR-puh*

SIZE: 3'h × 2'w
TYPE: Woody shrub
FORM: Upright
TEXTURE: Medium
GROWTH: Slow
LIGHT: High
MOISTURE: Moist
SOIL: Potting soil
FEATURES: Glossy foliage, fragrant flowers, edible fruit
USES: Blooming, fruiting accent
FLOWERS: ☐

Calamondin orange fills a room with the fragrance of orange blossoms.

SITING: With more than a half-day of direct sun, Calamondin orange will bloom at least twice a year and almost continuously provide attractive, pungent tiny oranges. The plant performs best at around 55–68°F and average humidity (30–60 percent). It tolerates higher temperatures but may not fruit.

CARE: Keep the soil moist but not soggy. Feed every 2–3 months with an acid plant food. Repot every 3 years but avoid too large a container. The plant has a shallow root system, so a wide pot is better than a deep one. To keep it looking good and producing well, thin to 3 sturdy stems. Although the plant may bloom periodically during the year, it may not produce fruit unless helped with pollination. Dust a small, soft paintbrush over the stamens of each flower; fruit should begin developing

Calamondin orange may be filled with blossoms, green fruit, and ripe fruit all at the same time.

in a few weeks. Shower the plants often to reduce pest problems. Plants benefit from spending the summer outdoors, especially for pollination. Gradually introduce them to a protected spot or they will drop leaves and abort fruits. Reverse the process when bringing them back indoors in fall (when outdoor temperatures drop below 50°F).

PROPAGATION: Seeds take a long time to make a sizable plant. The best way to ensure a fruiting specimen is to propagate by stem cuttings. Take the cuttings of semihardwood in early summer; root in sterile potting mix with rooting hormone and bottom heat.

PESTS AND DISEASES: Pests include aphids, mealybugs, spider mites, and scale, particularly if the humidity is low. Control insect populations with horticultural oil and frequent showers of water.

RELATED SPECIES: There are many citrus species and hybrid crosses with a flavor and size to suit every gardener. *Fortunella margarita* (kumquat) is related to Calamondin orange and is easy to grow indoors.

LEMON
Citrus limon *SIH-trus LYE-mun*

SIZE: 3'h × 2'w
TYPE: Woody shrub
FORM: Upright
TEXTURE: Medium
GROWTH: Slow
LIGHT: Bright
MOISTURE: Moist
SOIL: Potting soil
FEATURES: Glossy foliage, fragrant flowers, edible fruit
USES: Blooming, fruiting accent
FLOWERS: ☐

Lemon is an ideal plant for a bright spot, providing an architectural element as well as tasty fruit.

SITING: With at least a half-day of direct sun, lemon blooms at least twice a year and almost continuously provides fruit. It performs best at 55–68°F and average humidity (30–60 percent). Use a room humidifier, a pot-in-pot system, or a pebble tray to increase humidity.

CARE: Keep the soil moist but not soggy. Feed every 2–3 months with an acid plant food. Repot every 3 years but avoid too large a container. Being pot-bound is what keeps dwarf citrus dwarf. To keep it looking good and producing well, thin the plant to 3 sturdy stems. Although it may bloom periodically during the year, it may not produce fruit unless helped with pollination. Dust a small, soft paintbrush

Lemon blossoms are waxy white and intensely fragrant.

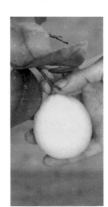

Thin all but one fruit per node to help develop large fruits.

over the stamens of each flower; fruit should begin developing in a few weeks. Shower the plants often to reduce pest problems. Plants benefit from spending the summer outdoors, especially for pollination. Gradually introduce them to a protected spot or they will drop leaves and abort fruits. Reverse the process when bringing them back indoors in fall (when outdoor temperatures drop below 50°F).

PROPAGATION: Seed-grown plants seldom produce fruit. The best way to ensure a fruiting specimen is to propagate by stem cuttings. Take the cuttings of semihardwood in early summer; root in sterile potting mix with rooting hormone and bottom heat. Provide a clear plastic tent for plenty of humidity while rooting.

PESTS: Pests include aphids, mealybugs, spider mites, and scale, particularly if the humidity is low. Control populations with horticultural oil and frequent showers.

RELATED SPECIES: Meyer lemon (*C. ×meyeri*) is one of the most commonly grown lemons for the home. *C. limon* 'Dwarf Ponderosa' has grapefruit-size lemons, yet the plant is small enough to be easily grown indoors.

ORANGE
Citrus sinensis SIH-trus sib-NEN-sis

Orange not only is a beautiful addition to the indoor garden but also provides you with tasty fruit.

SIZE: 3'h × 2'w
TYPE: Woody shrub
FORM: Upright
TEXTURE: Medium
GROWTH: Slow
LIGHT: High
MOISTURE: Evenly moist

SOIL: Potting soil
FEATURES: Glossy foliage, fragrant flowers, edible fruit
USES: Blooming, fruiting accent
FLOWERS: □

SITING: With at least a half-day of direct sun, orange plant will bloom at least twice a year and almost continuously provide attractive, tasty fruit. It performs best at 55–68°F. It tolerates higher temperatures but may not fruit. Keep the humidity at an average level (30–60 percent) with a room humidifier, pot-in-pot system, or pebble tray.

CARE: Keep the soil moist but not soggy. Feed every 2–3 months with an acid plant food. Repot every 3 years but avoid too large a container. To keep it looking good and producing well, thin the plant to 3 sturdy stems. Although it may bloom periodically during the year, it may not

Fertilize oranges and other citrus with a fertilizer designed for plants that need acid soil.

produce fruit unless helped with pollination. Dust a small, soft paintbrush over the stamens of each flower; fruit should begin developing in a few weeks. Shower the plants often to reduce pest problems. Plants benefit from spending the summer outdoors, especially for pollination. Gradually introduce them to a protected spot or they will drop leaves and abort fruits. Reverse the process when bringing them back indoors in fall (when outdoor temperatures drop below 50°F).

PROPAGATION: Seed-grown plants seldom produce fruit. The best way to ensure a fruiting specimen is to propagate by stem cuttings. Take the cuttings of semihardwood in early summer and root in sterile potting mix with rooting hormone and bottom heat. Provide a clear plastic tent for plenty of humidity while rooting.

PESTS AND DISEASES: Pests include aphids, mealybugs, spider mites, and scale. Control populations with horticultural oil and frequent showers.

RELATED SPECIES: The cultivar 'Valencia' is seedless and bears fruit up to 4" in diameter. 'Dwarf Washington' is easily peeled and delicious.

GLORYBOWER
Clerodendrum thomsoniae kler-oh-DEN-drum tom-SOHN-ee-eye

Glorybower can give you a striking hanging basket or even a wall of color when trained onto a trellis.

SIZE: 8'h × 5'w
TYPE: Woody vine
FORM: Trailing, upright
TEXTURE: Medium
GROWTH: Medium
LIGHT: High

MOISTURE: Moist
SOIL: Potting soil
FEATURES: Blossoms
USES: Hanging basket, trellis
FLOWERS: □ ■

SITING: Glorybower is a beautiful accent when in bloom from July through October. It needs bright, indirect light to develop flowers. Provide average (70–75°F) temperatures, not dropping below 55°F. It needs high humidity (above 60 percent).

CARE: Provide plenty of water during its active growing period, but hold back on watering and let dry somewhat during the winter. Repot every spring into a slightly larger container. Feed every 2 weeks with

When glorybower has finished its summer blooming, prune out the faded bracts to keep the plant attractive.

half-strength blooming plant food until its winter rest in November. Pinch regularly to avoid unkempt-looking growth. Although its natural inclination is to climb and you can train it to a trellis, it can be maintained in shrubby form by pruning. Prune back after flowering in fall. (It blooms on new wood.)

PROPAGATION: Take stem cuttings in spring and give plenty of humidity and bottom heat. Plants can also be started from seed.

PESTS AND DISEASES: Control mealybugs and spider mites by keeping the humidity high. Use horticultural oil if the populations get out of hand.

RELATED SPECIES: The cultivar 'Variegatum' has creamy white and pale green mottled leaves. Most species are more suited to the conservatory or growing outdoors in the South because of their large size. Butterfly flower, *C. ugandense* has blue flowers that hang down like butterflies.

CLIVIA

Clivia miniata KLI-vee-uh (KLY-vee-uh) min-ee-AH-tuh

Clivia, also known as Kafir lily, provides you with spectacular orange to red blossoms if kept pot-bound and somewhat dry.

SIZE: 1–2'h × 1–2'w
TYPE: Herbaceous
FORM: Vase-shaped
TEXTURE: Medium to coarse
GROWTH: Medium
LIGHT: High

MOISTURE: Dry
SOIL: Well-drained
FEATURES: Blossoms
USES: Blooming accent
FLOWERS: ■ ■ ■

SITING: Clivia prefers bright, indirect light all day. It will not tolerate direct afternoon sun. Provide daytime temperatures of 70°F or higher and nighttime temperatures not lower than 50°F. Drop the temperature during the rest period to just above 40°F.

CARE: Clivia roots are fleshy and store water, so they easily rot if overwatered. It's better to neglect a clivia than to overwater it. Feed monthly with a blooming plant food during active growth. In late fall give the plant a rest by withholding plant food and watering only enough to keep the leaves from wilting. Repot in spring just as it begins active growth. Well-drained potting soil is essential. Some gardeners

As a clivia grows, the bottom leaves may turn yellow. Simply prune these off by hand to keep the plant attractive.

pot clivia in orchid mix. Keep the same size pot; clivia needs to be pot-bound in order to bloom. The plants are top-heavy, so use a terra-cotta pot. Move clivia outdoors into light-dappled shade for the summer.

PROPAGATION: Propagate by separating the offsets from the parent plant. After flowering, remove the plant from the pot and gently tease the roots apart to separate the offsets. Pot them and give them plenty of water and light as they establish themselves. Clivia grown from seed takes a long time to reach blooming size. Sow seeds on sterile soil mix; press lightly into it, leaving the tops exposed. Keep warm and light. Pot the new plants about 8 months after sowing.

PESTS AND DISEASES: Remove scale and mealybugs by hand or with a cotton swab dipped in alcohol or horticultural oil.

RELATED SPECIES: *C. nobilis* has pendulous flowers. *C. miniata* var. *citrina* has clear yellow flowers; there are several cultivars of this variety. *C. gardenii* has pendulous flowers that are orange tipped in green.

CROTON

Codiaeum variegatum var. pictum Koh-dee-AY-um vair-eh-GAH-tum PIK-tum

Croton is perhaps one of the most colorful of all the houseplants. It will thrive if kept warm and humid.

SIZE: 2–6'h × 1–3'w
TYPE: Woody shrub
FORM: Rounded
TEXTURE: Coarse
GROWTH: Medium
LIGHT: High

MOISTURE: Evenly moist
SOIL: Potting soil
FEATURES: Variegated leaves
USES: Focal point, foliage

SITING: Croton needs bright light to keep its remarkable leaf coloration. In lower light the leaves fade and the plant will be stressed. Keep croton above 60°F at all times. It needs high humidity (65 percent or above) to keep its attractive form and to

deter spider mites. Grouping plants with croton as the focal point displays this plant well and keeps the humidity high.

CARE: Keep the soil evenly moist but not soggy. In winter, water when the soil begins to dry out; never let the soil completely dry. Feed every 2 months during the growing season with foliage plant food; do not fertilize in winter. Repot in spring if pot-bound (every few years). Remove yellow leaves and shower the plant monthly for aesthetics and insect control.

PROPAGATION: Propagate by softwood cuttings. Take cuttings in early summer. Stop the stem from "bleeding" by dusting it with charcoal. Remove all the leaves but one. If you are propagating a large-leaved variety, cut the leaf in half. Dust the cutting with rooting hormone

and insert it in sterile potting soil. Cover it with a plastic bag to keep high humidity. Croton can also be air-layered.

PESTS AND DISEASES: Pests include spider mites, mealybugs, and scale. Treat mealybugs and scale with horticultural oil. Use a forceful water spray to remove spider mites.

RELATED SPECIES: The cultivar 'Lauren's Rainbow' has ribbonlike emerald green leaves with a golden midrib. 'Goldfinger' has thin gold-hued leaves.

Corkscrew croton has interesting twisted leaves with plenty of colorful variegation.

Unless given quite bright light, croton leaves will tend to lose their beautiful colors.

COFFEE

Coffea arabica KAW-fee-uh uh-RAB-ih-kuh

Coffee seldom blooms or produces berries indoors, but the glossy green foliage is reason enough to grow the plant.

SIZE: 12"h × 3'w
TYPE: Woody shrub
FORM: Rounded
TEXTURE: Medium
GROWTH: Slow
LIGHT: High, indirect
MOISTURE: Evenly moist

SOIL: Potting soil
FEATURES: Glossy leaves, berries
USES: Focal point, blooming
FLOWERS: □

SITING: Coffee plant needs bright, indirect light (not direct sun) to produce its attractive, glossy red berries. It grows best at medium temperatures (60–75°F) and high humidity (65 percent or above).
CARE: Keep the soil evenly moist but not soggy. Feed every 2 weeks during the active growing season with half-strength foliage plant food. Feed monthly in winter. Feed every 2 months with acid fertilizer. Pinch off the growing tips periodically to keep the plant shrubby and attractive or prune more thoroughly once a year. Move outdoors in summer.
PROPAGATION: Propagate from cuttings or seed. Pick the ripe red berries, remove the pulp, and plant the seeds in sterile soil mix. Keep moist and humid until germination.
PESTS AND DISEASES: Wash spider mites from affected leaves with a spray of water.

Pinching out the growing tips of coffee will help the plant maintain an attractive shrubby shape.

GOLDFISH PLANT
Columnea spp. kah-LUM-nee-ah

Goldfish plants have bright red and yellow uniquely shaped flowers on deep shiny green foliage.

SIZE: 1'h × 3'w
TYPE: Gesneriad
FORM: Trailing
TEXTURE: Fine
GROWTH: Moderate
LIGHT: High to medium

MOISTURE: Evenly moist
SOIL: Potting soil
FEATURES: Hanging stems, glossy leaves
USES: Hanging basket
FLOWERS: ■■

SITING: Bright to medium light, away from direct sun, will keep goldfish plant looking its best. If the plant won't flower, move it into brighter but filtered light. Average to warm temperatures (60°F or more) and high humidity are needed for the plant to blossom. A pebble tray works well.
CARE: Keep the soil evenly moist but not soggy. When the plant is not actively growing, avoid wetting the foliage or it may develop water scarring. Reducing watering for 6–8 weeks may induce flowering. Feed every 2 weeks with half-strength plant food for blooming plants. Goldfish plant will drop leaves when it

Goldfish plant tends to have long trailing stems that should be pruned back periodically to keep the plant shrubby and attractive.

gets too cold or too dry or is overfertilized. Every month flush the soil with clear water to wash away fertilizer salts. Repotting is seldom necessary; goldfish plant blooms best when pot-bound. Prune long, wayward stems regularly to keep the plant full and appealing.
PROPAGATION: Propagate by stem or tip cuttings. Simply insert the cuttings into rooting hormone, then into sterile potting soil. Cover with plastic to boost humidity. Cuttings will root in a few weeks.
PESTS AND DISEASES: Pests include aphids, spider mites, and whiteflies. The plant is generally problem-free if cultural details are attended to.
RELATED SPECIES: *C. gloriosa* has purplish leaves covered with hairs and bright red flowers with a yellow throat. The cultivar 'Bonfire' has orange-yellow flowers. *C. microphylla* 'Variegata' has grayish leaves with creamy margins and scarlet flowers.

HAWAIIAN TI PLANT

Cordyline fruticosa (terminalis) KORE-dih-li-nee fru-tih-KOH-suh (ter-mih-NAHL-iss)

Hawaiian ti plant has been sold for many years as a symbol of good luck. It is also known as good luck plant or red dracaena.

SIZE: 4'h × 3'w
TYPE: Herbaceous
FORM: Upright
TEXTURE: Coarse
GROWTH: Slow
LIGHT: High, indirect

MOISTURE: Evenly moist
SOIL: Potting soil
FEATURES: Variegated leaves
USES: Architectural accent

SITING: Bright light will keep the ti plant healthy. Direct sun can cause the red and cream variegation in the leaves to fade. It prefers average temperatures (60–75°F), not below 55°F, and average humidity (30–65 percent).

CARE: Keep the soil evenly moist but not soggy. Reduce watering in winter but do not let it dry out. Feed only three times in summer. Repot infrequently; pot-bound plants produce shoots at the base. Remove yellowed leaves and shower monthly to reduce pest problems. Brown tips on the leaves indicate too little humidity. Brown spotting on the leaves may indicate a cold draft or underwatering.

PROPAGATION: Pieces of the cane or crown can be used for propagation. Cut out the crown, dust the base with rooting hormone, and set it in moist, sterile potting soil. For cane cuttings, take pieces 2–3" long, lay them on moist potting soil, and cover them with plastic to raise humidity. They should root in a few weeks.

PESTS AND DISEASES: Usually ti plant is pest free. However occasional pests include mealybugs, mites, and scale.

RELATED SPECIES: The cultivar 'Kiwi' has bright leaves with stripes of pink-red, yellow, and light green. 'White Baby Doll' has slender leaves with streaks of ivory and pink.

1 A stem cutting, called a ti log, quickly roots when placed on moist potting soil and covered with plastic.

2 Once the leaves sprout, remove the plastic and bring the plant into good light.

JADE PLANT

Crassula ovata (argentea) KRASS-yew-luh o-VAH-tuh (ar-JEN-tee-uh)

The succulent leaves and thick stems of jade plants are easily recognizable and give the home a southwestern flair.

SIZE: 2'h × 2'w
TYPE: Succulent
FORM: Rounded
TEXTURE: Medium
GROWTH: Slow
LIGHT: High
MOISTURE: Low
SOIL: Cactus

FEATURES: Thick leaves on thick stems
USES: Succulent garden, focal point
FLOWERS: ☐

SITING: Jade plant grows splendidly in high light. It grows in all temperatures but does best with low humidity (below 30 percent).
CARE: Let the potting mix dry out before watering, then soak thoroughly. Jade plant does well if not watered until the leaves begin to lose their shine, although it may drop its leaves if it dries out too much. Feed only three times in summer. It seldom needs repotting. But as the plant matures and gets top-heavy, it may be necessary to repot into a heavier soil mix and a heavier pot, or to prune it, to keep it from falling over and snapping off the succulent stems.
PROPAGATION: Propagate by stem cuttings, leaf cuttings, or seed.

PESTS AND DISEASES: Jade may have scale, but mealybugs are the most common problem. Overwatering causes stem rot.
RELATED SPECIES: 'Tricolor' has creamy white-and-rose-striped leaves. 'Sunset' has leaves tipped in gold. 'California Red Tip' has purple-edged reddish leaves. Silver jade plant (*C. argentea*) has grayish leaves with red margins.

1 To propagate a jade plant, cut off a leaf with the leaf bud at the base intact.

2 Dip the leaf-bud end of the leaf in rooting hormone and tap off the excess.

3 Insert the lower tip of the leaf cutting into sterile potting soil.

FIRECRACKER FLOWER
Crossandra infundibuliformis *kros-AN-druh in-fun-dib-bew-li-FOR-mis*

Firecracker flower explodes into bright impressive blossoms of yellow, red, or salmon.

SIZE: 2'h × 2'w
TYPE: Woody shrub
FORM: Rounded
TEXTURE: Medium
GROWTH: Medium
LIGHT: Medium to high

MOISTURE: Evenly moist
SOIL: Potting soil
FEATURES: Glossy leaves, bright flowers
USES: Focal point
FLOWERS: ■ ■ ■

SITING: Firecracker flower looks its best in bright, indirect light. It tolerates medium light but not direct sun. It prefers medium temperatures (60–75°F), not below 55°F in winter. Provide high humidity by placing the plant on a pebble tray or grouping it with other plants.

CARE: Keep the soil moist but not soggy. Feed weekly with half-strength foliage plant food from spring to early fall. Do not fertilize during the winter resting phase. Repot every 2–3 years as the plant outgrows its pot. Prune regularly to maintain shape. Remove spent flowers to keep the plant blooming from spring to fall.

PROPAGATION: Propagate by softwood cuttings or seed. Take stem cuttings in spring, dip in rooting hormone, and insert into sterile potting soil. Apply bottom heat.

PESTS AND DISEASES: Firecracker flower has few pests or diseases.

RELATED SPECIES: None are readily available.

As soon as the flower spikes fade, trim them off to keep the plant attractive and producing new blooms.

EARTH STAR
Cryptanthus bivittatus *krip-TAN-thus bib-vib-TAH-tus*

Earth star, a bromeliad, will keep its beautiful leaf color when provided bright light and warm temperatures.

SIZE: 6"h × 6–12"w
TYPE: Bromeliad
FORM: Mound
TEXTURE: Medium
GROWTH: Slow
LIGHT: High to medium

MOISTURE: Dry between waterings
SOIL: Epiphyte mix
FEATURES: Stiff, variegated leaves
USES: Focal point, dish garden, terrarium

SITING: Earth star shows its best leaf color in bright, filtered light. Provide warm to average temperatures (60°F and above) to keep the plant from rotting. This bromeliad looks best when grown in medium humidity (30–65 percent).

CARE: Let earth star dry out almost completely between waterings. Earth star may develop leaf spots in low humidity and root rot if it is overwatered. Feed with blooming plant formula three times in summer. Earth star has a minuscule root system that seldom outgrows a pot. If the plant flowers, remove the flower shoots as soon as they have faded and propagate new plants. The old plant will begin to deteriorate.

PROPAGATION: Propagate by removing the offsets that develop between the leaves and pot them. They will readily develop a root system merely by being in contact with moist soil.

PESTS AND DISEASES: Treat scale with horticultural oil.

RELATED SPECIES: The cultivar 'Pink Starlight' has bright pink, white, and green variegated leaves. *C. zonatus* 'Zebrinus' has reddish-brown leaves with silvery bands.

1

Offsets develop between the leaves of earth star, and these can be removed for propagating the plant.

2

After potting the offsets into sterile coarse potting mix, water them well. They will quickly develop roots.

FALSE HEATHER
Cuphea hyssopifolia KU-fee-uh hih-sop-ih-FOH-lee-uh

False heather, also known as Mexican heather, is adorned with soft lavender, white, or pink flowers.

SIZE: 8–14"h × 10"w
TYPE: Woody shrub
FORM: Upright
TEXTURE: Fine
GROWTH: Fast
LIGHT: High
MOISTURE: Evenly moist
SOIL: Potting soil
FEATURES: Tiny leaves, attractive flowers
USES: Blooming plant, focal point
FLOWERS: ▨ ▨ ☐

SITING: False heather thrives in bright light but tolerates full sun. Lower light reduces blooming. Provide average to cool temperatures (55–75°F) and average humidity (30 to 65 percent).
CARE: Keep the soil evenly moist. False heather will drop its leaves if the soil dries out. Feed with half-strength foliage plant food at every watering. Repot annually in spring before the blooming season. As soon as the plant has finished blooming, cut back by almost half to rejuvenate it.

PROPAGATION: Propagate by stem cuttings or from seed.
PESTS AND DISEASES: Pests include mealybugs, thrips, and whiteflies. If infestations are severe, discard the plant.
RELATED SPECIES: The cultivar 'Compacta' is a dwarf form. 'Rosea' has pink flowers, and 'Alba' has white flowers. All may be used as annual landscape plants in northern areas or as shrubs in the South. Cigar flower, *C. ignea*, is a soft-stemmed shrubby plant 1–2' tall with a spread of 1–3'. It develops 1-inch-long tubular red flowers with a white rim.

When false heather has finished blooming, cut the plant back by about half to rejuvenate it and promote new blossoms.

TEDDY BEAR VINE
Cyanotis kewensis sigh-a-NOTE-is cue-EN-sis

Teddy bear vine, a vining succulent plant covered with chocolate-colored hairs, is a favorite with children.

SIZE: 12" long
TYPE: Herbaceous
FORM: Trailing
TEXTURE: Fine
GROWTH: Fast
LIGHT: Medium
MOISTURE: Evenly moist
SOIL: Potting soil
FEATURES: Leaves with chocolate hairs
USES: Hanging basket

SITING: Give teddy bear vine medium light and average temperatures (60–75°F). This plant is easy to care for and tolerates medium to high humidity (30 percent or greater). Be sure to place it out of the way of traffic; the stems break easily. Velvety brown hairs on the leaves make the plant soft to the touch, giving rise to its common name.
CARE: The plant will tolerate dry conditions fairly well, but for optimum growth keep the soil evenly moist. Feed three times in summer with foliage plant food. Teddy bear vine is so succulent that the fragile stems do not fare well during repotting, and the roots do not grow quickly. It's best to leave the plant in its original pot. Although teddy bear vine can be pinched regularly to keep it shrubby, it doesn't branch well. It will eventually deteriorate, so new plants should be started regularly.

PROPAGATION: Start from stem cuttings. Simply take ends you pinch off during regular pruning, dip them in rooting hormone, and insert them in sterile potting soil. Extra humidity will speed rooting.
PESTS AND DISEASES: Mealybugs can be a problem. Control them with a labelled insecticide or by swabbing them with rubbing alcohol.
RELATED SPECIES: More succulent pussy ears (*C. somaliensis*) has larger leaves that clasp the plant's stem and are covered with silvery-gray hairs. It grows to 6" tall with a spread of 16". Teddy bear vine is distantly related to *Tradescantia* (see pages 133 and 134), but its hairs help it tolerate dry conditions better.

SAGO PALM
Cycas revoluta SIGH-kas rev-oh-LUTE-uh

Sago palms are easy to care for and although they are quite slow growing, they are extremely long-lived.

SIZE: 5'h × 4'w
TYPE: Cycad
FORM: Palmlike
TEXTURE: Coarse
GROWTH: Slow
LIGHT: High to medium
MOISTURE: Dry between waterings
SOIL: Cactus
FEATURES: Stiff architectural fronds
USES: Architectural accent

SITING: Sago palm (not a true palm) thrives in bright light, and even full sun. It also tolerates medium light. Any temperature and any humidity are fine. It grows extremely slowly but is very long-lived.

CARE: Let the soil dry out between waterings. The plant does not indicate when it is dry, so keep track of when it was watered. It tolerates drought but not overwatering. (Old leaves may turn yellow from overwatering.) Feed only once in spring and once in summer. If growing in low light, give it only half-strength plant food. (New leaves will turn yellow from

Sago palm lends a distinct, cleanly formal appearance to an interior landscape.

overfeeding.) Because it is so slow growing, it seldom needs repotting and actually looks best if pot-bound. Remove old fronds when necessary.

PROPAGATION: Propagate by separating the offsets, or "pups," that grow at the base or along the sides of mature plants. Remove them in early spring, late fall, or winter. Use a trowel to take small ones off the trunk or to separate larger ones from the base of the plant. Remove all the leaves and roots from each offset and set it aside to dry for a week. Then plant it in a cactus-type soil with half the offset below the soil level. Water it well and move it to a shady area. Allow the soil to dry before watering again. New leaves will appear in several months.

PESTS AND DISEASES: Treat scale with horticultural oil.

RELATED SPECIES: Queen sago palm (*C. circinalis*) has longer, softer fronds than *C. revoluta* and can reach 15' or more under ideal conditions.

CYCLAMEN
Cyclamen persicum SIGH-cla-men PER-sih-cum

Cyclamen, also known as florist's cyclamen, brightens up a room with its reflexed blossoms and variegated foliage.

SIZE: 6–10"h × 6–12"w
TYPE: Corm
FORM: Mounded
TEXTURE: Medium
GROWTH: Medium
LIGHT: Medium
MOISTURE: Dry between waterings
SOIL: Potting soil
FEATURES: Variegated, heart-shape leaves
USES: Blooming accent
FLOWERS: ■ ■ ■ □

SITING: Bright to medium indirect light will make the plant look its best. Cool temperatures (50–60°F) will prolong

cyclamen's blooming cycle. Provide average humidity (30–65 percent).

CARE: Allow the soil to dry only slightly before watering. Feed with half-strength food for blooming plants at every watering from fall until bud set. Repot in fall, keeping half the corm above the soil line.

Removing spent flowers and yellowed leaves regularly will keep cyclamen looking its best.

Remove faded flowers immediately to prevent seed formation, which shortens the blooming time. Also remove any faded leaves. Gently twist stems of leaves and flowers to remove. Yellow leaves indicate too warm a room or that the plant wilted severely at one time or was overwatered. Cyclamen is often treated as a throwaway plant because it is difficult to bring back into bloom. For the best success, set it under a shrub outdoors for the summer with the pot on its side. Water infrequently and expect the foliage to fade completely. Bring the pot back indoors as soon as temperatures cool in the fall. Repot and begin watering. Keep in a cool, bright spot and water as the soil dries slightly. Begin feeding as directed above.

PROPAGATION: Propagate from seed. The plant sets seed easily.

PESTS AND DISEASES: Cyclamen mites are a perennial problem. Spray with a miticide labeled for indoor use or discard severly infested plants.

RELATED SPECIES: There are hundreds of cultivars with flowers of every color and size. Many related species are grown outdoors and are not appropriate for indoor culture.

CYMBIDIUM ORCHID
Cymbidium spp. *sim-BID-ee-um*

There is nothing quite as breathtaking as a cymbidium orchid in bloom. This is 'Lavender Falls'.

SIZE: 1–3'h × 1'w
TYPE: Orchid
FORM: Upright
TEXTURE: Medium
GROWTH: Slow
LIGHT: High to medium

MOISTURE: Even
SOIL: Epiphyte
FEATURES: Flowers
USES: Focal point
FLOWERS: ☐ ■ ■
■ ■

SITING: Cymbidium orchid needs at least medium light to bloom and performs better in brighter, filtered light. Keep at 45–50°F most of the time. It can handle hot temperatures for short periods, but cold is essential to induce flowering.

Reduce the temperature to just above freezing in fall—a cool porch is ideal. Provide medium humidity (30–65 percent) and keep it away from drying winds to preserve the fragrant blossoms.

CARE: Cymbidium orchid is not hard to care for when grown in cool conditions. Keep the soil evenly moist except in winter, when water should be reduced as the growth slows. If you see tip burn, switch to distilled water. Feed with a dilute solution of standard plant food at every watering during active growth. When it

'Banff' produces sprays of delicate pink blooms.

'Mary Pinchess Del Rey' has gold blooms.

comes indoors in fall, feed with a blossom booster at every watering until the plant goes into its resting phase in winter. Repot when the plant begins to outgrow its pot and becomes unwieldy or when the potting mix begins to break down and you can no longer recognize individual pieces of bark. Tap the plant out of its pot and remove any withered roots. Let any broken roots air-dry for a few hours before potting. Remove faded leaves and flowers. Place outdoors in summer in a bright spot that is well protected from wind and direct sun.

PROPAGATION: Propagate by separating the pseudobulbs from one another; the new plants will bloom 2–3 years after propagation. The preferred method when the plant gets too large is repotting into a larger pot rather than dividing.

PESTS AND DISEASES: Scale and spider mites may be problems in poor cultural conditions.

RELATED SPECIES: There are hundreds of cymbidium cultivars. Newer miniature versions are popular for home use because of their smaller size and greater tolerance for heat.

DWARF PAPYRUS
Cyperus alternifolius *SIGH-pur-us al-tur-nih-FOHL-ee-us*

Dwarf papyrus, also known as umbrella plant, will win you over with its dancing leaflets that sit atop long, elegant stems.

SIZE: 3'h × 3'w
TYPE: Herbaceous
FORM: Vase-shaped
TEXTURE: Fine
GROWTH: Medium
LIGHT: High
MOISTURE: Wet

SOIL: Potting soil
FEATURES: Long stems, starry flowers
USES: Accent, aquatic
FLOWERS: ■

SITING: Provide dwarf papyrus with the highest indirect light possible. A south or west window is perfect as long as the light is slightly filtered, perhaps through a gauzy curtain. Because of its need for water, it is an ideal accent plant for an indoor water

feature. This plant tolerates cool to hot temperatures (50–85°F) and prefers medium (30–65 percent) humidity.

CARE: This unique-looking plant needs constantly wet soil. Use a pot with no drainage and keep the soil soaked, or stand the plant in a container of water. Be sure to use tepid water; cold water will rot the plant. Feed infrequently—about twice a year—with a general foliage

Dwarf papyrus performs well outdoors as a focal point in a water feature.

To propagate this plant invert a leaf in a container of water until new plants form.

houseplant food. Repot with average potting soil when the plant begins to creep out of its pot. Soil with too much organic matter will become sour and rot the roots. Remove any faded fronds. Wipe the leaves regularly with a dry, soft cloth.

PROPAGATION: Propagate by dividing the rhizome, but it's more interesting to take leaf cuttings. Cut one leaf with a small piece of stem attached and cut back the bracts by two-thirds. Invert the leaf in a container of water. New plants will form where the leaf meets the stem. Clip the new plants and pot them. Another easy way to propagate is to simply bend a stem over and pin the bracts down on wet sand in a new pot. Clip the new plant from the parent plant when rooted.

PESTS AND DISEASES: None.

RELATED SPECIES: The cultivar 'Gracilis' is a stiff-leaved dwarf form. Papyrus (*Cyperus papyrus*) grows to 7' tall.

JAPANESE HOLLY FERN

Cyrtomium falcatum sir-TOHM-ee-um fall-KAH-tum

Japanese holly ferns are handsome foliage plants that require medium light and cool to average temperatures.

SIZE: 1'h × 4'w
TYPE: Fern
FORM: Arching
TEXTURE: Medium
GROWTH: Medium to fast
LIGHT: Medium
MOISTURE: Even
SOIL: Potting soil
FEATURES: Glossy leaves
USES: Foliage

SITING: Japanese holly fern grows well in medium light, making it an excellent companion to many other plants. Its glossy leaves set off a blooming plant such as gardenia, columnea, or even a cattleya orchid. Provide cool to average temperatures (50–75°F) and keep the humidity high (above 65 percent). It will tolerate somewhat lower humidity but will look best when set on a moist pebble tray. Grouping it with other plants will also raise the humidity.

CARE: Keep the soil evenly moist but not soggy. Feed three times in summer with a general foliage plant food. Repot every year into sterile organic potting mix. Remove dead fronds.

PROPAGATION: Propagate by dividing the rhizome. This plant is also propagated fairly easily by spores, but it takes a while to grow into sizable plants.

PESTS AND DISEASES: Thrips are so difficult to control that it may be necessary to discard the plant. Treat mealybugs and scale with horticultural oil.

RELATED SPECIES: The cultivar 'Rochfordianum' (fringed holly fern) has closely fringed margins. *C. fortunei* is smaller than holly fern and more tolerant of cold.

1 Ferns reproduce by spores, borne in small cases on the backs of fronds.

2 Tap ripe spores out onto paper and then sprinkle them on moist soil mix.

3 Cover with glass or plastic to keep the interior moist until small plants form.

RABBIT'S FOOT FERN

Davallia fejeensis (Polypodium aureum) dub-VAHL-ya fee-jee-EN-sis (pahl-ee-POH-dee-um AW-ree-um)

Rabbit's foot fern, also known as hare's foot fern, makes a beautiful hanging basket.

SIZE: 8–12"h × 1–3'w
TYPE: Fern
FORM: Mounded
TEXTURE: Fine
GROWTH: Medium
LIGHT: High to medium
MOISTURE: Even
SOIL: Epiphyte mix
FEATURES: Fronds, creeping rhizomes
USES: Hanging basket

SITING: Rabbit's foot fern makes its best growth in bright, filtered light. It performs well in home temperatures from about 55°F at night to as high as 85°F during the day. It needs high humidity.

CARE: This epiphytic fern grows on the sides of trees in the wild, so keep it moderately moist. It has a resting period from October to February when it needs little water. Feed with a foliage plant food at half the recommended dose from April through September. Tip burn results from being fed too much. The fern's "rabbit's foot" rhizomes creep over the ground and hang over the sides of the pot. It's important not to cover the rhizomes with potting soil but rather to let them creep where they want. The rhizomes are succulent and can break, so instead of repotting the entire plant, push new potting mix between the rhizomes when the old potting mix breaks down. Rabbit's foot fern seldom needs pruning but may need yellowed fronds removed occasionally.

PROPAGATION: Propagate by rhizome division. Simply cut pieces of a rhizome and pin them to moist soil. This fern can also be propagated by spores.

PESTS AND DISEASES: Spider mites may be a problem if the humidity is low. Control them by showering the plant regularly and keeping humidity high. Browning fronds may result from low humidity.

RELATED SPECIES: Deer's foot fern (*D. canariensis*) has narrow triangular fronds. Polynesian foot fern (*D. solida*) has more leathery fronds. Squirrel's foot fern (*D. trichomanoides*) has diamond-shaped fronds.

1 This fern gets its name from the fuzzy rhizomes that creep over the edge of the pot.

2 Propagate this fern by placing a rhizome on moist sterile potting soil.

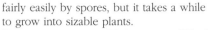

DENDROBIUM ORCHID
Dendrobium hybrids *den-DROH-bee-um*

Dendrobiums will bloom beautifully for you with bright light, warm temperatures, and regular fertilization.

SIZE: 2–6'h × 8–16"w
TYPE: Orchid
FORM: Upright
TEXTURE: Medium
GROWTH: Slow
LIGHT: High

MOISTURE: Even
SOIL: Epiphyte mix
FEATURES: Flowers
USES: Focal point
FLOWERS: □ ■ ■ ■

SITING: Give this orchid bright light with up to 50 percent sun, but shade it from direct sun. It requires a difference of 15–20°F between daytime and nighttime temperatures. Maintain a night temperature of 60–65°F and a day temperature of 80–90°F. Low temperatures may cause leaf drop. Dendrobium orchid needs 50–60 percent humidity.

CARE: Keep the soil evenly moist while in active growth. During the resting phase, allow to dry slightly between waterings. This plant thrives when grown outdoors in summer. Dendrobium needs regular fertilization to produce its magnificent blossoms. Feed weekly during the growing period. It blooms best when pot-bound. When the plant outgrows its pot, select a new one of a size that will allow only 1–2 years of growth. When the root ball is out of the pot, trim away any dead roots or shriveled pseudobulbs. Repot only when the plant is in active growth. Remove the occasional yellow leaf or papery sheath, which detracts from the overall beauty of the plant. Dendrobium flower spikes may need support. Before the buds open, anchor a sturdy stake securely beside the root ball. Tie the flower stem gently to the stake with soft twine using a loose figure eight.

PROPAGATION: Propagate by removing offsets when the plant is actively growing. Divided plants may take several years before they bloom. Some species can be propagated simply by laying the offsets on damp moss.

PESTS AND DISEASES: Control orchid scale with horticultural oil.

RELATED SPECIES: Choose the evergreen types for beauty year-round. These are grouped into the "cane," Farmeri, and Formosum groups.

***Dendrobium chrysotoxum* has fragrant yellow blooms**

To support the blossom spike, tie it gently to an orchid stake with soft twine.

DUMB CANE
Dieffenbachia amoena *dee-fin-BAH-kee-uh uh-MEE-nuh*

Dumb canes are absolutely carefree plants when given medium light, average temperatures, and occasional fertilization.

SIZE: 3–6'h × 1–3'w
TYPE: Herbaceous
FORM: Upright
TEXTURE: Coarse
GROWTH: Medium
LIGHT: Medium

MOISTURE: Dry
SOIL: Potting soil
FEATURES: Foliage
USES: Architectural accent, foliage

SITING: Dumb cane takes average conditions and easily tolerates some neglect. Provide medium light and average temperatures (60–75°F). Keep it out of drafts and drying winds. It tolerates medium humidity (30–65 percent) but looks much better in higher humidity.

CARE: Allow the soil to dry out slightly before watering; it tolerates an occasional missed watering. Wilting causes severe leaf loss. Feed mature plants three times in summer with a foliage plant food. Feeding more often may cause succulent growth that is not sturdy enough to tolerate dryness; it also makes the plant top-heavy and causes it to outgrow its pot. Repot annually in spring when the plant is young. As the plant ages, it begins to look sloppy, so take cuttings or air-layer to produce new plants. In summer, remove old canes to force new ones at the cut. Wipe the leaves frequently to keep them looking fresh and pest free. Be aware when pruning that the sap is toxic if ingested and may be irritating to the skin.

PROPAGATION: Dieffenbachia naturally loses its bottom leaves, which gives ample opportunity for air-layering. It can also be propagated easily by stem cuttings.

PESTS AND DISEASES: Watch for spider mites, mealybugs, and scale if grown in low humidity.

RELATED SPECIES: 'Hilo' looks much like a canna with large dark green leaves and a thick white midrib.

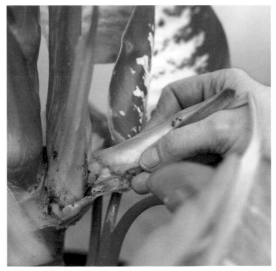

To keep dumb canes looking pristine, remove any yellowing or browning leaves and leaf sheaths.

SPOTTED DUMB CANE
Dieffenbachia maculata *dee-fin-BAH-kee-uh mak-yew-LAH-ta*

The striking spotted dumb cane is a simple plant to maintain as long as you keep it out of drafts and provide medium light.

SIZE: 5'h × 3'w
TYPE: Herbaceous
FORM: Upright
TEXTURE: Coarse
GROWTH: Medium
LIGHT: Medium
MOISTURE: Dry
SOIL: Average
FEATURES: Foliage
USES: Architectural accent, foliage

SITING: Provide medium light and average temperatures (60–75°F) for spotted dumb cane. Keep it out of drafts. It tolerates medium humidity (30–65 percent) but looks much better in higher humidity.
CARE: Allow the soil to dry out slightly before watering. Feed three times in summer with a foliage plant food once it is mature. Repot annually in spring when it is young. In summer remove old canes to force new ones at the cut. Wipe the leaves frequently to keep them looking fresh and pest free. Be aware when pruning that the sap is toxic if ingested and may be irritating to the skin.

PROPAGATION: Propagate by stem cuttings or air-layering.
PESTS AND DISEASES: Watch for spider mites, mealybugs, and scale when grown in low humidity.
RELATED SPECIES: The cultivar 'Tropic Snow' has beautiful splotches through the center of the leaf. Almost half the leaf of 'Camille' is colored ivory.

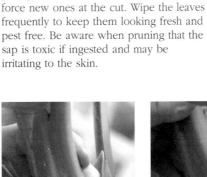

1 To air-layer a dumb cane, cut a notch in the cane near the top tuft of leaves.

2 Dust the notch with rooting hormone and prop the cut edges apart.

3 Wrap with damp sphagnum moss and enclose in plastic until roots form.

DUMB CANE
Dieffenbachia picta *dee-fin-BAH-kee-uh PIK-tuh*

This dumb cane shows another of the myriad of leaf variations and shapes available for the home interior.

SIZE: 2–3'h × 1–2'w
TYPE: Herbaceous
FORM: Upright
TEXTURE: Coarse
GROWTH: Medium
LIGHT: Medium
MOISTURE: Dry
SOIL: Potting soil
FEATURES: Variegated leaves
USES: Architectural accent, foliage

SITING: Dumb cane takes average conditions and tolerates some neglect. Provide medium light and average temperatures (60–75°F). Keep it out of drafts and drying winds. It tolerates medium humidity (30–65 percent) but looks much better in higher humidity.
CARE: Allow the soil to dry out slightly before watering. Avoid wilting, which causes severe leaf loss. Feed three times in summer with a foliage plant food once it is mature. Repot annually in spring when it is young. In summer remove old canes to force new ones at the cut. Wipe leaves frequently to keep them pest free and looking fresh. Be aware when pruning that the sap is toxic if ingested and may be irritating to the skin.
PROPAGATION: Propagate by stem cuttings.
PESTS AND DISEASES: Spider mites, mealybugs, and scale can be problems when grown in low humidity.
RELATED SPECIES: There are hundreds of cultivars to suit every taste.

1 Dumb canes elongate and lose their lower leaves. Cut them back occasionally to make them more attractive.

2 Once a plant has been cut back, new growth will emerge from dormant buds alongside the cut stem.

DUMB CANE
Dieffenbachia seguine *dee-fin-BAH-kee-uh sub-GEEN*

Dumb canes make a beautiful statement in the home because of their brightly variegated leaves and large size.

SIZE: 3–6'h × 1–3'w
TYPE: Herbaceous
FORM: Upright
TEXTURE: Coarse
GROWTH: Medium
LIGHT: Medium

MOISTURE: Dry
SOIL: Potting soil
FEATURES: Foliage
USES: Architectural accent, foliage

SITING: Dumb cane is fairly carefree, which is the main reason it is such a staple in the interior plant industry. It takes average conditions and easily tolerates some neglect. It gives a dynamic tropical look to any interior space. Provide medium light and average temperatures (60–75°F). Keep it out of drafts and drying winds. It tolerates medium humidity (30–65 percent) but looks much better with higher humidity. It looks attractive when the pot-in-pot method is used to increase humidity; the two-pot combination helps weight the plant, which tends to be top-heavy.
CARE: Allow the soil to dry out slightly before watering. It will tolerate an occasional missed watering, but wilting will cause severe leaf loss. Feed only three times in summer with a foliage plant food once it is mature. Feeding more often may cause succulent growth that is not sturdy enough to tolerate dryness. It also makes

the plant become top-heavy and likely to outgrow its pot. Repot annually in spring when the plant is young. As it ages, it begins to look sloppy, so take cuttings or air-layer to produce new plants. In summer, remove old canes to force new ones at the cut. Wipe the leaves frequently to keep them pest free and looking fresh. Be aware when pruning that the sap is toxic if ingested and may be irritating to the skin. Dumb cane is not a plant to have in a home with young children and chewing pets.
PROPAGATION: Dieffenbachia naturally loses its bottom leaves, which gives ample opportunity for air-layering. It can also be propagated fairly easily by stem cuttings.
PESTS AND DISEASES: Spider mites, scale, and mealybugs thrive in low humidity.
RELATED SPECIES: *Dieffenbachia* 'Hilo' looks much like a canna with dark green leaves and a white midrib.

VENUS FLYTRAP
Dionaea muscipula *dye-oh-NEE-uh myew-SIP-yew-luh*

These plants are naturally found in bogs, so simulate these conditions by repotting them into pure sphagnum moss mixed with sand.

Venus flytraps are must-haves for the plant collector because they certainly will stimulate conversation.

SIZE: 6–8"h × 6–8"w
TYPE: Herbaceous
FORM: Rounded
TEXTURE: Medium
GROWTH: Medium
LIGHT: High to medium

MOISTURE: Even
SOIL: Mossy
FEATURES: Insect traps
USES: Terrarium, conversation piece

SITING: Venus flytrap does well in medium to high light but not direct sunlight. A healthy plant grown with enough light will have reddish to pink traps. The plant is a challenge to grow. It thrives in average to cool temperatures (55–75°F) but needs a dormant period from November to March in which the temperature is reduced to 38–45°F. The easiest way to accomplish this is to put it in a perforated plastic bag in a refrigerator and reduce watering, but don't let it dry out. It does not need light

at this time. Venus flytrap needs high humidity; a terrarium is ideal.
CARE: Venus flytrap needs plenty of moisture to help it thrive. It grows best when planted in long-fibered sphagnum

moss mixed with sand. Use distilled water or rainwater only and change the water often. Venus flytrap does not need to be fed. (It feeds itself!) A spider, pill bug, or fly every month or so is enough. Traps that close empty will reopen in a day or two. Venus flytrap sends up a flower stalk in spring with tiny white flowers and black seeds. Most growers pinch out this stalk as soon as it appears, to enhance formation of traps and to keep the plant vigorous. Older leaves regularly blacken and die. Remove them; new ones will be produced quickly.
PROPAGATION: Remove a leaf at the base of the rhizome and set it in a mix of half sand and half peat moss. Keep watered and humidified until tiny plants form at the base, usually in 6 weeks or more. Separate the plants and discard any that have rotted. Pot them up individually.
PESTS AND DISEASES: If new leaves appear distorted, look for aphids. Wash off with a strong spray of water or handpick.
RELATED SPECIES: The cultivar 'Akai Ryu' has much redder traps than the species.

GREEN DRACAENA

Dracaena deremensis *druh-SEEN-uh dair-uh-MEN-sis*

Green dracaena is a stunning architectural plant for use in either medium or low light.

SIZE: 4–10'h × 3'w
TYPE: Herbaceous
FORM: Upright
TEXTURE: Coarse
GROWTH: Medium
LIGHT: Low to medium

MOISTURE: Low to medium
SOIL: Potting soil
FEATURES: Tall stems, variegated leaves
USES: Architectural accent

SITING: Green dracaena grows beautifully in low to medium light and average home temperatures (60–75°F). It benefits from a drop of about 10 degrees at night. It tolerates drying out but not low humidity.

CARE: Allow the soil to dry out slightly between waterings, especially when grown in low light. It will rot easily if the soil remains soggy. Low humidity may cause leaf tips to brown. Brown tips may also develop from fluoride in the water or excess plant food. Leaves curl downward

Leaf tips may brown when the humidity is low, so change the cultural situation and trim the brown off the leaves.

when temperatures are too low. This can eventually kill the plant. Feed only every couple of months. It has a smallish root system and does well in a small pot. Repot into a heavy container when it becomes top-heavy. Remove yellowed leaves. Cut back stems to produce new tufts of leaves along the stems and give a more lush look.
PROPAGATION: Propagate from 2–3" stem cuttings or by air-layering. Make a simple cut and force in a toothpick or skewer to separate the two sides.
PESTS AND DISEASES: Spider mites can be a problem in low humidity. Frequent showers or wiping the leaves will prevent their getting out of hand. Mealybugs may appear in leaf axils. A sour smell in the soil indicates root rot, especially in low light; dry the plant out somewhat and repot to correct the situation.
RELATED SPECIES: The cultivar 'Janet Craig' is the foliage plant industry standard. The leaves are very dark green, and the plant may reach 10' high. 'Warneckei' (striped dracaena) is 4' high with narrow white-striped leaves. It doesn't suffer tip burn as readily as 'Janet Craig'.

CORN PLANT

Dracaena fragrans *druh-SEEN-uh FRAY-gruns*

Variegated corn plant is the most widely grown form. It has a central yellow band on each leaf.

SIZE: 4–10'h × 2'w
TYPE: Herbaceous
FORM: Upright
TEXTURE: Coarse
GROWTH: Medium
LIGHT: Low to medium

MOISTURE: Dry
SOIL: Potting soil
FEATURES: Tall stems, variegated leaves
USES: Architectural

SITING: Corn plant is ideal in a darker corner of the home. It grows best in average home temperatures (60–75°F) and benefits from a drop of about 10 degrees at night. It can tolerate drying out but not low humidity or drying winds.

CARE: Allow it to dry out between waterings. Feed only every couple of months. It has a smallish root system and does well in a small pot. Repot into a heavy container when it becomes top-heavy. Very low humidity may cause tip burn. Brown tips may also develop if fluoride is present in the water or when excess plant food is provided. Leaves curl downward when temperatures are too

To produce new tufts of leaves, make a cut in the stem and force the cut edges apart with a toothpick.

low. This can eventually kill the plant. Remove yellowed leaves. Cut stems to produce new tufts of leaves along the stems and give them a more lush look.
PROPAGATION: Propagate from 2–3" stem cuttings or by air-layering.
PESTS AND DISEASES: Spider mites can be a problem in low humidity, although frequent showers or wiping the leaves will prevent their getting out of hand. Mealybugs may infest corn plant. A sour smell in the soil indicates root rot, especially in low light. Dry the plant out somewhat and repot to correct the situation.
RELATED SPECIES: The cultivar 'Massangeana' (variegated corn plant) has yellow bands along the leaves. A former species, *D. deremensis*, grows wider and has more stems than corn plant. The glossy dark leaves meet the stem in graceful arches. *D. deremensis* 'Janet Craig' is the foliage plant industry standard. The leaves are very dark green, and the plant may reach 10' high. 'Warneckei' (striped dracaena) is 4' high with narrow white-striped leaves. It doesn't suffer tip burn as readily as 'Janet Craig'.

MADAGASCAR DRAGON TREE

Dracaena marginata druh-SEEN-uh mar-jin-AH-tuh

Madagascar dragon tree tolerates the low humidity of most homes.

SIZE: 2–6'h × 2–4'w
TYPE: Herbaceous
FORM: Upright
TEXTURE: Coarse
GROWTH: Slow to medium
LIGHT: Low to medium

MOISTURE: Dry
SOIL: Potting soil
FEATURES: Variegated foliage
USES: Architectural accent

SITING: Madagascar dragon tree grows best in average home temperatures (60–75°F). It tolerates lower humidity than other dracaenas. Its attractive foliage, large size, and interesting stems make an ideal backdrop for smaller plants.
CARE: Allow the soil to dry out about an inch below the soil level between waterings. Growing it with more moisture can cause rotting roots and leaf drop. Reducing water makes the stems stronger, although if you intend to induce bends in the stems, they need to be pliable. Feed only every couple of months. Repot only when it becomes top-heavy or the roots begin to creep out of the drainage holes.

Spruce up the soil in a pot of Madagascar dragon tree by covering the soil with decorative mulch such as stones or shredded bark.

It's natural for this dracaena to periodically shed leaves, but extremely low humidity or drying out too much will cause many lower leaves to drop. To produce quirky, meandering stems, start with a young plant and suspend weights from the stems at different places. Produce the same effect by tipping the pot on its side, forcing a stem to change direction, then tipping the pot a different way for several weeks. Because Madagascar dragon tree has such long, bare stems, it is a perfect candidate for attractive mulch in the pot.
PROPAGATION: Propagate from 2–3" stem cuttings or air-layer.
PESTS AND DISEASES: Spider mites can be a problem in low humidity, although frequent showers or wiping the leaves will prevent population explosions. A sour smell in the soil indicates root rot. Dry the plant out somewhat and repot to correct the situation.
RELATED SPECIES: The cultivar 'Tricolor' has pink, green, and white leaves. It is the most commonly seen dragon tree in commercial settings.

SONG OF INDIA

Dracaena reflexa (Pleomele reflexa) druh-SEEN-uh ree-FLEX-uh (PLEE-oh-meel ree-FLEX-uh)

Song of India, also known as pleomele, makes a dramatic statement with its attractively variegated leaves.

SIZE: 7–8'h × 3–4'w
TYPE: Herbaceous
FORM: Upright
TEXTURE: Medium
GROWTH: Medium
LIGHT: High, indirect

MOISTURE: Even
SOIL: Potting soil
FEATURES: Erect stems, clasping leaves
USES: Architectural

SITING: This dracaena grows better in bright, indirect light than in the low to medium light preferred by other dracaenas. Because of its large size, it makes a dramatic statement as an architectural feature in the home or office setting. Provide average home temperatures (60–75°F) with a drop of about 10 degrees at night. This plant can tolerate drying out somewhat, but it will not tolerate low humidity or drying winds. Although it is often used as a single plant in commercial settings, it needs average humidity (around 30–65 percent), so group it with other plants. Its attractive foliage and large size make it an ideal backdrop for smaller plants.
CARE: Keep the soil more evenly moist than other dracaenas, but if growing in lower-than-ideal light, make sure the soil does not become soggy. Reducing water somewhat makes the stems even sturdier and stronger. Winter water reduction helps keep the roots from rotting. Feed with a foliage plant food once a month. If growing in less than ideal light, reduce feeding to once every couple of months. Because of its smallish root system, it does well in a small pot. Repot into a heavy container when it becomes top-heavy. Leaves curl downward when temperatures are too low. This can eventually kill the plant. Very low humidity may cause tip burn. Trimmed tips will eventually turn brown again, so remove affected leaves when necessary.
PROPAGATION: Propagate from 2–3" stem cuttings or air-layer. If the plant blooms, new plants can be started from seed. Root cuttings are sometimes successful as well.
PESTS AND DISEASES: Spider mites can be a problem in low humidity, although frequent showers or wiping the leaves will prevent their getting out of hand. Mealybugs may attack plants. A sour smell in the soil indicates root rot, especially in low light. Dry the plant out somewhat and repot to correct the situation.
RELATED SPECIES: The cultivar 'Variegata' has yellow-edged leaves. 'Song of Jamaica' has buff to yellow stripes. 'Song of India' has bright yellow stripes.

LUCKY BAMBOO
Dracaena sanderiana *drub-SEEN-uh san-dur-ee-AHN-uh*

Lucky bamboo, also known as ribbon plant, can be grown in water or soil and takes little care except for regular fertilizing.

SIZE: 4–12"h × 2–6"w
TYPE: Herbaceous
FORM: Upright
TEXTURE: Medium
GROWTH: Fast
LIGHT: Medium

MOISTURE: Wet
SOIL: Potting soil
FEATURES: Twisted stems, variegated leaves
USES: Focal point

SITING: Lucky bamboo needs bright light to thrive, but it will not tolerate any sun. Browning leaves indicate too much direct light. It can be grown in lower light but may become leggy. It needs average temperatures (60–75°F) and average humidity (30–65 percent).
CARE: Lucky bamboo is often grown as a hydroponic plant, with the stems set in water and held upright with decorative stones. When grown this way, it is critical to use water that has no minerals, especially fluoride, and to change the

water every 3–5 days. The plant can also be grown in soil as long as the soil remains wet at all times. Start the canes in water; as soon as they develop a mass of roots, pot them in rich soil. Lucky bamboo must be fertilized, especially when grown in water. Use a half-strength foliage plant food every 2 weeks whether grown in

Lucky bamboo can be formed into unique shapes by manipulating the light source or wiring stems.

water or soil. Some gardeners grow the plant in water with a Siamese fighting fish in the same bowl; the fish provides the fertilizer. It is important not to add plant food or the fish might be harmed. The canes are often grouped together or twisted and shaped to give the plant an unusual appearance. You can twist and shape your own stems simply by manipulating light. Put a young plant in a darkened spot with a single light source directed at the stem. The plant will respond by growing toward the light.
PROPAGATION: These plants are traditionally propagated as 2–3" cane cuttings. A piece of cane is cut, waxed to keep out fungus, and sold. You can propagate your own plants simply by breaking a cane into pieces and putting them in water.
PESTS AND DISEASES: Lucky bamboo plants that are shipped in water from Southeast Asian countries may have tiger mosquito larvae in the water. If your plant came in water, dump the water on dry ground and replenish with fresh water.

GOLD DUST DRACAENA
Dracaena surculosa *drub-SEEN-uh sir-kyew-LOH-suh*

Gold dust dracaena is carefree like other dracaenas and has the added attraction of gold-spattered foliage.

SIZE: 2–3'h × 2–3'w
TYPE: Herbaceous
FORM: Mound
TEXTURE: Medium
GROWTH: Medium
LIGHT: Medium

MOISTURE: Dry
SOIL: Potting soil
FEATURES: Flecked leaves
USES: Focal point

SITING: Gold dust dracaena needs more light than most dracaenas to keep its beautiful variegation. It grows best in average home temperatures (60–75°F) and benefits from a drop of about 10 degrees at night. It can tolerate drying out somewhat but will not tolerate low humidity or drying drafts. It needs average humidity (around 30–65 percent), so group it with other plants. Its attractive foliage and large size make it an ideal accent for smaller plants. This variegated type, in particular, is an attractive backdrop for smaller-leaved plants.
CARE: Allow the soil to dry out slightly between waterings, especially when grown in low light. It will rot easily if the soil remains soggy. Reducing water somewhat makes the stems even sturdier and stronger. Winter water reduction helps keep the roots from rotting. Feed once a month with a foliage plant food. It does well in a small pot. Repot into a heavy

container when it becomes top-heavy. Leaves curl downward when temperatures are too low. This can eventually kill the plant. Very low humidity may cause tip burn. Trimmed tips will eventually turn brown again, so remove affected leaves when necessary.
PROPAGATION: Propagate from 2–3" stem cuttings or air-layer. If the plant blooms, new plants can be started from seed. Root cuttings are sometimes successful as well.
PESTS AND DISEASES: Spider mites can be a problem in low humidity, although frequent showers or wiping the leaves will control them. If the plant flowers, mealybugs may appear. A sour smell in the soil indicates root rot, especially in low light. Dry the plant out somewhat and repot to correct the situation.
RELATED SPECIES: The cultivar 'Florida Beauty' has leaves that are flecked with yellow and white, with little green visible.

PINEAPPLE DYCKIA
Dyckia brevifolia *DIK-ee-uh brev-ih-FOH-lee-uh*

Pineapple dyckia, like other bromeliads, needs high light, average temperatures, and low humidity.

SIZE: 1'h × 2'w
TYPE: Bromeliad
FORM: Horizontal
TEXTURE: Coarse
GROWTH: Slow
LIGHT: High
MOISTURE: Low

SOIL: Cactus mix
FEATURES: Colorful leaves
USES: Focal point, cactus garden
FLOWERS: ■

SITING: Although pineapple dyckia is a bromeliad, it acts more like a cactus. It is found in rocky, dry soils, which hints at its tolerance of neglect. It needs high light and does beautifully in direct sun—the perfect plant for a western or southern windowsill. High light shows off the striking coloration of the leaves, particularly the undersides. Pineapple dyckia is not fussy but does best with nighttime temperatures of 50–55°F and daytime temperatures above 68°F. Being a succulent, pineapple dyckia performs best with low humidity. Be sure to place this plant out of the way of traffic, because the spines can cause a painful stab.

CARE: This plant is ideal for a situation in which it might be neglected or plant care is performed only every 2 weeks or so. Allow the soil to dry fairly well between waterings. Root rot might occur if the plant is grown in low light and kept too moist.

Feed only once a year with an all-purpose plant food. Repotting is seldom necessary because of the small root system. Grow it in a heavy terra-cotta pot to keep it well anchored. Remove any yellow leaves. Shower the plant occasionally, because it is prone to collect dust. Move it outdoors for the summer. If grown well, it may produce a bloom spike with bright orange flowers.

PROPAGATION: Dyckia produces multiple crowns, so it is easy to divide to produce more plants. If your plant blooms, you can collect seed for propagating. Sprinkle ripe seed on moist soil mix and tent with glass or plastic until germinated.

PESTS AND DISEASES: Even when neglected, dyckia has no pest problems.

RELATED SPECIES: *D. fosteriana* grows to only 6–12" wide and has beautiful spines and silvery leaves. *D. cinerea* has broad, succulent leaves and yellow flowers.

HEN-AND-CHICKS
Echeveria spp. *ay-shuh-VER-ee-uh*

Carefree hen-and-chicks plants have been favorites in indoor and outdoor gardens for many years.

SIZE: 6-36"h × 12"w
TYPE: Succulent
FORM: Mounded
TEXTURE: Medium
GROWTH: Medium
LIGHT: High

MOISTURE: Low
SOIL: Cactus mix
FEATURES: Succulent leaves
USES: Dish garden, cactus garden

SITING: Hen-and-chicks is the perfect houseplant for someone who travels. It withstands neglect and continues to thrive. The only requirement is good light. In summer when it is growing actively, half a day of direct sun is best, with some shading from afternoon sun. In winter all-day sun is preferred. Provide average to hot temperatures (60°F and above) and low to average humidity (60 percent and below).

CARE: Provide plenty of water in spring and summer and little in fall and winter.

Overwatering will cause root rot. If the plant fills the pot, water from the bottom to avoid scarring the leaves. Feed only once a year with a general houseplant food. This succulent plant has a very small root system and will seldom need repotting. If varieties that have a rosette top get too tall, simply cut off the top with a couple of inches still attached, set it aside to callus for a few days, then set it in some cactus mix. It will root in 2–3 weeks. Discard the original plant.

PROPAGATION: Most species of *Echeveria* readily produce offsets. Detach from the parent plant, set on a pot of cactus mix, and water. They will send out roots quickly. For types that produce stolons, cut the stolon and pot.

PESTS AND DISEASES: Wipe away mealybugs with a cotton swab dipped in alcohol.

RELATED SPECIES: 'Chocolate' has apple green leaves that mature to dark bronze tones from autumn to spring. 'Wavy Curls' has silver leaves with frilled edges.

Use leaf cuttings to start new echeveria plants.

After several weeks new roots will form at the base of the leaf, and later a new shoot will sprout.

GOLDEN BARREL CACTUS
Echinocactus grusonii *ee-KINE-ob-kak-tus grub-SONE-ee-eye*

(top-left cactus photo)

Golden barrel cactus is the perfect complement to a decor with a southwestern flavor.

SIZE: 1'h × 1'w
TYPE: Cactus
FORM: Round
TEXTURE: Coarse
GROWTH: Slow
LIGHT: High
MOISTURE: Low

SOIL: Cactus mix
FEATURES: Golden spines
USES: Cactus garden, accent
FLOWERS: ▪

SITING: Golden barrel cactus is an appealing design element for Southwestern decor. As with all cacti, golden barrel cactus needs high light. If the light is perfect, small, attractive yellow flowers will arise from the woolly center. The preferred temperature is from 50–85°F or higher. It prefers low humidity. This is a plant to grow on a dry, exposed windowsill. Keep the plant out of traffic, because its spines can inflict painful wounds.

The plant likes it dry and hot, and mulching the soil with small stones mimics the desert from which it comes.

CARE: Golden barrel cactus needs little water most of the time. Let it dry out completely between waterings, then soak it just as a desert rain would do. It must have perfect drainage. Root rot may occur in overly wet soil and low light. In winter give it a cooler, drier resting time. Feed three times in summer with a general-purpose plant food. Repot only when the plant creeps beyond the edge of the pot, making it difficult to get water to the soil. The spines might make you think twice about repotting, but it can be done without injury. Prepare a larger terra-cotta pot with soil to receive the cactus. Take an old piece of carpet or something thick enough to avoid puncture and wrap it around the cactus. Lift it gently out of its pot and lower it into the new pot.
PROPAGATION: Propagate by seed. Because the plant seldom produces flowers indoors, obtain seed from a supplier.
PESTS AND DISEASES: Mealybugs may appear at the base of the spines. They are hard to remove physically, so dab them with horticultural oil on a cotton swab.
RELATED SPECIES: *E. g.* var. *alba* has white spines.

GOLDEN POTHOS
Epipremnum aureum (Scindapsus aureus) *eb-pib-PREM-num AWR-ee-um (sin-DAP-sus AWR-ee-us)*

Golden pothos is also known as devil's ivy or Ceylon creeper. It grows well even in dark corners.

SIZE: 3–10'h × 1–3'w
TYPE: Herbaceous
FORM: Vine
TEXTURE: Medium
GROWTH: Medium
LIGHT: Low to medium

MOISTURE: Dry
SOIL: Potting soil
FEATURES: Variegated leaves
USES: Hanging basket, upright accent

SITING: This plant grows equally well in low and medium light. It prefers average temperatures (60–75°F) but will tolerate cooler periods. It needs high humidity (60–70 percent). When grown on a bark pole or slab, watering the slab helps the aerial roots hold on and provides more ambient humidity for the plant.
CARE: Allow the soil to dry after being thoroughly soaked. Feed once or twice a year with a general foliage plant food. Repot only every 2–3 years as the roots fill the pot. Prune as needed to keep the plant symmetrical. Pinch off the tips frequently to keep the plant shrubby. Pull off the occasional brown or yellow leaf. To train this plant onto a bark pole or slab, insert the pole next to the root ball and drape the vines on it. Use hairpins or plant pins to bring the vine in contact with the pole. Keeping the pole moist will encourage aerial roots to form and attach themselves to the pole.
PROPAGATION: Propagate from stem cuttings rooted in water or soil. Cut the vines you prune into 3–5" pieces with one leaf attached. Little knobs along the stem will produce roots when in contact with soil or water. You can also layer golden pothos by pinning the vines down to soil; once the roots form, cut the plant from the parent plant.
PESTS AND DISEASES: Treat scale with horticultural oil.

1 **Propagate from stem cuttings taken at any time during the year.**

2 **Dip cuttings in rooting hormone for faster rooting.**

3 **Insert cuttings in sterile potting soil and cover with plastic until roots form.**

SATIN POTHOS

Epipremnum pictum (Scindapsus pictus) *eh-pih-PREM-num PIK-tum (sin-DAP-sus PIK-tus)*

Satin pothos makes a stunning trailing plant on a mantel.

SIZE: 3–6'h × 1–2'w
TYPE: Herbaceous
FORM: Vine
TEXTURE: Medium
GROWTH: Medium
LIGHT: Low to medium

MOISTURE: Dry
SOIL: Potting soil
FEATURES: Satiny leaves
USES: Hanging basket, upright accent

SITING: Satin pothos is a stunning ground cover when used with large specimens such as weeping fig. It grows equally well in low and medium light. It prefers average temperatures (60–75°F) but will tolerate brief cooler periods. It requires high humidity (60–70 percent).

CARE: Allow the soil to dry after being thoroughly soaked. Feed once or twice a year with a general foliage plant food.

Bright light highlights the silvery variegation of satin pothos.

Repot every 2–3 years. In low light the plant will grow much more slowly and can be left in the same pot for several years. If the vines are allowed to grow long, they may begin to shed leaves and become bare with only a few leaves at the ends. In this case cut off the stems close to the crown and allow the plant to rejuvenate itself. Pull off the occasional brown or yellow leaf and give the plant a shower periodically. To train this plant onto a bark pole or slab, insert the pole next to the root ball and drape the vines on it. You may need to occasionally pinch and reattach vines, but once the aerial roots form, the plant will keep itself upright.
PROPAGATION: Root stem cuttings in water or soil. Simply cut the vines you prune into 3–5" pieces with one leaf attached. Little knobs along the stem will produce roots when in contact with soil or water. You can also layer satin pothos by pinning the vines down to soil; once the roots form, cut the plant from the parent plant.
PESTS AND DISEASES: Treat scale with horticultural oil.
RELATED SPECIES: The cultivar 'Argyraeus' has more silvery markings than the species.

FLAME VIOLET

Episcia spp. *ee-PIS-ee-ah*

Flame violets are related to African violets and have many of the same requirements.

SIZE: 4–6"h × 2'+w
TYPE: Gesneriad
FORM: Vine
TEXTURE: Fine
GROWTH: Medium
LIGHT: High to medium

MOISTURE: Medium
SOIL: Potting soil
FEATURES: Foliage, blossoms
USES: Hanging basket
FLOWERS: ■ □ □ ■

SITING: Flame violet needs bright, indirect to medium light; it will scorch in full sun. This gesneriad requires average to warm temperatures (65°F and up). Avoid hot or cold drafts to prevent leaf damage. Humidity levels of 50 percent or above will keep the plant from being stressed. It benefits from a pot-in-pot system.
CARE: Water when the soil surface feels dry. Keep moist but not soggy. Feed with half-strength foliage plant food at every watering. Once a month flush out fertilizer salts with several applications of clear water. Remove yellowed leaves and pinch out stolons as needed to keep the plant

neat. Leaf margins turn brown if humidity is low or soil moisture level is low. Plants will die back severely if overwatered or if they get too cold. Check the plant's root system periodically by removing it from the pot. Flame violet likes to be somewhat pot-bound, but if it is extremely pot-bound, repot into a container about an inch bigger. Use organic African violet mix if possible.
PROPAGATION: Root from stolon cuttings. Plantlets are produced at the tips of the plant, so simply pinch out a stem and place the plantlet on sterile soil mix. Keep it moist and covered until the plant roots. You may need to pin the plantlet to keep it in contact with the soil mix.
PESTS AND DISEASES: Flame violet may have aphids or mealybugs when stressed. Control by hand-picking or dabbing with alcohol.
RELATED SPECIES: There are many cultivars with all colors of leaves and types of variegation.

Flame violets may develop splotches on their leaves if watered with cold water.

JAPANESE EUONYMUS
Euonymus japonicus yew-AH-nih-mus juh-PAH-nih-kus

Japanese euonymus is a low-maintenance plant with glossy green foliage that provides beautiful foil to blooming plants.

SIZE: 6'h x 4'w
TYPE: Shrub
FORM: Round
TEXTURE: Medium
GROWTH: Medium
LIGHT: High to medium

MOISTURE: Even
SOIL: Potting soil
FEATURES: Glossy leaves
USES: Backdrop, topiary, bonsai

SITING: Japanese euonymus is a carefree plant if given enough moisture. Site it in a spot with medium to high but indirect light. Give it average to cool temperatures (55–75°F) to keep the growth slowed and prevent it from getting too large to handle.

Average humidity (30–65 percent) will keep Japanese euonymus looking its best.
CARE: Give it evenly moist soil, although the soil surface can dry out slightly. Feed only three times in summer. If the plant is being used as a bonsai specimen, give it more regular feeding, because the root system and soil base are minimal. It tolerates and is stimulated by pruning,

These plants tolerate drastic pruning and thus make great topiaries, bonsais, or miniature hedges.

so it can be sheared into topiary shapes or used for bonsai. The variegated leaf forms make a pleasing backdrop for a large flowering plant such as hibiscus or parlor maple. The tiny-leaved varieties are often trimmed as hedges and small topiary for dollhouse or miniature-train displays. Regular spraying with water keeps dust at a minimum and prevents spider mite population explosions.
PROPAGATION: Propagate by semihardwood stem cuttings. Take cuttings in late spring to early summer; remove all but one or two leaves, dip in rooting hormone, and insert in moist potting soil. Cover with plastic to keep the humidity high while rooting. The plants may take 6 weeks to develop roots.
PESTS AND DISEASES: Control scale with horticultural oil. Aphids will occasionally occur on new growth and can be easily handpicked.
RELATED SPECIES: Cultivars may be standard size or miniature. The cultivar 'Aureo-variegata' has large leaves with yellow blotches and green edges. *E. j. microphyllus* 'Albovariegatus' has tiny leaves splashed with white.

CROWN-OF-THORNS
Euphorbia milii yew-FOR-bee-uh MIL-ee-eye

Crown-of-thorns will reward you with year-round pink, salmon, red, or white blossoms if given high light and low humidity.

SIZE: 1–3'h x 2–3'w
TYPE: Succulent
FORM: Rounded
TEXTURE: Medium
GROWTH: Medium
LIGHT: High

MOISTURE: Low
SOIL: Cactus mix
FEATURES: Bracts
USES: Dry garden, focal point
FLOWERS: ■■□□■

SITING: Crown-of-thorns needs full sun for continuous bloom. It will tolerate part shade for vegetative growth only. It grows in cool to hot temperatures (50°F and up) and needs low humidity, usually easy to achieve in warmer temperatures.

CARE: Crown-of-thorns will not tolerate wet soil, so let it dry considerably between waterings. Then soak it well, let drain, and empty the plant saucer. Feed only three times in summer. It needs a rest period in winter, so water less and give it no plant food. It seldom needs repotting because of its small root system. If you do repot, use a cactus-type soil mix and a terra-cotta pot to allow the soil to drain well and breathe. To maintain a shrubby form or to contain the size, prune the plant tips periodically.

Propagate by taking stem tip cuttings that are 3-4 inches long. Wash the milky sap off the cutting and let it air dry for a day or two before potting it in cactus potting mix.

Be aware that the sap from all *Euphorbias* is an irritant and can be toxic, so be sure to wash your hands immediately after pruning. It's also a good idea to wash off the cut ends of the plant after pruning to remove excess sap.
PROPAGATION: Propagate by stem tip cuttings. Simply snip off a stem tip, rinse off the sap, and let it sit for a day or two to form a callus. Then insert it in cactus mix and water. Keep the soil slightly moist but not soggy or the plant will rot without producing roots. Plants can also be propagated by division and seed but not as easily as with stem-tip cuttings.
PESTS AND DISEASES: Crown-of-thorns may attract aphids and mealybugs; handpick or dab with alcohol. Overwatering causes root rots, stem rots, and perhaps leaf yellowing. Leaf drop may occur.
RELATED SPECIES: 'Koeninger's Aalbaumle' is a dwarf.

POINSETTIA
Euphorbia pulcherrima *yew-FOR-bee-uh pul-KER-ib-muh*

Poinsettia is a traditional holiday plant that can be brought back into bloom the following year with a great deal of effort.

SIZE: 6–12"h × 12"w
TYPE: Herbaceous
FORM: Mounded
TEXTURE: Medium to coarse
GROWTH: Medium

LIGHT: High
MOISTURE: Dry
SOIL: Potting soil
FEATURES: Bracts
USES: Focal point
FLOWERS: ■■□

SITING: Keep poinsettia away from warm or cold drafts from radiators, air registers, or open doors and windows. Give it 60–70°F temperatures during the day and nighttime temperatures around 55°F. Average home humidity (30–60 percent) is fine for this plant.

CARE: Water when the soil is slightly dry to the touch. If the plant pot is wrapped in foil, punch holes in the bottom and put the pot in a saucer. There is no need to fertilize while the bracts remain red through the holiday season. If you plan to keep the poinsettia as a houseplant and get it to rebloom, begin feeding in February once a month with a foliage houseplant food. Cut the stems back to about 4–6" high in March to force new growth. In April repot into a slightly larger container. Move it outdoors after nighttime temperatures are above 60°F. Pinch out the growing shoots once or twice to keep the plant compact. Water regularly and feed

When selecting a poinsettia to purchase, make sure the true flowers in the center of the plant look healthy and fresh.

every 2 weeks with a foliage plant food while outdoors. Before nighttime temperatures fall below 55°F, bring indoors to a sunny window. Starting in September, give the plant more than 12 hours of darkness nightly to initiate flower buds.

PROPAGATION: Propagate by stem tip cuttings. Prepare the best stems by pinching them back in early June. The shoots that are produced will be ready to cut in mid-July to early August. Cut 2½–3" tips with one or two leaves. Dip in rooting hormone and insert no more than an inch deep in sterile soil mix.

PESTS AND DISEASES: Whitefly is the worst pest. Check your plant carefully for the tiny larvae that look like small, transparent, oblong bubbles on the undersides of the leaves. If you find them, isolate the plant and treat with horticultural oil.

RELATED SPECIES: The cultivar 'Amazone Peppermint' has pink and white marbled bracts. 'Freedom Marble' has white bracts with soft pink highlights. 'Hollypoint' has green and gold variegated foliage with bright red bracts.

AFRICAN MILK TREE
Euphorbia trigona *yew-FOR-bee-uh try-GOHN-uh*

African milk tree, also known as candelabra plant, requires the same culture as most cacti. But keep it out of direct sun.

SIZE: 4–6'h × 2'w
TYPE: Succulent
FORM: Upright
TEXTURE: Coarse
GROWTH: Fast
LIGHT: High

MOISTURE: Low
SOIL: Cactus mix
FEATURES: Spiny stems
USES: Desert theme, architectural accent

SITING: African milk tree resembles a cactus in every way except that it is not a cactus! It needs bright light but does not handle full sun as well as a cactus would.

It tolerates 55–90°F temperatures, but below 50°F there may be some leaf scarring. Low humidity (below 30 percent) is best.

Although African milk tree looks like a cactus, the succulent leaves borne along the stem indicate that it is not a true cactus.

CARE: Water when the soil is dry to the touch; keep drier in winter during its resting phase. Water stress can cause the plant to drop its tender leaves. This doesn't harm the plant, and as soon as it is watered it will produce leaves again. Feed only three times in summer with foliage plant food. Repot whenever it starts to get top heavy into a terra-cotta pot an inch larger in diameter. African milk tree scars easily, so prune lightly. Occasionally pinch out stem tips to make the stems branch. Remember that African milk tree sap is an irritant and can be toxic, so use gloves and wash the cut ends after pruning.

PROPAGATION: Propagate by stem cuttings. Pinch off the slender stems and set aside to dry and callus for a day or so. Insert the cuttings into moist cactus mix for rooting.

PESTS AND DISEASES: African milk tree has no serious pests.

RELATED SPECIES: The cultivar 'Red' has pink to red stems in high light. *E. tetragona* has four-angled stems.

PERSIAN VIOLET

Exacum affine ECK-suh-cum uh-FIN-ee

Persian violets provide beautiful color indoors. They can be cut back and planted in the outdoor garden as an annual.

SIZE: 10"h × 10"w
TYPE: Herbaceous
FORM: Round
TEXTURE: Fine
GROWTH: Medium
LIGHT: Medium

MOISTURE: Even
SOIL: Potting soil
FEATURES: Flowers
USES: Focal point
FLOWERS: ■■□

SITING: Persian violet thrives in medium light. For the longest display of its starry pastel flowers, purchase a plant that is in tight bud and keep it in a cool room (55–65°F). Average humidity (30–65 percent) will keep the plant looking good, so place it on a pebble tray in dry situations. Place plants where you can enjoy their perfumey fragrance.

CARE: Keep the plant's soil evenly moist but not soggy, especially when grown in cool temperatures. Feed with half-strength plant food for blooming plants at every watering. Remove the spent blossoms regularly to prolong bloom. It is almost impossible to bring Persian violet back into bloom in the home because in its native Middle Eastern range it is an annual flower or short-lived perennial. When it is finished blooming, the foliage deteriorates. Most gardeners discard the plant, although it can be cut back, planted in the garden in full sun, and treated as an annual. It may develop new buds and bloom for the rest of the summer outdoors.

PROPAGATION: Propagate Persian violet from seed. Seeds will germinate in 2–3 weeks at 65°F.

PESTS AND DISEASES: Pests include mealybugs, aphids, and spider mites. They can be handled easily by handpicking or dabbing with horticultural oil. Botrytis blight and root rot may be problems when moisture is excessive.

RELATED SPECIES: Many cultivars are available with lavender, pink, and white flowers. There are also some double-flowered cultivars.

TREE IVY

×*Fatshedera lizei* fats-HED-ur-uh LIZ-ee-eye

Tree ivy, also known as fat-headed Lizzy, is an unusual plant specimen with large glossy leaves.

SIZE: 3–6'h × 3'w
TYPE: Vine
FORM: Upright
TEXTURE: Medium
GROWTH: Medium
LIGHT: Medium to low

MOISTURE: Dry
SOIL: Potting soil
FEATURES: Glossy leaves
USES: Focal point, backdrop

SITING: Although tree ivy will produce its stunning glossy bright green leaves in low light, medium light will keep it looking its best. Keep it somewhat cool (55–65°F) and use the pot-in-pot method for maintaining average humidity (30–60 percent).

CARE: Water when the soil just begins to dry out, making sure to soak it well and drain it well. If it gets too dry, it will go dormant and drop its leaves. The original plant will not recover completely after drying out, so cut off the stem tips and root them. Keeping the plant too moist, especially in lower light, may cause root

Although tree ivy doesn't naturally climb, you can train it onto an upright support by tying the vines to the support with soft twine or twist tie.

rot. Feed only three times in summer with a foliage houseplant food at regular strength. Repot annually to keep it thriving; you can skip a year if the plant is grown in lower light where the growth is slowed. Pot in average potting mix and go up only an inch in pot size. Although tree ivy will clump or mound if pinched regularly, training it onto a stake makes a much better-looking plant. Tie the plant to a stake. Pinch the tips regularly to force it to branch into an attractive, upright plant.

PROPAGATION: Propagate by stem cuttings. Take 3–5" cuttings, dip into rooting hormone, and insert into sterile potting soil. They will root in a few weeks. Or pin a vine to the soil at a node with a hairpin; when roots form at the node, clip it from the parent plant.

PESTS AND DISEASES: Spider mites can be serious pests. Watch for mealybugs in the axils of the large leaves. Swab with alcohol or horticultural oil.

RELATED SPECIES: The cultivar 'Annemieke' has wavy edges. 'Aurea' has light green leaves with white splotches. 'Variegata' has variegated leaves.

JAPANESE ARALIA

Fatsia japonica FAT-see-uh juh-PON-ih-kuh

Japanese aralias are perfect plants for dark corners where some tropical interest would be appreciated.

SIZE: 6'h × 6'w
TYPE: Shrub
FORM: Round
TEXTURE: Coarse
GROWTH: Slow
LIGHT: Low
MOISTURE: Dry
SOIL: Potting soil
FEATURES: Leaves
USES: Foliage, backdrop

SITING: Japanese aralia is ideal for low-light situations. It can be grown in medium light but will grow more quickly and outgrow its pot. It tolerates temperature extremes and will thrive in drafty spots, such as in front of a sliding glass door. It needs only low to average humidity.

CARE: Allow the soil to dry out between waterings in low light, but keep the soil more evenly moist when grown in medium light. Feed only three times in summer with a foliage houseplant food to keep it in bounds. Repot annually while it is growing to reach intended size. Once it has achieved the desired size, repot only

These naturally large plants can be kept within bounds by regular pruning of long shoots that develop.

every 2–3 years. Train it to a stake or leave it shrubby. To maintain it as a shrubby, mounded plant, pinch out the tips regularly to promote branching. Keep it shorter than its normal 6' height by selective pruning. If leaves turn yellow and fall, the plant either is overwatered or is receiving too much heat. Put it in a cooler spot and let it dry out and the plant will most likely recover. If the leaves are pale and the leaf edges are brown, the plant is not receiving enough water. Large plants in particular need plenty of water to keep them healthy.

PROPAGATION: Propagate by taking stem cuttings in midsummer. They will root faster if rooting hormone is used. Provide a plastic tent to increase humidity while rooting. This plant can also be propagated by seed or by air-layering.

PESTS AND DISEASES: Pests include scale, mites, and mealybugs. Give the plant a regular shower to keep the large, attractive leaves looking their best and to reduce mite populations.

RELATED SPECIES: The cultivar 'Moseri' is much more compact than the species. 'Variegata' has white-edged leaves.

WEEPING FIG

Ficus benjamina FYE-kus ben-ja-MYE-nuh

SIZE: 6–18'h × 2–10'w
TYPE: Tree
FORM: Vase-shaped
TEXTURE: Medium
GROWTH: Medium
LIGHT: Medium to high
MOISTURE: Dry
SOIL: Potting soil
FEATURES: Specimen
USES: Architectural accent

Weeping fig may be grown with braided multiple trunks.

SITING: Weeping fig needs medium to high light and average home temperatures (60–75°F). It tolerates lower light, but growth will be open and sparse. Give the plants average humidity (30–60 percent).
CARE: Allow the soil to dry out slightly between soakings. Feed up to three times in summer with a foliage houseplant food. If the plant is at the maximum size that your space can handle, reduce fertilizing

to once a year. To maintain the attractive weeping shape, prune major branches instead of just branch tips. Be aware that the milky sap exuded from cuts can be irritating and will stain clothes. To train

Weeping figs are sensitive to climate changes, which make their leaves yellow. Remove these yellowed leaves regularly.

stems into unusual shapes such as braids, start with very young saplings and plant three or more to a pot. Repot every third year or so. Prune the roots and crown by about a third at the same time and put the plant back into its original pot.
Weeping fig is well known for dropping its leaves whenever climatic conditions change. If you move your plant outdoors for the summer, place it in shade and gradually move it to a sunnier location. Reverse the process in autumn. This plant also drops leaves whenever the season changes but soon will put out plenty of new leaves.

PROPAGATION: Propagate by stem cuttings just like any other woody plant. Take cuttings in summer and provide rooting hormone and humidity.

PESTS AND DISEASES: The most common pest is scale, which is easily handled by a routine spraying of horticultural oil.

RELATED SPECIES: The cultivar 'Exotica' has twisted leaf tips. 'Golden King' has gray-green leaves with ivory and light green margins. 'Starlight' has creamy margins on gray-green leaves. 'Citation' is a bush form with curled leaves.

MISTLETOE FIG

Ficus deltoidea var. diversifolia FYE-kus del-TOY-dee-uh dib-vur-sib-FOLE-ee-uh

Mistletoe fig has diminutive foliage that makes it a tidy, attractive plant for the home interior.

SIZE: 3'h × 2'w
TYPE: Shrub
FORM: Rounded
TEXTURE: Coarse
GROWTH: Slow
LIGHT: Medium to high

MOISTURE: Dry
SOIL: Potting soil
FEATURES: Leaves
USES: Accent, backdrop

SITING: Provide medium to high light and average home temperatures (60–75°F). Mistletoe fig tolerates lower light, but growth will be open and sparse. Give the plants average humidity (30–60 percent), accomplished most easily for large plants with a pot-in-pot system.

CARE: Allow the soil to dry out slightly between soakings. In lower light, reduce watering somewhat. Feed three times in summer with foliage houseplant food if you want the plant to put on growth. If it is at the maximum size that your space can handle, reduce fertilizing to once a year, particularly if you repot it. Mistletoe fig can reach 6' or more when trained as a standard. Always prune at a node, where you can see which direction the remaining bud is facing. This plant tolerates pruning so well that it is a good candidate for topiary and is often used for bonsai as

well. Be aware that the milky sap exuded from cuts can be irritating and will stain clothes. Pick up the small yellow-green fruits and remove yellow leaves. Turn the pot a quarter turn at every watering to keep the plant symmetrical. About every third year or so, repot the plant. Prune the roots and crown by about a third at the same time and put the plant back into its original pot. This will keep the plant at a reasonable size for the home.

PROPAGATION: Propagate by stem cuttings. Take cuttings in summer and provide rooting hormone and humidity. This plant can also be air-layered.

PESTS AND DISEASES: Treat scale by routinely spraying the plant with horticultural oil. Use a drop cloth because this quantity of oil can make a mess on the floor.

RUBBER TREE

Ficus elastica FYE-kus ee-LAS-tib-kuh

Rubber trees have long been used to add a tropical flair to the home, with their large glossy leaves and sturdy stems.

SIZE: 4–6'h × 3–4'w
TYPE: Shrub
FORM: Upright
TEXTURE: Coarse
GROWTH: Medium
LIGHT: High to medium

MOISTURE: Even
SOIL: Potting soil
FEATURES: Foliage
USES: Architectural accent

SITING: Provide medium to high light and average home temperatures (60–75°F). Rubber tree tolerates lower light, but growth will be open and sparse. Give it average humidity (30–60 percent).

CARE: Keep the soil slightly more moist than other figs when in active growth. Allow to dry out slightly between soakings in winter. In lower light, reduce watering somewhat. Feed three times in summer with a foliage houseplant food if you want the plant to put on growth. If it is at the maximum size that your space can handle,

reduce fertilizing to once a year. Although rubber tree can get large, it can be pruned substantially to keep it smaller and in bounds. Always prune at a node where you can see which direction the remaining bud is facing. This allows you to effectively shape the plant. Rubber tree naturally loses

Rubber tree leaves are large and few, so dusting is easy. Dusting enhances the beauty of the plant and prevents a myriad of problems.

its lower leaves but may send out new leaves at the nodes of the old ones. Giving the plant a slight nick above a node will force new leaves faster. Be aware that the milky sap exuded from cuts can be irritating and will stain clothes. Repot every third year or so. Prune the roots and crown by about a third at the same time and put the plant back into its original pot. This will keep the plant at a reasonable size for the home. Wipe off the large leaves to keep them looking attractive and to discourage spider mites.

PROPAGATION: Propagate by stem cuttings. Take cuttings in summer and provide rooting hormone and humidity. Rubber tree can be effectively air-layered when the stem gets bare at the bottom. When you cut off the newly rooted top portion, the old stem will produce new shoots from its base.

PESTS AND DISEASES: Treat scale by routinely spraying the plant with horticultural oil.

RELATED SPECIES: The cultivar 'Doescheri' has creamy white variegated leaves; 'Robusta' is much more compact. 'Burgundy' has reddish leaves.

FIDDLELEAF FIG

Ficus lyrata *FYE-kus lye-RAH-tuh*

Fiddleleaf fig has uniquely shaped large leaves and can grow to a large size.

SIZE: 20–30'h × 10'w
TYPE: Tree
FORM: Upright
TEXTURE: Coarse
GROWTH: Slow
LIGHT: High to medium

MOISTURE: Even
SOIL: Potting soil
FEATURES: Leaves, bark
USES: Accent

SITING: Provide medium to high light and average home temperatures (60–75°F). Fiddleleaf fig tolerates lower light, but growth will be open and sparse. Give it average humidity (30–60 percent).
CARE: Keep the soil evenly moist when in active growth; allow to dry out slightly between soakings in winter. In lower light, reduce watering. Fiddleleaf fig will drop its leaves if it is overwatered. Feed three times in summer with a foliage houseplant food. If the plant is at the maximum size that your space can handle, reduce fertilizing to once a year. The plant has a tendency to

Fiddleleaf figs are easily air-layered when the plant gets leggy with sparse leaves at the bottom.

grow unbranched, so pinch out the tips of the stems of young plants to force side buds to develop. Be aware that the milky sap exuded from cuts can be irritating and will stain clothes. To increase its size, every third year or so repot into a slightly larger container. Once the plant has reached the maximum size for your space, prune the roots and crown back by about a third when you repot it and put the plant back into its original pot.
PROPAGATION: Propagate by stem cuttings. Take cuttings in summer and provide rooting hormone and humidity. Fiddleleaf fig can also be air-layered.
PESTS AND DISEASES: Treat scale, mealybugs, and spider mites by routinely spraying the plant with horticultural oil. Use a drop cloth because this quantity of oil can make a mess on the floor.
RELATED SPECIES: The cultivar 'Compacta' is a dwarf form with closely spaced leaves and short petioles, giving it a much less coarse appearance.

ALII FIG

Ficus maclellandii (binnendykii) 'Alii' *FYE-kus mack-luh-LAN-dee-eye (bin-en-DYE-kee-eye)*

Alii fig leaves resemble willow leaves, gracefully hanging from the upright stems. It is also known as banana leaf fig.

SIZE: 9'h × 6'w
TYPE: Tree
FORM: Upright
TEXTURE: Medium
GROWTH: Medium
LIGHT: High to medium

MOISTURE: Even
SOIL: Potting soil
FEATURES: Willowlike leaves
USES: Architectural accent

SITING: Provide medium to high light and average home temperatures (60–75°F). Alii fig tolerates lower light, but growth will be open and sparse. Give the plant average humidity (30–60 percent).

CARE: Keep the soil evenly moist when in active growth; allow to dry out slightly between soakings in winter. In lower light, reduce watering somewhat. Alii fig will drop its leaves if overwatered. Feed three times in summer with a foliage houseplant food if you want the plant to put on

Alii figs grow quickly enough that it may be necessary to prune back long, wayward stems occasionally.

growth. If it is at the maximum size that your space can handle, reduce fertilizing to once a year, particularly if you repot it. Although Alii fig can get large, it can be pruned substantially to keep it smaller and in bounds. To maintain the attractive rounded crown, prune at a node where you can see in which direction the remaining bud is facing. This allows you to make the plant symmetrical instead of sending out wayward branches toward the ceiling. Be aware that the milky sap exuded from cuts can be irritating and will stain clothes. Repot every third year or so. Prune the roots and crown by about a third at the same time, then put the plant back into its original pot. This will keep the plant at a reasonable size for the home.
PROPAGATION: Propagate by stem cuttings. Take cuttings in summer and provide rooting hormone and humidity.
PESTS AND DISEASES: Treat scale, mealybugs, and spider mites by routinely spraying the plant with horticultural oil.
RELATED SPECIES: The cultivar 'Amstel Gold' has wide golden margins. 'Amstel Queen' has larger leaves that are matte green.

INDIAN LAUREL FIG

Ficus microcarpa (retusa nitida) FYE-kus my-kroh-KAR-puh (reh-TOO-suh NIH-tih-duh)

Indian laurel fig has a more upright shape than weeping fig and is more tolerant of lower light. This is a variegated form.

SIZE: 4–12'h × 6'w
TYPE: Tree
FORM: Rounded
TEXTURE: Medium
GROWTH: Medium
LIGHT: High to medium

MOISTURE: Dry
SOIL: Average
FEATURES: Foliage
USES: Architectural accent

SITING: Provide medium to high light and average home temperatures (60–75°F). Indian laurel fig tolerates lower light, but growth will be open and sparse. Give the plants average humidity, accomplished for large plants with a pot-in-pot system.
CARE: Allow the soil to dry out slightly between soakings. In lower light, reduce watering somewhat. Feed three times in summer with a foliage houseplant food if you want the plant to put on growth. If it is at the maximum size that your space can handle, reduce fertilizing to once a year, particularly if you repot it. Although Indian laurel fig can get large, it can be pruned substantially to keep it smaller and in bounds. Although its form isn't weeping as is *Ficus benjamina,* you prune it in the same way. Prune major branches instead of just branch tips and prune at a node where you can see in which direction the remaining bud is facing. This keeps the plant rounded instead of allowing it to send out wayward branches toward the ceiling. Be aware that the milky sap exuded from cuts can be irritating and will stain clothes. To train stems into unusual shapes such as braids, loops, and twists,

Indian laurel fig has a naturally rounded top, and occasional pruning is necessary to head back shoots to keep this form.

start with very young saplings and plant three or more to a pot. Repot every third year or so. Prune the roots and crown by about a third at the same time and put the plant back into its original pot. This will keep the plant at a reasonable size for the home. Plants grown in ideal conditions may produce small, hard figs. These will not detract from the plant but can cause a litter problem if not picked up. Indian laurel fig will drop its leaves whenever climatic conditions change. If you move your plant outdoors for the summer, place it in shade and gradually move to brighter light. Reverse the process in fall when you bring the plant back indoors. This plant also drops its leaves whenever the season changes but will soon put out plenty of new leaves.
PROPAGATION: Take stem cuttings in summer and provide rooting hormone and humidity.
PESTS AND DISEASES: Treat scale by routinely spraying the plant with horticultural oil. Use a drop cloth, because this quantity of oil can make a mess on the floor.
RELATED SPECIES: The cultivar 'Green Gem' has darker, coarser leaves than the species. 'Hawaii' has a dense crown and light gray-to-white-margined leaves. 'Variegata' has a yellow midrib on dark green leaves.

OAKLEAF FIG

Ficus montana (quercifolia) FYE-kus mahn-TAN-uh (kwair-sih-FOH-lee-uh)

Oakleaf fig is a great plant to use as a ground cover in a container with a larger plant.

SIZE: 6"h × 18"w
TYPE: Woody ground cover
FORM: Ground cover
TEXTURE: Coarse
GROWTH: Slow
LIGHT: Low

MOISTURE: Even
SOIL: Average
FEATURES: Oaklike leaves
USES: Planter, ground cover, hanging basket

SITING: Oakleaf fig thrives in low light and average home temperatures (60–75°F). Give this unique plant average humidity and keep it out of cold or warm drafts. It is perfectly suited to use as a ground cover with a large potted fig, where it will be shaded by a large crown.
CARE: Keep the soil evenly moist but not soggy. In winter reduce watering somewhat. Feed three times in summer with a foliage houseplant food. Pinch to make it branch; otherwise, no pruning is needed unless you want to change the form of the plant. Be aware that the milky sap exuded from cuts can be irritating and will stain clothes. Repot every 2–3 years, going up only an inch in pot size each time. Once the plant reaches its mature size, prune the roots and crown by about a third at repotting time, then put the plant back into its original pot. This will keep the plant at a reasonable size for the home. Wipe off the leaves periodically to keep them looking shiny and attractive and keep pests controlled. Plants in ideal conditions may produce small, hard figs. These will not detract from the plant but can cause a litter problem if not picked up.
PROPAGATION: Take stem cuttings in summer and provide rooting hormone and humidity.
PESTS AND DISEASES: A well-grown oakleaf fig will have few insect problems.

CREEPING FIG
Ficus pumila FYE-kus PEW-mill-uh

Tiny-leaved creeping fig grows long, trailing stems that make it a perfect candidate for a hanging basket or as ground cover.

SIZE: 3"h × 24"w
TYPE: Herbaceous
FORM: Vine
TEXTURE: Fine
GROWTH: Medium
LIGHT: Medium to low

MOISTURE: Even
SOIL: Organic
FEATURES: Trailing stems
USES: Hanging basket, ground cover, topiary

SITING: Provide medium to low light and average home temperatures (60–75°F). Give the plant higher humidity than other figs by placing pots on moist pebbles or using the pot-in-pot method for hanging baskets. Creeping fig lends a soft texture when used as a ground cover under large, bold-leaved plants.

CARE: Keep the soil evenly moist to prevent shedding of leaves. Choose a companion that likes the same conditions when using the fig as a ground cover. Feed three times in summer with a foliage houseplant food or at every other watering with half-strength plant food. Pinch it regularly to keep the long, trailing vines looking good. Be aware that the milky sap exuded from cuts can be irritating and will stain clothes. Repot every third year or so.

Select a vine and pin it to moist soil at a node where it will take root. Once rooted, sever it from the main plant.

Prune the roots and crown by about a third at the same time, then put the plant back into its original pot. Because creeping fig tolerates pruning so well, it is commonly used for topiary. The slender stems bend easily, and the small leaves make a perfect soft covering for a topiary frame. Fill the frame with sphagnum moss and keep it damp. The vines root and hold themselves to the frame.

PROPAGATION: Propagate by stem cuttings. Take cuttings in summer and provide rooting hormone and humidity. Creeping fig also is easily propagated by layering. Pin a vine to moist soil at a leaf node. Within a few weeks the plant should be well rooted and can be severed from the parent plant.

PESTS AND DISEASES: Creeping fig may have scale, mealybugs, or spider mites. Start new plants annually to prevent these problems from getting out of hand.

RELATED SPECIES: The cultivar 'Curly' has oakleaf-shaped chartreuse leaves. 'Minima' has very fine-textured dark-green leaves and is often the choice for topiary. Creeping fig is used to climb walls in conservatories, because the vines cling to rough surfaces. 'Snowflake' makes a dense mat with bright-green leaves and white margins.

MOSAIC PLANT
Fittonia albivenis verschaffeltii fit-TOH-nee-uh all-bih-VEN-is ver-schaf-FELT-tee-eye

Mosaic plant, also known as nerve plant for the netted veins on its leaves, thrives in the humid conditions of a terrarium.

SIZE: 3–6"h × 12–18"w
TYPE: Herbaceous
FORM: Mounded
TEXTURE: Fine
GROWTH: Medium
LIGHT: High to medium

MOISTURE: Even
SOIL: Organic
FEATURES: Prominently veined leaves
USES: Terrarium, hanging basket, ground cover

SITING: Mosaic plant thrives in medium or bright but well-filtered light. It will not

tolerate sun or drying winds. Moderate to warm temperatures (65°F and above) are best; the plant may suffer if temperatures fall below this. Provide at least 60 percent humidity, whether with a pebble tray or

Place mosaic plant on damp pebbles to increase the humidity surrounding the plant.

pot-in-pot. The plant's small size makes it superb for a terrarium or for grouping with other plants to raise the humidity. If tempted to put it on the windowsill because of its diminutive size, be sure it receives no direct sun.

CARE: Keep the soil evenly moist but not soggy. Wet soil can cause rot. Pinch off the growing tips regularly to keep the plant shrubby and pleasing in appearance. If the plant is in ideal conditions, it may produce small yellow flowers. They don't add to the beauty of the plant and may even detract from its appearance, so some gardeners pinch them off.

PROPAGATION: Propagate by division, seed, or stem cuttings. Take tip cuttings in spring or layer stems in midsummer. Provide plenty of humidity with both methods.

PESTS AND DISEASES: Treat mealybugs with a cotton swab and alcohol.

RELATED SPECIES: Nerve plant (*F. a.* Argyroneura Group) has silver veins. 'Nana' ('Minima') has smaller leaves. The variety *pearcei* has carmine veins.

FUCHSIA
Fuchsia triphylla 'Gartenmeister Bonstedt' *FEW-shub try-FILL-uh*

Gartenmeister Bonstedt fuchsia offers coppery leaves and soft salmon blossoms. It is also known as lady's eardrops.

SIZE: 2–3'h × 2–3'w
TYPE: Shrub
FORM: Draping
TEXTURE: Medium
GROWTH: Medium
LIGHT: High
MOISTURE: Dry
SOIL: Potting soil
FEATURES: Colored foliage
USES: Hanging basket
FLOWERS: ■

SITING: This plant benefits from bright, indirect sunlight to keep its maroon foliage at full color. In lower light it turns greenish bronze and doesn't blossom as well. Keep it somewhat warm (60–70°F) and provide average humidity (30–65 percent).

CARE: Although fuchsia seems fussy and in need of much moisture, it actually needs to dry out slightly between waterings. To prepare for its winter rest, extend the time between waterings starting in fall. Feed every 2–4 weeks with a foliage plant food. Reduce feeding about 2 weeks before the plant will come in for the winter. Hot, dry conditions will cause flower buds to drop. This plant benefits from being outdoors during the summer and can even be grown in the ground outdoors as a butterfly magnet. To bring indoors for winter, cut the plant back severely and keep it in a

Pinch out faded flowers to keep the plant blossoming for a longer time.

cool (45–55°F) location for the duration of the winter. A cool porch that doesn't freeze is ideal. Water only enough to keep the potting soil from becoming completely dry. In spring move the plant into a warmer location and begin watering. As soon as new growth appears, repot the plant using new potting soil. Put it back into the same pot. Pinch each branch tip after it has produced two sets of leaves. This will keep the plant shrubby and attractive. Pinch periodically throughout the summer, but stop pinching a month before frost occurs.
PROPAGATION: Propagate by softwood cuttings in spring. Take 4–5" cuttings, dip in rooting hormone, and insert in sterile potting mix. Cover with a plastic tent to keep the humidity high.
PESTS AND DISEASES: Whiteflies are common on fuchsia, usually coming to roost on plants outdoors for the summer. Before bringing the plant in for winter, treat the entire plant with horticultural oil, even if you don't see signs of the small whiteflies.
RELATED SPECIES: 'Firecracker' has cream and green foliage and salmon-orange flowers. 'Mary' has scarlet blossoms.

GARDENIA
Gardenia augusta *gar-DEEN-yuh aw-GUST-uh*

Gardenias are prized for their intensely fragrant waxy white blossoms set off by deep glossy green foliage.

SIZE: 18–24"h × 18"w
TYPE: Shrub
FORM: Round
TEXTURE: Medium
GROWTH: Medium
LIGHT: Medium
MOISTURE: Even
SOIL: Potting soil
FEATURES: Foliage, blossoms
USES: Focal point, fragrance
FLOWERS: □

SITING: Gardenias need medium light, average home temperatures (65–75°F), and high humidity. For best results, place a small humidifier next to the plant.
CARE: Keep evenly moist. Feed every 2 weeks during spring and summer with half-strength acid plant food. The plant benefits from spending the summer outdoors, where it is best placed in partial shade. When the plant comes indoors in fall, reduce feeding to once a month. Be prepared for the plant to lose leaves when it comes back indoors. If you provide good conditions, the plant will leaf out again. Gardenia may drop its flower buds before opening when the plant is in low humidity or too-low light, is overwatered or underwatered, or is moved. No flower buds may mean the plant is too warm. Repot annually into organic soil to help retain moisture and use a plastic pot to avoid evaporation through its walls. Prune in late winter or early spring after blooming.
PROPAGATION: Propagate by stem cuttings taken in summer when semihardened. Use rooting hormone and very high humidity to root the cuttings.

PESTS AND DISEASES: Gardenias are prone to several insects, particularly when the humidity is not high enough. Watch for scale, mealybugs, aphids, and spider mites.
RELATED SPECIES: The cultivar 'Shooting Star' has smaller, single blossoms. 'Grif's Select' is more compact than the species. 'Prostrata' grows more horizontally and is often used for bonsai.

Gardenias must be fed with an acid fertilizer to keep the leaves healthy and the blossoms continuous.

OX TONGUE

Gasteria spp. *gas-TARE-ee-uh*

Lawyer's tongue is an unlikely name for this beautifully marked succulent. Another common name is cow tongue.

SIZE: 3–12" x 6–18"
TYPE: Succulent
FORM: Upright
TEXTURE: Coarse
GROWTH: Slow
LIGHT: High

MOISTURE: Dry
SOIL: Cactus mix
FEATURES: Unique leaves
USES: Dish garden, focal point

SITING: Ox tongue tolerates adverse conditions as long as it is in high light. It thrives in temperatures of 50–85°F and requires low humidity (below 30 percent). The succulent leaves are easily scarred, so place ox tongue out of the way of traffic.

CARE: Ox tongue requires many of the same conditions as cactus and other succulents. Allow to dry between soakings during active growth and dry out a bit more during winter rest. Fertilize only once a year in summer with foliage plant food. Wipe off the leaves occasionally to keep them looking pristine and to keep dust to a minimum. Remove the occasional scarred

Ox tongue plants have striking flecked leaves with several shades of green spots.

leaf or faded flower spike. Clump-forming species need to be divided and repotted when the pot fills with many small plants. Use fast-draining cactus mix. Smaller species may need some soil added occasionally, but their small root system will seldom fill a pot. If you choose to move ox tongue outdoors for the summer, place it where it will get morning and late afternoon sun but not direct midday sun.

PROPAGATION: Depending on the species, ox tongue can be propagated by division, offsets, or seed.

PESTS AND DISEASES: The plant is virtually pest free. But check it periodically for mealybugs, and treat with a cotton swab dipped in alcohol or horticultural oil.

RELATED SPECIES: *G. armstrongii* is a small plant that is perfect for the windowsill. Its pleated leaves have downward-pointing tips. *G. excelsa* resembles an aloe or yucca. Lawyer's tongue (*G. liliputana*) has flat, overlapping leaves with white spots.

TAHITIAN BRIDAL VEIL

Gibasis geniculata (pellucida) *jib-BAY-sis jen-ik-yoo-LAH-tuh (pel-LOO-sih-duh)*

Tahitian bridal veil is a stunning vining plant that engulfs its container with tiny leaves and delicate white blossoms.

SIZE: 6"h x 2'w
TYPE: Herbaceous
FORM: Trailing
TEXTURE: Fine
GROWTH: Fast
LIGHT: High
MOISTURE: Dry

SOIL: Potting soil
FEATURES: Leaves, blossoms
USES: Hanging basket, terrarium
FLOWERS: □

SITING: Tahitian bridal veil is a striking plant when grown well. It needs high light to keep it compact and shrubby. Average to warm temperatures (65–85°F) will keep the plant looking good. Cooler temperatures slow its growth and make the leaves hang limply. Provide average humidity (30–65 percent).

CARE: Let the soil dry out slightly between waterings. If given too much water or allowed to sit in water, the stem will rot. Feed once a month with foliage plant food to keep it from becoming too succulent and prone to fungal rots. It grows fairly quickly, so repot annually. To keep the plant in the same size pot, divide when you repot, and pot the divisions as separate plants. Pinch off the growing tips every few weeks to keep the plant compact and shrubby. Pinch stems that are blocked from light or they will begin to die. If the stems do become bare and leggy, cut back all the stems to a few inches and start the plant over. Remove faded and dried leaves and flower stalks by giving the plant a solid shake to dislodge them.

PROPAGATION: Propagate from stem cuttings or by layering. The plant stems root readily at the leaf nodes, so start new

plants in soil or water. Tahitian bridal veil is also easily divided. The root ball is unusually dense, so remove the plant from the pot and use a serrated knife to cut the root ball in half or thirds. Cut back the stems at this time to help the plant recover.

PESTS AND DISEASES: Aphids can be somewhat hard to control in the mass of foliage. Dislodge with a periodic strong spray of water.

The stems of Tahitian bridal veil will become leggy and bare, so pinch them regularly and cut them back to a few inches to completely rejuvenate the plant.

GUZMANIA
Guzmania lingulata *gooz-MANE-yuh lin-gyu-LAH-tuh*

Guzmania is an easy-to-care-for bromeliad that requires only high humidity to keep it looking good.

SIZE: 1–2'h × 1–2'w
TYPE: Bromeliad
FORM: Vase shape
TEXTURE: Medium
GROWTH: Slow
LIGHT: High to medium
MOISTURE: Dry

SOIL: Epiphyte mix
FEATURES: Striped leaves, colorful bracts
USES: Focal point, blooming
FLOWERS: ■□

SITING: Guzmania shows its best leaf color in bright, filtered light. Provide average to hot temperatures (60°F and above) to prevent rotting. High humidity (above 65 percent) is crucial to keep this bromeliad looking good.
CARE: Let the soil dry out almost completely between waterings and keep the "vase" full of water. Every couple of months, empty and refill the vase to keep the water fresh. Feed with blooming plant formula three times in summer. Repot only when the potting mix begins to break down and no longer has recognizable chunks of bark. Guzmania can be grown on a slab, but high humidity is essential.
PROPAGATION: Propagate by removing the offsets or side shoots when they are about one-third the size of the parent plant. Take the plant out of the pot and gently pull off each offset, making sure it has some roots. You can also propagate guzmania by seed in spring. Collect the seeds as they ripen and place them on moist paper towels in a covered plastic container until they germinate.
PESTS AND DISEASES: Treat scale and spider mites with horticultural oil. The plant may develop leaf spots in low humidity and root rot if overwatered.
RELATED SPECIES: The cultivar 'Variegata' has white-striped leaves. 'Empire' has bright green leaves and scarlet flowers. 'Marjan' has yellow flowers. *G. lingulata* var. *minor* has a smaller overall stature and smaller leaves.

1 Guzmanias produce "pups," small plants at the base of the mother plant, which can be separated to form new plants.

2 After pulling off a pup with some roots, pot it into damp, sterile potting soil and place it in a protected spot for several days.

PURPLE PASSION
Gynura aurantiaca *guy-NOOR-uh aw-ran-tee-AH-kuh*

Purple passion is also known as purple velvet plant, an apt name considering the fuzzy purple hairs covering its foliage.

SIZE: 6"h × 2'w
TYPE: Herbaceous
FORM: Trailing
TEXTURE: Medium
GROWTH: Medium
LIGHT: High to medium

MOISTURE: Evenly moist
SOIL: Potting soil
FEATURES: Leaves with purple hairs
USES: Hanging basket
FLOWERS: ■

SITING: Purple passion needs bright to medium light to keep its intense purple color and dense form. When grown in the proper light, it remains stocky and thick. If grown in too little light, the plant becomes leggy. Adaptable to a cool window, purple passion tolerates cool to average temperatures (55–65°F) and average humidity (30–60 percent). A pot-in-pot system helps maintain adequate humidity.
CARE: Keep evenly moist during active growth; reduce watering and allow the soil to dry slightly in winter. Feed three times in summer with foliage plant food. You can repot the plant annually, but it isn't necessary. After a couple of years, the plant may get ragged, so start a new plant every year to keep an attractive specimen. Pinch it regularly to keep it stocky.
PROPAGATION: Propagate by stem cuttings in water or soil. You will get an attractive plant faster if you place several cuttings in a single pot. Use rooting hormone and keep the humidity higher than usual while the plant is developing roots.
PESTS AND DISEASES: Treat mealybugs with a cotton swab dipped in alcohol or horticultural oil. Avoid spraying the entire plant with oil so the hairs don't mat.
RELATED SPECIES: The cultivar 'Purple Passion' is the standard plant. The species is seldom available.

Pinch out the stem tips regularly to keep the plant looking shrubby and attractive. Also pinch out flower buds because they have an unpleasant odor.

ZEBRA HAWORTHIA

Haworthia fasciata huh-WAR-thee-yuh fas-kee-AH-tuh

Zebra haworthia's striking foliage will remain attractive with the same conditions given to cactus.

SIZE: 5–6"h × 5–6"w
TYPE: Succulent
FORM: Mounded
TEXTURE: Medium
GROWTH: Slow
LIGHT: High
MOISTURE: Dry

SOIL: Cactus mix
FEATURES: Foliage with white bands
USES: Dish garden, focal point
FLOWERS: □ ■

SITING: This plant is perfect for the windowsill that receives no direct sun. It prefers filtered bright light. Direct sun will cause the leaf tips to brown. It performs best in average to high temperatures (65°F and above). It needs low humidity (below 30 percent).

CARE: Allow the soil to dry slightly between waterings when the plant is in active growth and let it dry to an inch below the soil surface during rest times. More water than this will rot the roots. Zebra haworthia grows most actively from March through May, then goes into a summer rest until August. In September it resumes growth. Feed only three times during the active growth periods with a general foliage plant food. Repotting is seldom necessary unless the offsets spill out of the pot or crowd one another in the pot. Use a fast-draining cactus mix for repotting the plant or potting up divisions. Occasionally spray off the leaves to keep them looking clean and healthy.

PROPAGATION: Propagate zebra haworthia by separating the offsets that appear frequently. Use a knife to separate the offsets from the parent plant and pot them up in cactus mix. Roots should appear fairly quickly.

PESTS AND DISEASES: Treat mealybugs and scale with horticultural oil.

RELATED SPECIES: *H. attenuata* looks quite similar to zebra haworthia and is sometimes considered synonymous with it. *H. ×cuspidata* has fat, clumping leaves that form 4" rosettes. Window plant (*H. cymbiformis*) has pale green succulent leaves with translucent tips resembling windows into the plant. *H. reinwardtii* has dense, upright, tightly clasped leaves.

ALGERIAN IVY

Hedera canariensis HEH-der-uh kuh-nar-ee-EN-sis

Algerian ivy, one of the sturdiest of the ivies, will thrive in cool conditions and medium light.

SIZE: 10"h × 5'w
TYPE: Vine
FORM: Trailing
TEXTURE: Medium
GROWTH: Medium
LIGHT: Medium

MOISTURE: Evenly moist
SOIL: Potting soil
FEATURES: Glossy leaves
USES: Hanging basket, ground cover

SITING: Algerian ivy is a vigorous plant that grows thickly enough and long enough to make a living curtain. Provide medium light and cool temperatures (55–65°F) for the best growth. Cooler temperatures make the reddish petioles redder still, an attractive accent. Provide medium to high humidity (60 percent and above) to deter spider mites.

CARE: Keep the soil evenly moist. In winter allow it to dry out a bit, but not too much or the plant will begin to brown. Feed with foliage plant food according to label directions. Algerian ivy does not branch well, so pinching may keep the plant within bounds but will not produce a thick, shrubby specimen. Algerian ivy doesn't require frequent repotting; plants can be grown in the same pot for years. If you want to rejuvenate it somewhat, repot into a larger container every 2–3 years. Old plants become woody and leggy, so start new plants from cuttings every few years. If the vines lose their leaves at the base, simply cut the vines off short. They will produce more leaves fairly quickly. If the leaf tips turn brown, raise the humidity and check for spider mites.

PROPAGATION: Propagate from stem cuttings or by layering. The vines will produce roots at the leaf nodes, so pin a vine with the node touching the soil. When the plant roots in a couple of weeks, sever it from the parent plant and pot.

PESTS AND DISEASES: Ivies have an inherent problem with spider mites, especially if grown in low humidity. Wash off the plant often, raise the humidity, and treat the mites with horticultural oil. Ivies may have scale as well, which can also be treated with horticultural oil. If leaves of variegated ivies lose their variegation, give them more light (but not direct sun).

RELATED SPECIES: The cultivar 'Gloire de Marengo' is a standard variegated ivy with golden yellow and light gray variegation. Other cultivars are not widely available.

Algerian ivy makes an attractive accent when planted as ground cover in the container of a large plant.

ENGLISH IVY

Hedera helix *HEH-der-uh HEE-licks*

English ivy comes in many leaf shapes, sizes, and colors, with something to please every gardener.

SIZE: 6–8"h × 2'w
TYPE: Vine
FORM: Trailing
TEXTURE: Medium
GROWTH: Medium
LIGHT: High

MOISTURE: Evenly moist
SOIL: Organic
FEATURES: Leaves
USES: Hanging basket, ground cover, topiary

SITING: English ivy is vigorous when given bright, indirect light during the summer and some direct sun during the winter. It thrives in cool temperatures (55–65°F), which bring out the best color and keep the plant stocky and attractive. Provide medium to high humidity (60 percent and above) to deter spider mites.

CARE: Keep the soil evenly moist. Avoid letting the plant dry out too much or it will begin to brown. Feed with foliage plant food according to label directions. Frequent pinching produces a thick, shrubby plant. Repot about every 2 years.

English ivy can be trained onto a trellis or topiary frame with a little assistance and gentle ties.

As older stems become woody and leggy and lose their bottom leaves, prune them hard. If the leaf tips turn brown, raise the humidity and check for spider mites. English ivy is an excellent candidate for topiary because it branches well. If leaves of variegated ivies lose their variegation, give them more light (but not direct sun).

PROPAGATION: Propagate from stem cuttings or by layering. The vines produce roots at the leaf nodes, so pin a vine with the node touching the soil and wait a couple of weeks for the plant to root, then sever it from the parent plant and pot.

PESTS AND DISEASES: Ivies have inherent problems with spider mites, especially if grown in low humidity. Wash the plant often, raise the humidity, and treat the mites with horticultural oil. Ivies may have scale as well, which can also be treated with horticultural oil.

RELATED SPECIES: The American Ivy Society classifies cultivars according to leaf shape and leaf type. 'Needlepoint' has tiny green leaves and makes an attractive topiary, 'Romanze' has gold-variegated leaves and wavy margins. 'Harrison' has large triangular leaves with white veins.

RED FLAME IVY

Hemigraphis alternata *hem-uh-GRAF-iss al-ter-NAH-tuh*

Red flame ivy will keep its lovely red leaves when given medium light and kept away from drying winds and cold drafts.

SIZE: 6"h × 18"w
TYPE: Herbaceous
FORM: Mounded
TEXTURE: Medium
GROWTH: Medium
LIGHT: Medium
MOISTURE: Evenly moist

SOIL: Potting soil
FEATURES: Maroon leaves
USES: Hanging basket
FLOWERS: ☐

SITING: Red flame ivy needs medium light; high or low light will cause the plant to decline. It will tolerate average to high temperatures (60°F and above) but must be kept away from drying winds and cold drafts. Medium to high humidity (30 percent and higher) will keep the foliage in peak condition. A pot-in-pot system works well in a hanging basket.

CARE: Keep the soil evenly moist. Allowing it to dry out may cause the leaf edges to brown. Feed only three times in summer with foliage plant food. Repot annually; the plant has a vigorous root system. Red flame ivy branches well when pruned, so pinch out the growing tips regularly to keep the plant shrubby and thick. If the

Pinch out the stem tips regularly to keep the plant shrubby and attractive. The tips can be easily rooted to make new plants.

stems become leggy and bare, cut the plant back severely to rejuvenate it. Occasionally pull off browned leaves and give the plant a shower once a month.

PROPAGATION: Root by stem cuttings or by layering. Stem cuttings will root in water or soil, but you will get the fastest, healthiest plant if you start them in soil. Use rooting hormone and provide warmth and high humidity. These plants root well, so take cuttings to grow in a well-protected spot in the outdoor garden.

PESTS AND DISEASES: Mealybugs and spider mites may be problems when the plant is grown in low humidity.

RELATED SPECIES: Purple waffle plant (*H. a.* 'Exotica') has puckered purple leaves. *H. repanda* is a prostrate plant with small leaves and tiny white flowers. 'Red Equator' has small metallic green leaves with red underneath and a more compact habit.

ROSE MALLOW

Hibiscus rosa-sinensis hih-BIS-kus ROZE-uh sih-NEN-sis

Rose mallow is also known as Chinese rose or hibiscus. It makes an intensely tropical statement with its magnificent flowers.

SIZE: 6'h × 4'w
TYPE: Woody shrub
FORM: Upright
TEXTURE: Coarse
GROWTH: Medium
LIGHT: High
MOISTURE: Evenly moist
SOIL: Potting soil
FEATURES: Flowers
USES: Focal point
FLOWERS: ■ ■ ■
           □ ■

SITING: Rose mallow needs bright light to produce flowers. It grows well in cool to average temperatures (55–70°F) and must have high humidity to keep the buds from dropping and to keep spider mites at bay. Avoid drying winds and cold drafts.

CARE: Keep the soil evenly moist. Feed twice a month from April through September with foliage plant food. Repot annually in spring. If you want rose mallow to increase in size, pot into a container an inch larger after loosening any wrapping roots. Otherwise, root-prune and put the plant back into the same pot. Establish three or four main branches and remove all others at the base. Cut back these main branches by one-third. The plant blooms on new wood,

Cut back rose mallow substantially to keep an attractive shape, stimulate new growth, and promote profuse bloom.

so pruning in this way will produce plenty of new shoots for blooming. Pinch off the growing tips in early spring to force more flowers along the stems. Leaves yellow when they are old or if the plant is under stress. Conditions that are too dry, too moist, or too cold will cause leaf drop. Usually the leaves return quickly when the conditions are corrected. This plant benefits from spending the summer outdoors in bright, indirect light.

PROPAGATION: Propagate by taking semihardwood cuttings in summer. Use rooting hormone, bottom heat, and high humidity for rooting. The plants can also be layered by pinning a nicked stem to moist potting soil.

PESTS AND DISEASES: Spider mite populations can explode when the plant is grown in dry conditions. Regular rinsing will help deter them.

RELATED SPECIES: Cultivars come with single and double flowers, bicolored flowers, small and large leaves, and variegated foliage. When choosing a plant, keep in mind that coarse texture and large flowers can dominate your houseplant display.

AMARYLLIS

Hippeastrum spp. hip-ee-AS-trum

Amaryllis, treasured for its holiday blooms, produces a magnificent stalk of massive tubular flowers in many different shades.

SIZE: 18"h × 12"w
TYPE: Bulb
FORM: Upright, vase shape
TEXTURE: Coarse
GROWTH: Medium
LIGHT: High
MOISTURE: Dry
SOIL: Potting soil
FEATURES: Funnel-shaped flowers
USES: Focal point, holiday accent
FLOWERS: ■ □ ■
           ■ ■

SITING: While the plant is developing new leaves and sending up its flower stalk, give it bright light. It grows well in average temperatures (60–75°F), although cooler temperatures will prolong the bloom.

CARE: Plant bulbs with ⅓ to ½ of the bulb above the soil line. Allow the top inch of soil to dry between waterings. Feed weekly during the growing season. Remove faded flowers then pull the stalk once it softens and yellows. When all danger of frost has passed, sink the pot in a sunny spot in the garden. In early September, pull the pot out of the ground. Stop watering and bring the pot indoors to a dry, dark, cool spot for at least 2 months. When you are ready to force it into bloom, bring the plant into warmth, replace the top inch of soil, and water. As soon as foliage appears, move the plant into the preferred light conditions and begin fertilizing. Within 6–8 weeks,

flower stalks should emerge. Stake the stalk if your plant needs it.

PROPAGATION: Amaryllis produces bulblets as it ages; these can be separated and potted. Offsets bloom sooner when left attached to the original bulb. You can also divide bulbs, but be sure that each division has part of the basal plate.

PESTS: Amaryllis bulbs and leaves can be bothered by fungal disease, which is difficult to treat. If you see signs of disease, it's best to discard the bulb.

RELATED SPECIES: Butterfly amaryllis (*H. papilio*) has an elegant lime green flower with maroon markings.

1 Amaryllis bulbs are often sold dry, ready to be potted and forced into bloom.

2 Place the bulb with the top one-third above the soil.

3 Water in well and place in a warm location until shoot growth begins.

DROP TONGUE

Homalomena rubescens *bome-ub-lo-MANE-ub roo-BES-sens*

Drop tongue has an unusual name for a very attractive foliage plant that is a wonderful choice in low-light situations.

SIZE: 18"h × 12"w
TYPE: Herbaceous
FORM: Mounded
TEXTURE: Medium
GROWTH: Slow
LIGHT: Medium to low
MOISTURE: Evenly moist
SOIL: Potting soil
FEATURES: Heart-shape leaves
USES: Foliage, low light

SITING: Drop tongue is a popular plant for use in foliage displays because of its attractive, glossy leaves. Its tolerance of low light makes it useful in darker areas of the home; however, if given medium light the plant looks better. Drop tongue thrives in medium to high temperatures (65°F and above) and requires high humidity (above 65 percent). Avoid drying winds and cold drafts.

CARE: Keep the soil evenly moist. Drying out only slightly can cause the plant to decline. If growing in low light, make sure the soil doesn't become soggy. Feed only three times in summer with foliage plant food. Repot annually; the roots quickly fill the pot and the plant loses its ability to take up water. The flowers are insignificant; pinching them off makes the foliage more lush. Wash the leaves monthly to keep the plant looking its best.

PROPAGATION: Propagate by dividing the root ball. Simply split the root mass down the middle or pull off sections with roots attached.

PESTS AND DISEASES: Treat mealybugs and spider mites with horticultural oil. Neither should get out of hand in high humidity.

RELATED SPECIES: 'Emerald Gem' is an industry standard with compact growth and glossy leaves. Silver shield (*H. wallisii*) has variegated large leaves. *H. picturata* has broad leaves with silver-green markings.

1 When drop tongue fills its pot with roots, remove the root ball from the old pot and loosen the roots gently.

2 Place the plant in a larger pot or root prune it and return it to the same pot to keep it the same size.

3 Water in the repotted plant to moisten the soil and remove air pockets.

KENTIA PALM

Howea forsteriana *HOW-ee-yub for-stare-ee-AH-nub*

Kentia palm is the largest of the interior palms, making an extraordinary statement in a vast room.

SIZE: 10'h × 10'w
TYPE: Palm
FORM: Upright, arching
TEXTURE: Coarse
GROWTH: Slow
LIGHT: Medium to low
MOISTURE: Evenly moist
SOIL: Potting soil
FEATURES: Fronds
USES: Architectural accent

SITING: Kentia palm is majestic in stature and tolerant of a wide range of conditions. It grows as wide as it is tall, so make sure you have a suitable site. Provide medium to low light (it grows slowly in low light and will be somewhat open). It does well in cool temperatures (50–60°F) but also tolerates average temperatures (65–75°F). Provide average humidity (30–60 percent) to deter spider mites.

CARE: Provide evenly moist soil; the plant should not sit in water. In winter it goes through a rest period, so reduce water somewhat. Feed only three times in summer with foliage plant food. Repot when the plant becomes difficult to water, but go up only an inch or two in pot size to avoid a lot of soil and few roots to fill it. Remove the occasional dead frond. Avoid tying the fronds together as the plant widens. Selectively remove fronds if necessary. Brown tips usually indicate dry soil, low humidity, or soluble salt build-up in the soil. Because this palm does not grow many fronds, trim the brown tips rather than removing the entire frond. If the fronds have spots, the plant may be in light that is too bright, or there may be a problem with chemicals in the water.

PROPAGATION: Propagate by seed, which must be attained from a seed supplier.

PESTS AND DISEASES: Spider mites can be a problem, but washing the leaves regularly will help prevent infestations. The leaves are few, so this is not a daunting task. Watch also for mealybugs. Treat with rubbing alcohol.

RELATED SPECIES: Sentry palm (*H. balmoreana*) is slower growing and more susceptible to pests, so it is seldom available for houseplant use.

WAX PLANT

Hoya carnosa HOY-yuh kar-NOH-suh

Wax plant comes with several different types of leaves and flower colors. It is also known as hoya.

SIZE: 3–4"h × 4'w	**SOIL:** Potting soil
TYPE: Vine	**FEATURES:** Waxy
FORM: Trailing	leaves
TEXTURE: Medium	**USES:** Hanging
GROWTH: Fast	basket, topiary
LIGHT: High	**FLOWERS:** ☐ ■ ■
MOISTURE: Dry	

SITING: Hoya is an attractive vining plant that, if grown in adequate light, has waxy flowers with a sweet scent at night. It is slow to begin blooming, but flowers annually once it starts to bloom. Plants will tolerate some morning sun but not midday sun. Cool to medium temperatures (55–75°F) will keep the plants stocky; avoid placing them in cold drafts.

CARE: Water wax plant only after the top half-inch of soil has dried. Feed three times in summer with foliage plant food.

Repot as infrequently as possible. It has a smallish root system and does not take repotting well. Use an average soil that is very well drained. Overwatering will cause leaves to drop. It is possible to pinch off growing tips to make the plant branch, but be aware that it is difficult to recognize the flowering spikes and you may delay flowering. After the plant blooms, allow faded flowers to fall off, but don't remove the flower stalk; the plant will rebloom on the same stalk. Hoya can be trained to grow upright but will need trellising, because its only means of support is vines twining among themselves.

PROPAGATION: Propagate by stem cuttings. Take 3–5" cuttings anytime during active growth; strip all but one leaf, dip in rooting hormone powder, and insert in

sterile soil. Bottom heat and high humidity will ensure rooting. Wax plant can also be propagated by layering. Simply pin a stem to the soil at a leaf node and keep the soil mix moist until the plant forms roots. When rooted, sever from the parent plant.

PESTS AND DISEASES: Mealybugs are frequently a problem, especially on the curly-leaved varieties. Treat by dabbing with a cotton swab dipped in alcohol or horticultural oil.

RELATED SPECIES: The cultivar 'Krinkle Kurl' (Hindu rope) has oddly curved leaves clustered along the stems. 'Exotica' has pink and light green variegated foliage. String bean plant (*H. longifolia*) has long, narrow leaves and an elegant appearance. Imperial wax plant (*H. imperialis*) has huge leaves and large red-brown flowers.

The vining nature of wax plant makes it a good candidate for training onto a topiary form as well as use in a hanging basket.

The flowers of wax plant are uniquely shaped, waxy, and delightfully fragrant, somewhat reminiscent of honey.

COMPACT WAX PLANT

Hoya compacta HOY-yuh kom-PAK-tuh

Compact wax plant is a diminutive variety that is perfect for a windowsill or small hanging basket.

SIZE: 3–4"h × 1'w	**SOIL:** Potting soil
TYPE: Vine	**FEATURES:** Waxy
FORM: Trailing	leaves
TEXTURE: Medium	**USES:** Hanging
GROWTH: Fast	basket, topiary
LIGHT: High	**FLOWERS:** ☐ ■ ■
MOISTURE: Dry	

SITING: Hoya is an attractive vining foliage plant, and in adequate light it has waxy flowers with reflexed petals and a sweet scent at night. Compact wax plant is smaller all around than the species, making it perfect for small baskets and windowsills. Provide bright light. Hoya will tolerate some morning sun but not midday sun. Cool to medium temperatures (55–75°F) will keep the plant stocky; avoid cold drafts.

CARE: Water compact wax plant only after the top half-inch of soil has dried. Feed three times in summer with foliage plant food. Repot as infrequently as possible. Hoya has a smallish root system and does not take repotting well. Use an average soil that is very well drained. Overwatering will cause leaves to drop. It is possible to pinch off growing tips to make the plant branch, but be aware that it is difficult to recognize the flowering spikes, and you may delay

flowering. After the plant blooms, allow faded flowers to fall off, but leave the flower stalk alone; the plant will rebloom on the same stalk. Hoya can be trained to grow upright but will need trellising, because its only means of support is vines that twine among themselves.

PROPAGATION: Propagate by stem cuttings. Take 3–5" cuttings anytime during active growth; strip all but one leaf, dip in rooting hormone powder, and insert in sterile soil. Bottom heat and high humidity will ensure rooting. Hoya can also be propagated by layering. Simply pin a stem to the soil at a leaf node and keep the soil mix moist until the plant forms roots. When rooted, sever from the parent plant.

PESTS AND DISEASES: Mealybugs are frequently a problem, especially on the curly-leaved varieties. Treat by dabbing with a cotton swab dipped in alcohol or horticultural oil.

BEAUTIFUL HOYA

Hoya lanceolata ssp. *bella*   HOY-yuh lan-see-oh-LATE-uh BELL-uh

Beautiful hoya is adorned with diamond-shaped leaves and soft pink and white blossoms. It is also known as miniature wax plant.

SIZE: 3–4"h × 4'w
TYPE: Vine
FORM: Trailing
TEXTURE: Medium
GROWTH: Fast
LIGHT: High
MOISTURE: Dry

SOIL: Potting soil
FEATURES: Waxy leaves
USES: Hanging basket, topiary
FLOWERS: □ ▪

SITING: Hoya is an attractive vining foliage plant, but in adequate light it has waxy flowers with reflexed petals and a sweet scent at night. Beautiful hoya is diminutive in stature with diamond-shape leaves and bicolored white and pink flowers. Provide bright light. Hoya will tolerate some morning sun but not midday sun. Cool to medium temperatures (55–75°F) will keep the plant stocky; avoid cold drafts.

CARE: Water only after the top half-inch of soil has dried. Feed three times in summer with foliage plant food. Repot as infrequently as possible. Hoya has a smallish root system and does not take repotting well. Use an average soil that is very well drained. Overwatering will cause leaves to drop. It is possible to pinch off growing tips to make the plant branch, but be aware that it is difficult to recognize the flowering spikes, and you may delay flowering. After the plant blooms, allow spent flowers to fall, but do not remove the flower stalk; the plant will rebloom on the same stalk. Hoya can be trained to grow upright but will need trellising, because the only means of support is vines that twine among themselves.

PROPAGATION: Propagate by stem cuttings. Take 3–5" cuttings anytime during active growth; strip all but one leaf, dip in rooting hormone powder, and insert in sterile soil. Bottom heat and high humidity will ensure rooting. Hoya can also be propagated by layering. Pin a stem to the soil at a leaf node and keep the soil mix moist until the plant forms roots. When rooted, sever from the parent plant.

PESTS AND DISEASES: Mealybugs are frequently a problem, especially on the curly-leaved varieties. Treat by dabbing with a cotton swab dipped in alcohol or horticultural oil.

RELATED SPECIES: The cultivar 'Variegata' has lime green variegation.

POLKA DOT PLANT

Hypoestes phyllostachya   hi-poh-ES-teez fill-oh-STAK-yuh

Polka dot plant, also known as freckle face, is a favorite for its uniquely colored foliage that adds a bright splash of color.

SIZE: 24"h × 9"w
TYPE: Herbaceous
FORM: Mounded
TEXTURE: Fine
GROWTH: Fast
LIGHT: High
MOISTURE: Evenly moist

SOIL: Potting soil
FEATURES: Variegated leaves
USES: Accent, dish garden
FLOWERS: ▪

SITING: Polka dot plant has green leaves with pink markings that are made more pronounced when the plant is grown in bright light. It will not tolerate direct sun but does well in a protected bright window. Provide average temperatures (60–75°F) and high humidity (60 percent and above).

CARE: Provide evenly moist soil so the edges of the leaves don't brown. Feed only three times in summer with foliage plant food and repot annually. Trim back regularly so the plant does not become leggy and floppy. Pinch out the growing tips every few weeks to keep the plant shrubby and full. If the stems do become leggy, prune the plant back hard, and new growth at the soil level will come back strong fairly quickly. The flower stalks arise from the base of the plant. Some gardeners feel that they detract from the plant and pinch them off at the base. However, if you want to start new plants from seed, let them grow and ripen their seeds.

PROPAGATION: Propagate by cuttings at any time. The plants can be started fresh from seeds as well. When the stalks begin to dry and the seeds are ripe, collect the seeds and sow immediately on fresh, sterile potting mix. Keep the soil slightly moist but not soggy and cover with glass or plastic to increase the humidity until the seeds germinate. When the seedlings are several inches tall, transplant into pots.

PESTS AND DISEASES: Treat mealybugs and whiteflies with horticultural oil.

RELATED SPECIES: 'Wine Red' has dark red spots. Splash Select Series has bright red, rose, white or pink speckles.

To grow polka dot plants from seed, sow the seed on the top of fresh potting mix, sprinkle with soil, and water gently.

After watering, cover the seeds with glass or plastic to keep the seeds moist. Remove the cover once seeds germinate.

BLOODLEAF

Iresine herbstii *eye-REH-see-nee HERB-stee-eye*

Bloodleaf provides an intense focal point with its bright maroon and pink leaves. It is also known as chicken gizzard.

SIZE: 2'h × 1'w
TYPE: Herbaceous
FORM: Upright
TEXTURE: Medium
GROWTH: Medium
LIGHT: High, indirect

MOISTURE: Evenly moist
SOIL: Potting soil
FEATURES: Brightly variegated leaves
USES: Foliage, accent

SITING: Given the right light conditions, bloodleaf is a spectacular foliage accent with bright maroon leaves and stems. If this plant is not in the brightest light, the leaves tend to fade and become dull. The light needs to be filtered or the leaves will bleach out and the edges will brown.

Provide average warmth (60–75°F) during the growing season and slightly cooler conditions in winter (not below 55°F however). It prefers average to high humidity (above 30 percent). Provide extra humidity by setting the pot on a tray of moist pebbles.

Bloodleaf branches well, so periodically pinch out the stem tips to keep the plant shrubby and full.

CARE: Keep evenly moist during the active growing season; reduce watering somewhat in winter and allow the soil surface to dry slightly to prevent rot. Feed three times in summer with foliage plant food. Repot annually and pinch the plant frequently to keep it shrubby and full.

PROPAGATION: Propagate in winter and spring by herbaceous stem cuttings. Take 3–5" cuttings; remove all but one leaf, dip in rooting hormone, and insert in sterile potting soil. Cover with plastic to keep in humidity and check daily for rotting. When plants are rooted, remove the plastic cover, pinch the growing tip, and transplant into pots. Bloodleaf can also be propagated by dividing the root ball.

PESTS AND DISEASES: Bloodleaf may have spider mites in low humidity and aphids as new growth begins. Treat both with insecticidal soap.

RELATED SPECIES: 'Aureoreticulata' has green leaves with yellow veins and red stems. 'Brilliantissima' has bright crimson foliage with pink-red veins. *I. lindenii* has black-red foliage shaped like willow leaves. 'Purple Lady' is a dark purple ground cover that grows to 6" high.

JASMINE

Jasminum polyanthum *JAZ-mi-num pah-lee-ANTH-um*

Jasmine intoxicates you with its fragrance, so put it in a sunny window where the warmth will intensify the perfume.

SIZE: 4'h × 4–6'w
TYPE: Vine
FORM: Trailing
TEXTURE: Fine
GROWTH: Medium
LIGHT: High
MOISTURE: Evenly moist

SOIL: Potting soil
FEATURES: Fragrant blooms
USES: Hanging basket, topiary
FLOWERS: ☐

SITING: It's a must to site this plant in a spot where you can enjoy the intensely fragrant blossoms. Giving it a sunny window will help it bloom, and the

warm sun will release the intoxicating scent. Jasmine grows in average temperatures (60–75°F) but sets flower buds only if grown for a time in fall between 40 and 60°F. Give this plant average to high humidity (above 30 percent). A humidifier helps provide moisture as well as air circulation, which keeps the plant leaves fungus free.

Jasmine requires bright light to develop its highly fragrant white blooms.

CARE: Keep evenly moist during active growth; water sparingly in winter. Feed once a month during active growth and not at all in winter. Move outdoors in bright light during the summer. Leaving it outdoors until temperatures reach about 40°F will set the flower buds. After it has bloomed in late winter, repot the plant and prune it back hard to avoid tangling. It will need some support such as a trellis or topiary frame, or it can be grown in a hanging basket. Prune it often to keep it looking good.

PROPAGATION: Propagate by taking stem cuttings in spring or by layering anytime. To layer, pin a stem to moist soil at a leaf node. When roots have formed, separate the plant from the parent plant.

PESTS AND DISEASES: Spider mites are a frequent pest, so wash the plant often to keep populations low.

RELATED SPECIES: Arabian jasmine (*J. sambac*) has large flowers and is used to flavor jasmine tea. Common jasmine (*J. officinale*) has white flowers and does not vine quite as much.

KALANCHOE

Kalanchoe blossfeldiana *kuh-LAN-cho (kal-an-KO-ee) bloss-fell-dee-AH-nah*

Kalanchoe takes little care and will bloom continuously for months with all shades of pink, red, yellow, or white blossoms.

SIZE: 6–12"h × 6–12"w
TYPE: Succulent
FORM: Upright
TEXTURE: Medium
GROWTH: Slow

LIGHT: High
MOISTURE: Dry
SOIL: Cactus mix
FEATURES: Flowers
USES: Accent plant
FLOWERS: ■ ■ ■ □

SITING: Grow kalanchoe in full morning or afternoon sun, avoiding midday sun. It performs best in average home temperatures (60–75°F) but will tolerate cold and heat for short periods. It needs only low to average humidity (30–60 percent).

CARE: Kalanchoe takes little care; it blooms for a long time with little attention. Water when the soil feels dry. Plants that are underwatered will turn reddish and shrivel, and the flowers and leaves will drop prematurely. Overwatering fosters rot and falling leaves. Feed only when new growth begins. Use a foliage plant food at half strength every 2 weeks. Remove faded leaves and flowers and wash the leaves occasionally. It is difficult to bring kalanchoe back into blossom in the home.

As flowers fade, pinch out the old blossoms and stalks to force the plant to produce more flower buds.

New plants grown from cuttings will bloom better than old plants that have already blossomed.

PROPAGATION: Propagate by stem cuttings. Cut a 3" section of stem, remove all but one leaf, and set aside to callus for 2–3 days. Then dip in rooting hormone and insert in sterile potting mix.

PESTS AND DISEASES: Few pests bother kalanchoe. Mealybugs are easily taken care of with a cotton swab dipped in alcohol or horticultural oil.

To force a kalanchoe into bloom again once it has finished will require an elaborate routine of light and darkness.

MOTHER OF THOUSANDS

Kalanchoe daigremontiana *kuh-LAN-cho (kal-an-KO-ee) deh-gre-mon-tee-ANN-uh*

Mother of thousands derives its name from the tiny plantlets all along each leaf. It is also known as air plant.

SIZE: 3'h × 3'w
TYPE: Succulent
FORM: Upright
TEXTURE: Medium
GROWTH: Medium
LIGHT: High

MOISTURE: Dry
SOIL: Cactus mix
FEATURES: Plantlets along margins
USES: Architectural accent

SITING: Grow mother of thousands in full morning or afternoon sun, avoiding midday sun. High light will cause leaf edges to turn red, an attractive feature. Lower light will cause the plants to be leggy and spindly. It performs best in average home temperatures (60–75°F)

but will tolerate cold and heat for short periods. It needs only low to average humidity (30–60 percent).

CARE: Mother of thousands takes little care. It is a succulent so it doesn't need a lot of water, but it should be watered when the soil is dry to the touch. This may take 1–2 weeks, depending on the type of pot and the temperature in which the plant

The plantlets along the leaves will fall by themselves, but you can remove them, and set them on moist soil to start new plants.

is grown. Plants that are underwatered will turn reddish and shrivel, and the flowers and leaves will drop prematurely. Overwatering or letting the plant sit in water will foster rot and falling leaves. Feed three times in summer with half-strength foliage plant food. Repot when the roots fill the pot. Remove faded leaves and flowers and wash the leaves occasionally.

PROPAGATION: This kalanchoe is called mother of thousands because small plantlets form along the margins of every leaf. These tiny plantlets give the plant a unique look; as they mature, they fall off and start new plants automatically. To produce new plants, place a pot with moist soil beneath a leaf, or remove an entire leaf and place it on the surface of the soil. The plantlets will send out new roots fairly quickly.

PESTS AND DISEASES: Few pests bother kalanchoe. Mealybugs are easily taken care of with a cotton swab dipped in alcohol or horticultural oil.

RELATED SPECIES: Chandelier plant (*K. delagoensis*) has rounded, succulent leaves with bulbils on the edges.

PANDA PLANT
Kalanchoe tomentosa *kuh-LAN-cho (kal-an-KO-ee) toh-men-TOH-suh*

Panda plant's soft, fuzzy leaves thrive in warm, dry conditions. It is also known as pussy ears.

SIZE: 20"h × 20"w	**MOISTURE:** Dry
TYPE: Succulent	**SOIL:** Cactus mix
FORM: Mounded	**FEATURES:** Fuzzy leaves
TEXTURE: Medium	
GROWTH: Medium	**USES:** Dish garden, focal point
LIGHT: High	

SITING: Panda plant has a unique texture that contrasts nicely with spiky cactus. Grow panda plant in full morning or afternoon sun, avoiding midday sun. High light will cause the leaf edges to turn red, an attractive feature. Lower light will cause it to beome leggy and spindly. Panda plant performs best in average home temperatures (60–75°F) but will tolerate cold and heat for short periods. It needs only low to average humidity (30–60 percent).

CARE: Panda plant, like the other kalanchoes, takes little care. Kalanchoes are succulents and don't need a lot of water, but they should be watered when the soil feels dry. This may take 1–2 weeks, depending on the type of pot and the temperature in which the plant is grown. Plants that are underwatered will turn reddish and shrivel, and the flowers and leaves will drop prematurely. Overwatering or letting the plant sit in water will foster rot and falling leaves. Feed three times in summer with half-strength foliage plant food. Repot when the roots fill the pot. Remove faded leaves and flowers and wash the leaves occasionally.

PROPAGATION: Propagate by stem cuttings. Cut a 3" section of stem, remove all but one leaf, and set aside to callus for 2–3 days. Then dip in rooting hormone and insert in sterile potting mix. Do not cover and water sparingly until the cuttings root. When new growth starts, feed as directed above. The plants can also be propagated by leaf cuttings.

PESTS AND DISEASES: Few pests bother kalanchoes. Mealybugs are easily taken care of with a cotton swab dipped in alcohol or horticultural oil.

RELATED SPECIES: Felt bush (*K. beharensis*) 'Maltese Cross' has cupped, curly leaves with brown felt on their upper surface and silver undersides.

SWEET BAY
Laurus nobilis *LOR-us no-BILL-us*

Sweet bay is also known as Roman laurel or bay tree. It makes a magnificent houseplant with its glossy green foliage.

SIZE: 4'h × 3'w	**MOISTURE:** Evenly moist
TYPE: Woody shrub	
FORM: Upright	**SOIL:** Potting soil
TEXTURE: Medium	**FEATURES:** Fragrant foliage
GROWTH: Slow	
LIGHT: Medium to high	**USES:** Foliage backdrop, culinary

SITING: Sweet bay is a plant worth having for its culinary value and for its fragrant foliage. Bay performs best in medium to high light and thrives in cool to average temperatures (50–75°F) and low to average humidity (30–60 percent). It is an excellent choice for an architectural plant in a cool foyer or porch.

CARE: Keep the soil evenly moist when the plant is in active growth and somewhat dry during its winter rest. Soil that is too wet in winter will cause leaf yellowing and leaf drop. Feed infrequently to keep the foliage oils strong for flavoring and to control the size. (It can grow to 40' in the wild.) Repot when roots fill the pot; prune the roots to put the plant back in the same pot. Prune off some of the crown to reduce the stress of root pruning. Sweet bay can be sheared into hedges and topiary shapes. It benefits from spending the summer outdoors in a bright but indirectly lit spot.

PROPAGATION: Propagate by taking 4–6" cuttings in early summer after the new growth has hardened somewhat. Remove all but one or two leaves, dip in rooting hormone, and insert in sterile potting soil. Cover with a plastic tent for extra humidity. Be aware that sweet bay is difficult to root.

PESTS AND DISEASES: Control scale with horticultural oil. Moving the plant outdoors in summer allows natural predators to keep scale in check. Be sure to wash carefully any leaves you use for cooking.

RELATED SPECIES: The cultivar 'Aurea' has yellowish young foliage. 'Angustifolia' has willow-shaped leaves. 'Undulata' leaves have wavy margins.

The leaves of sweet bay can be used straight from the plant for seasoning food and will surprise you with much more flavor than the dried ones from the grocery.

LIVING STONES

Lithops spp. *LITH-ups*

Living stones' succulent leaves resemble small stones or rocks.

SIZE: 2"h × 4"w
TYPE: Succulent
FORM: Round
TEXTURE: Medium
GROWTH: Slow
LIGHT: High
MOISTURE: Low

SOIL: Cactus mix
FEATURES: Leaves resemble stones
USES: Dish garden, cactus garden
FLOWERS: ■☐

SITING: These oddities of the plant world have evolved to have only one pair of leaves that are plump water storage organs. They resemble stones in their natural habitat so are left alone by grazing animals. When grown in high light, they produce a daisylike flower from between the two leaves. In lower light, they stretch, lose their stonelike appearance, and can die. Give living stones direct sun, cool to hot temperatures, and low humidity (below 30 percent), and they will live a long time. Keep the plant at 50–55°F in winter. It will not tolerate stagnant air, so keep it well ventilated, using a fan if necessary to create air movement.

CARE: Living stones needs very little water. Even more than cactus, it will quickly rot if overwatered. Water only when the soil feels dry. At the end of October, cease watering and let the plant dry completely. For the next few months, it will produce a new set of leaves, consuming the moisture from the old pair, which will shrivel. Avoid watering the plants during this time. When new leaves appear in early spring, begin

Living stones grow best in the same conditions as cactus—hot and dry—and benefit from an attractive stone mulch.

watering again. Soak the soil well, allow it to drain completely, then let it dry out a bit before watering again. The general rule is when in doubt about watering, don't. Feed the plants with foliage plant food once a year when the new leaves are fully formed. Living stones has a minuscule root system, so it doesn't need repotting. Once the old leaves and flower stalk have shriveled, use tweezers to remove them. Occasionally wipe off the leaves.

PROPAGATION: Living stones is traditionally propagated from seed. If your plant produces a flower, you can harvest your own seed. Otherwise, order from a supplier. Sprinkle the seeds on moist potting mix and provide bottom heat. Germination can take from 2–14 days. When the seedlings are about 6 months old, they are sturdy enough to pot up.

PESTS AND DISEASES: Mice can be troublesome for plants that spend the summer outdoors.

RELATED SPECIES: Species and cultivars vary widely in their leaf markings.

CHINESE FAN PALM

Livistona chinensis *liv-ib-STONE-uh chib-NEN-sis*

Chinese fan palms have a magnificent stature, useful in a vast room where an architectural accent is needed.

SIZE: 12'h × 12'w
TYPE: Palm
FORM: Vase
TEXTURE: Coarse
GROWTH: Medium
LIGHT: High

MOISTURE: Dry
SOIL: Potting soil
FEATURES: Fan-shape fronds
USES: Architectural accent

SITING: Chinese fan palm looks its best when given bright light and some direct sun. In lower light its magnificent fronds fade to lime green and generally look unhealthy. It thrives in average temperatures (60–75°F) and average humidity (30–60 percent). Make sure you have plenty of room for these large plants. They are not easily kept to smaller proportions, and the fronds will appear ragged if they brush against walls, windows or furniture.

CARE: Allow the soil to dry about an inch deep before watering. Soak the plant well and discard the runoff. The plant should not sit in water. Yellow leaves may result from underwatering; brown spots on the leaves can come from overwatering or chemicals in the water. Feed with foliage plant food every month to maintain good color. Palms of all types perform best when somewhat pot-bound, so you will seldom have to repot a Chinese fan palm. Occasionally remove browned leaves at the bottom and snip the brown tips off the fronds.

PROPAGATION: Propagate by seed, available from suppliers.

PESTS AND DISEASES: Spider mites may appear if the plant is grown in low humidity. Wash the leaves frequently to control these pests. Scale insects can be easily taken care of with a cotton swab dipped in horticultural oil.

RELATED SPECIES: Other species are grown as outdoor landscape plants. *Livistona chinensis* is the only one that is grown as a houseplant.

JEWEL ORCHID
Ludisia discolor lew-DEE-see-uh dis-CUH-ler

Jewel orchid has rich velvety maroon foliage that is wonderful even without the stalks of dainty white miniature orchids.

SIZE: 6"h × 12"w
TYPE: Orchid
FORM: Trailing
TEXTURE: Medium
GROWTH: Slow
LIGHT: Medium to low
MOISTURE: Evenly moist

SOIL: Potting soil
FEATURES: Velvety maroon leaves
USES: Focal point, hanging basket, terrarium
FLOWERS: ☐

SITING: This terrestrial orchid is lovely as an addition to a dish garden or as a display piece for the foliage alone. It is easy to grow. The tall spikes hold tiny, perfectly formed white and yellow blossoms. Jewel orchid grows well in medium light and tolerates low light. It needs warmth (70°F or above) and high humidity (above 60 percent) to look its best.

CARE: Keep the soil evenly moist year round. Feed once a month with foliage plant food diluted to half strength. Seldom does jewel orchid need repotting, because it has a fairly small root system. If you

The white flower spikes are set off by the darker striped foliage.

choose to move the plant outdoors in summer, keep it in low light under a tree or shrub where it will receive rain and air movement but no direct sun. Remove the occasional dead leaf and old leaf sheaths to avoid giving scale insects a place to hide.

PROPAGATION: Stem cuttings root readily; the plant can also be layered. The creeping stems automatically root at the nodes, so find a rooted one and sever it from the main plant. Or pin one and wait for it to root. The plant can also be divided.

PESTS AND DISEASES: Scrape off scale insects with your finger and gently wash the leaves frequently. Horticultural oil may harm the plant.

RELATED SPECIES: The *Ludisia discolor* called "type form" has almost black leaves and silvery veins.

SNOWBALL CACTUS
Mammillaria bocasana mam-mil-AIR-ee-uh bok-uh-SAHN-uh

Snowball cactus is easy to grow, and although it looks soft and lush, the hairs hide spines that can prick.

SIZE: 4–6"h × 6–12"w
TYPE: Cactus
FORM: Mounded
TEXTURE: Coarse
GROWTH: Slow
LIGHT: High

MOISTURE: Low
SOIL: Cactus mix
FEATURES: Fuzzy, interlocking hairs
USES: Cactus garden, focal point
FLOWERS: ■

SITING: Snowball cactus is easy for the beginner to grow. Its soft, cuddly look is deceiving; the interlocking hairs that give the fuzzy appearance actually cover hooked central spines that can catch a finger easily. As with all cacti, snowball cactus needs high light. If light in the home is perfect, it produces rings of flowers, followed by red fruits. Provide average to hot (65°F and above) temperatures in spring and summer and cool (50–60°F) temperatures in winter. It prefers low humidity. This is a plant to grow on a dry, exposed windowsill. This location will keep the plant out of traffic, where its spines can inflict painful wounds.

CARE: Snowball cactus needs little water most of the time. Let it dry out completely between waterings, then soak it just as a desert rain would do. It must have perfect drainage, however, or it will rot. Low light also may cause it to rot. In winter give this cactus a cooler, drier resting time. Feed three times in summer with a general-purpose plant food. Repot annually.

PROPAGATION: Propagate by seed and division of the crown as it splits.

PESTS AND DISEASES: Mealybugs may appear beneath the hairs. Dab them with horticultural oil on a cotton swab.

RELATED SPECIES: *M. b.* ssp. *eschauzieri* has longer hairs and pale yellow flowers. *M. densispina* remains as a single ball.

1 The crown of snowball cactus splits into many "snowballs." These offsets can be separated to form new plants.

2 Pot the offsets in a fast-draining cactus mix and set them in a protected place until they form roots.

PRAYER PLANT

Maranta leuconeura *muh-RAN-tuh lew-co-NEW-ruh*

Prayer plant is well recognized by its beautifully variegated foliage in shades of green and maroon.

SIZE: 12"h × 12"w
TYPE: Herbaceous
FORM: Mounded
TEXTURE: Coarse
GROWTH: Slow
LIGHT: Low to medium

MOISTURE: Evenly moist
SOIL: Potting soil
FEATURES: Striped leaves
USES: Foliage, dish garden
FLOWERS: □

SITING: Prayer plant is a must-have in a foliage plant collection because of its unique coloration and interesting habit of folding up vertically in the evening. In perfect conditions the plant produces small white flowers with purple spots. This slow-growing plant takes little care if given low to medium light. It thrives in average home temperatures (60–75°F) and tolerates hot temperatures as well. Provide average humidity (30–60 percent); if the leaves begin to brown on the edges, increase the humidity with a pebble tray or humidifier.

CARE: Keep the soil evenly moist. Feed three times in summer with all-purpose foliage plant food. Repot only when it is difficult to water the plant, usually once every couple of years. Remove any dead leaves. Wash the leaves monthly to keep spider mites at bay and to maintain the leaves' attractive colors. The plant may suffer from root rot if overwatered. Leaves will turn pale in too much light and will curl and brown if the plant is too cool or in a draft.

PROPAGATION: Propagate by dividing the root ball, by cutting off rhizomes and potting them, or by stem cuttings.

PESTS AND DISEASES: Spider mites and mealybugs may become pests on prayer plant, but usually only in low humidity.

RELATED SPECIES: 'Massangeana' has dark olive leaves with a silver midrib and veins.

Herringbone plant (*M. l.* var. *erythroneura*) has olive to black leaves with bright red markings.

Prayer plant has a habit of folding its leaves upright at night, resembling praying hands.

SENSITIVE PLANT

Mimosa pudica *mim-OH-suh PEW-di-kuh*

Sensitive plants are perfect conversations pieces with their soft gray-green leaflets and pink plumy blossoms.

SIZE: 18"h × 18"w
TYPE: Woody shrub
FORM: Mounded
TEXTURE: Fine
GROWTH: Fast
LIGHT: Medium to high
MOISTURE: Evenly moist

SOIL: Potting soil
FEATURES: Leaflets fold up when touched
USES: Conversation piece
FLOWERS: ■

SITING: Sensitive plant is a wonderful plant for a child to enjoy. It is soft textured and has the delightful habit of folding its leaves up tightly when stroked. It does have small spines, so it's wise to be cautious. If grown in high light, it may produce pink puffball flowers, a delight to children. The plants thrive at temperatures of 65–80°F. If temperatures fall below this range, the leaves will yellow and drop.

The plant's leaves fold when it is softly touched or brushed, giving rise to its alternate common name, touch-me-not.

CARE: To keep sensitive plant from dropping its leaves, keep the soil moist except during the winter rest period, when watering should be reduced somewhat. This plant can draw nitrogen from the air and fix it in its roots. It needs infrequent feeding—only once or twice a year with a foliage plant food. Sensitive plant will grow woody with age. Repot annually until it becomes unattractive, then discard the plant. Remove faded leaves.

PROPAGATION: Sensitive plant is easily started from the seeds that are produced prolifically when the plant blooms. When the pods ripen, remove the seeds and soak them for 24 hours in hot water. After the seeds have swelled, plant them in sterile potting soil and keep the humidity high until the seeds germinate. Plants can also be propagated by semihardwood stem cuttings, although the success rate for this method is limited.

PESTS AND DISEASES: Spider mites can be a problem, especially in low humidity, so keep the humidity up and give the plant a monthly shower to keep populations low.

RELATED SPECIES: No other *Mimosa* species is grown indoors.

SPLIT-LEAF PHILODENDRON
Monstera deliciosa mon-STAIR-uh deh-lih-see-OH-suh

Split-leaf philodendron is also known as Swiss-cheese plant or monstera.

SIZE: 10'h × 10'w
TYPE: Vine
FORM: Upright
TEXTURE: Coarse
GROWTH: Slow
LIGHT: Low to medium
MOISTURE: Dry
SOIL: Potting soil
FEATURES: Cut leaves
USES: Architectural accent
FLOWERS: ■□

SITING: Monstera is a large plant that needs the proper site to look good. If it is grown upright, the leaf shapes will change from juvenile to mature. Monstera has heavy stems with long pinkish aerial roots. If grown in the right conditions, it may produce greenish-white flowers followed by edible fruits that taste somewhat like custard when ripe. (All other parts of the plant are toxic to ingest, and the fruits may be irritating to some people.) Grow monstera in low to medium light, average home temperatures (60–75°F), and low humidity (below 30 percent).

CARE: Allow it to dry somewhat between waterings during active growth, then let it dry out a bit more during the winter rest. Feed three times in summer with foliage

The thick aerial roots can be attached to a moss or bark pole to train the philodendron to have a more upright appearance.

plant food at regular strength and repot infrequently. Prune regularly to maintain a particular size, although trying to make it much smaller is seldom successful. Give the plant monthly showers to keep the glossy leaves clean and reduce the incidence of spider mites. Small leaves or leaves with no splits may indicate that the light is too low. Browning leaves indicate too much water. Do not cut off the aerial roots. Direct them back into the potting soil or into a moss pole to give the plant some support. Otherwise it will lean and become unwieldy in the home. Moss poles are a simple way to train the plant, and the damp moss gives the plant some moisture and nutrients.

PROPAGATION: Propagate by stem cuttings and layering. Simply cut off a stem tip with an aerial root and pot it. If a stem has an aerial root already in the soil, sever the new plant and pot it.

PESTS AND DISEASES: Spider mites, scale, and whiteflies can be deterred by frequently wiping and washing the leaves.

RELATED SPECIES: The cultivar 'Variegata' has creamy yellow patches that revert to green. 'Albovariegata' has white patches.

SWEET MYRTLE
Myrtus communis MUR-tiss kuh-MUNE-iss

Sweet myrtle is a lovely fine-textured plant with glossy dark leaves and attractive diminutive blossoms.

SIZE: 6'h × 3'w
TYPE: Woody shrub
FORM: Upright
TEXTURE: Fine
GROWTH: Slow
LIGHT: Medium to high
MOISTURE: Evenly moist
SOIL: Potting soil
FEATURES: Glossy leaves, attractive flowers
USES: Topiary, bonsai
FLOWERS: □■

SITING: Sweet myrtle is a popular plant for topiary and bonsai because of its adaptation to shearing. The glossy leaves are attractive enough by themselves when the plant is grown in medium light; if the plant is grown in bright, indirect light, it will often produce voluminous small, starry pink or white blossoms. The plants tolerate cool to average home temperatures (55–75°F) and high humidity (above 60 percent). Use a pebble tray or pot-in-pot system to boost the humidity.

Myrtle accepts pruning quite well and is an excellent candidate for training as a bonsai or topiary accent.

CARE: Keep the soil evenly moist. It may lose its leaves if allowed to dry out, and may show some tip chlorosis if the soil is not well drained. When grown in high light, myrtle will suffer if even one watering is missed. Feed with foliage plant food according to label directions. Repot annually or at least every 2 years. It may be worth root-pruning when you repot to keep the plant within bounds. Sweet myrtle naturally gets large but can be kept small by regular pruning. It will tolerate pruning all the way back to stubs and will leaf out again quickly, which is why it is popular for topiary.

PROPAGATION: Propagate by semihardwood cuttings in early summer. Cuttings must be rooted in high humidity. The plants can be propagated by seed as well.

PESTS AND DISEASES: Sweet myrtle can have a myriad of problems, especially when grown in lower light and lower humidity. Watch for spider mites, scale, mealybugs, and whiteflies. All can be controlled with horticultural oil.

RELATED SPECIES: The cultivar 'Variegata' has creamy white margins. 'Microphylla' has tiny leaves and grows to only 2' high.

GUPPY PLANT
Nematanthus spp. *nee-muh-TAN-thuss*

Guppy plants offer striking glossy foliage and unusually shaped brightly colored blossoms on vining stems.

SIZE: 2–4'h × 2–4'w
TYPE: Gesneriad
FORM: Trailing
TEXTURE: Fine
GROWTH: Moderate
LIGHT: Bright to medium

MOISTURE: Dry
SOIL: Potting soil
FEATURES: Glossy leaves, flowers
USES: Hanging basket
FLOWERS: ■ ■ □

SITING: Bright to medium light, away from direct sun, will keep guppy plant looking its best. If the plant won't flower, move it into higher filtered light. Provide temperatures of 65–80°F for the plant to blossom. In winter, reduce temperatures to 50–55°F and reduce watering. High humidity is a necessity, as with most gesneriads. A pebble tray works well to achieve this.

CARE: Guppy plant is somewhat epiphytic, so allow the soil to dry slightly between waterings. When the plant is not actively growing, avoid wetting the foliage or it may develop fungal leaf spots. Reducing watering for 6–8 weeks may induce flowering. Feed every 2 weeks with half-strength plant food for blooming plants during active growth. Every month flush the soil with clear water to wash away fertilizer salts. Repotting is seldom needed; guppy plant blooms best when pot-bound.

Prune wayward stems regularly to keep the plant full and appealing. Guppy plant will drop its leaves when it gets too cold or too dry or is overfertilized.

PROPAGATION: Propagate by stem or tip cuttings. When you prune long stems to keep the plant looking good, simply insert the cuttings in rooting hormone, then into sterile potting soil. Cover with plastic to keep the humidity up, and in a few weeks the cuttings will be rooted.

PESTS AND DISEASES: Watch for aphids, spider mites, and whiteflies. The plant will generally not have a problem unless cultural details are neglected.

RELATED SPECIES: *N. crassifolius* has dangling orange-red blossoms. *N. corticola* has orange flowers that dangle on pedicels (flower stalks) 3–4" long. *N. gregarious* 'Golden West' has variegated foliage. 'Christmas Holly' has intensely glossy foliage and bright red flowers.

BLUSHING BROMELIAD
Neoregelia carolinae *nee-oh-reg-EEL-ee-uh kair-oh-LIN-ay*

Blushing bromeliads have attractive variegated foliage that turns bright pink at the base as the plant begins to blossom.

SIZE: 1–2'h × 1–2'w
TYPE: Bromeliad
FORM: Vase-shaped
TEXTURE: Medium
GROWTH: Slow
LIGHT: High to medium

MOISTURE: Dry
SOIL: Epiphyte mix
FEATURES: Striped leaves, colorful vase
USES: Focal point, blooming
FLOWERS: ■ □

SITING: Blushing bromeliad shows its best leaf color in bright, filtered light. The "vase" turns from pinkish to bright crimson when the plant begins to flower. It will not tolerate direct sun. It does well in medium light, although it will not be as symmetrical and tight and the leaves may fade somewhat. Provide average to hot temperatures (60°F and above) to prevent rotting. High humidity (above 65 percent) will keep this bromeliad looking good.

CARE: Let the soil dry out almost completely between waterings, and keep the vase full of water. Every couple of months, empty and refill the vase to keep the water somewhat fresh. Feed with blooming plant food three times in summer, or add half-strength formula to

These epiphytes are best kept moist by keeping the vase formed by the leaf bases filled with water.

the vase every month. Blushing bromeliad has a minuscule root system that will seldom outgrow a pot. Repot only when the potting mix begins to break down and no longer has recognizable chunks of bark. This bromeliad can be grown on a slab, but high humidity is essential. The plant may develop leaf spots in low humidity and root rot if overwatered.

PROPAGATION: Propagate by removing the offsets or side shoots when they are about one-third the size of the parent plant. (They will not root if taken when too young.) Take the plant out of the pot and gently pull off each offset, making sure it has some roots. Pot up the offsets and keep them in a warm, bright spot until they establish themselves. Water daily. A plant started this way should bloom in 1–2 years. You can also propagate blushing bromeliad by seed in spring. Collect the seeds as they ripen and place them on moist paper towels in a covered plastic container. Check daily for mold, and leave the lid off briefly for air exchange. When the plant has 5 leaves, it is ready to pot. Expect a blooming plant in 6–8 years.

PESTS AND DISEASES: Treat scale and spider mites with insecticidal soap.

RELATED SPECIES: The cultivar 'Tricolor' is most commonly grown. Its leaves have a chartreuse center, dark green margins, and blushing pink in the center of the vase, which turns carmine red when it blossoms.

BOSTON FERN

Nephrolepis exaltata neh-froh-LEP-iss ex-all-TAH-tuh

Boston fern, also known as sword fern, has been a favorite for centuries with its arching fronds and delicate foliage.

SIZE: 2'h × 4'w
TYPE: Fern
FORM: Arching
TEXTURE: Fine
GROWTH: Fast
LIGHT: Medium

MOISTURE: Evenly moist
SOIL: Potting soil
FEATURES: Arching fronds
USES: Hanging basket, focal point

SITING: Boston fern has a lush, rich appearance in medium to bright, indirect light and average home temperatures (60–75°F). It needs high humidity (above 60 percent). A common site for these moisture lovers is in a bathroom, where the humidity is naturally high. Dropping leaflets are typical.

CARE: Keep the soil moist but well drained. Feed three times in summer, or with foliage plant food according to label directions. Boston fern fills a pot quickly and should be repotted annually with fresh potting soil. Regular root pruning

Most ferns need plenty of humidity. Insert one pot inside another filled with moist sphagnum moss to raise moisture levels.

will also keep the plant vigorous. It drops brown leaflets constantly, especially in drafts, so give the plant a good shaking to dislodge the dead leaflets. Any change in a cultural condition will cause leaf drop. Prune out any brown fronds at the base of the plant. Wash the leaves often to keep pests at bay and to keep the plant looking its best.

PROPAGATION: Propagate by dividing the crown. Pull the plant from its pot, cut the crown apart at its obvious joints, and repot the portions. To propagate from spores, wait until the spore cases on the back of the fronds ripen, then tap the spores onto a piece of paper. Scatter the spores on moist, sterile potting mix and cover the container with glass or plastic.

PESTS AND DISEASES: Boston fern is susceptible to scale and mealybugs. Treat both pests with horticultural oil.

RELATED SPECIES: Erect sword fern (*N. cordifolia*) has more fronds that stand more upright than Boston fern. 'Fluffy Ruffles' has curly fronds. 'Dallas' is more compact and does better in low light. 'Golden Boston' has golden-yellow fronds.

BUNNY EAR CACTUS

Opuntia microdasys o-PUN-tee-uh my-crow-DAY-siss

SIZE: 18–24"h × 18–24"w
TYPE: Cactus
FORM: Upright
TEXTURE: Coarse
GROWTH: Slow
LIGHT: High
MOISTURE: Low
SOIL: Cactus mix
FEATURES: Flattened "ears" with yellow spines
USES: Cactus garden, Southwest theme
FLOWERS: ■ ■ ■

Bunny ear cactus can give you a carefree southwestern focal point provided that it gets high light and low humidity.

SITING: Bunny ear cactus needs full sun to bloom. The yellow or sometimes pink or red flowers are often followed by edible fruits. Keep the plant warm (65–85°F) when in active growth and provide cooler temperatures (55–60°F) during its dormant period in winter. Provide low humidity (20–30 percent) to keep it looking its best.

High humidity often causes leaf scarring. Be sure to site this plant away from traffic. The large spines are troublesome to passersby, and the smaller glochids (barbed hairs) that are formed in each tubercle (nodule of spines) are just as irritating, because they stick easily into skin and clothing.

CARE: Let the soil dry out considerably between waterings during active growth,

These cactus tolerate pruning for propagating new plants or for shaping.

and even more so during the dormant stage. Feed with half-strength plant food only after flower buds form. Bunny ear cactus has a small root system, like other cacti, so repotting is seldom necessary. This is one of the few cactuses that can be pruned. Do so by removing a pad. If pruned in summer, new growth will start forming at the cut. When pruning or handling bunny ear cactus, grasp the ears with gloves or several layers of newspaper to avoid having the glochids become imbedded in your skin. The most common problem with bunny ear cactus is root rot from overwatering. Occasionally a plant will die from overwatering yet remain standing until someone knocks it over and finds that it is rotted away inside.

PROPAGATION: Propagate by stem cuttings. Remove a pad and let it sit for several days to callus. Then set it in potting mix.

PESTS AND DISEASES: Mealybugs and scale may be hidden under the spines. Aphids may appear on the flowers.

RELATED SPECIES: *O. m.* var. *albospinna* has white glochids. *O. m.* var. *rufida* has reddish brown glochids.

SWEET OLIVE

Osmanthus fragrans oz-MAN-thus FRAY-grans

Sweet olives are a must-have for fragrance year-round even though the plant itself is a subtle addition to a foliage plant collection.

SIZE: 1–2'h × 1'w
TYPE: Woody shrub
FORM: Rounded
TEXTURE: Medium
GROWTH: Slow
LIGHT: High to medium
MOISTURE: Dry

SOIL: Potting soil
FEATURES: Glossy leaves, fragrant blossoms
USES: Fragrance, foliage
FLOWERS: ☐

SITING: This unassuming plant will knock you over with its citrusy, jasminelike scent. It tolerates full sun, indirect bright light, and even medium light; average to high temperatures (60°F and above); and

average to low humidity (60 percent and below).

CARE: Water once a week and feed with foliage plant food once or twice a year. Repot only every 2–3 years. Move outdoors

The tiny white or cream blossoms of sweet olive are intensely fragrant, with hints of citrus and jasmine.

to a protected spot in summer. Pruning is unnecessary, because even the branches that have few leaves will bear flowers. In fact, pruning what looks like dead wood will prune the flowering wood, so it's best left alone. Sweet olive does benefit from periodic washing of the leaves. If you forget to water for a long while, it will still have green leaves. However, one shake and they will all fall.

PROPAGATION: Propagate from semihardwood cuttings, although the success rate is not high. In early summer after the new growth has hardened somewhat, take 3–4" cuttings, remove all but one leaf, dip in rooting hormone, and insert in sterile potting soil. Tent with plastic until the cuttings have rooted.

PESTS AND DISEASES: Spider mites may be a problem in very dry locations but can be controlled with regular spraying. Scale may also appear. Treat with horticultural oil.

RELATED SPECIES: The cultivar 'Aurantiacus' has orange flowers. *O. ×fortunei,* a hybrid cross between *O. fragrans* and *O. hererophyllus,* has the same leaves as *O. fragrans* but larger flowers.

FALSE HOLLY

Osmanthus heterophyllus oz-MAN-thus het-ur-oh-FILL-us

False holly has striking hollylike leaves that make an delightful statement in a foliage plant collection.

SIZE: 1–2'h × 1'w
TYPE: Woody shrub
FORM: Rounded
TEXTURE: Medium
GROWTH: Slow
LIGHT: High to medium

MOISTURE: Dry
SOIL: Potting soil
FEATURES: Hollylike leaves
USES: Foliage, focal point
FLOWERS: ☐

SITING: False holly tolerates full sun, indirect, bright light, and even medium light; average to high temperatures (60°F and above); and average to low humidity (60 percent and below).

CARE: Water once a week, and feed with foliage plant food once or twice a year. Repot every 2–3 years. Move outdoors to a protected spot in summer. Prune only to shape the plant. False holly does benefit from periodic washing of the leaves. The plant remains green even when dried out, so don't rely on leaf changes to remind you to water. It's possible to forget to water for a long while and the plant will still have green leaves. However, one shake and they will all fall.

PROPAGATION: Propagate from semihardwood cuttings, although the

success rate is not high. In early summer take 3–5" cuttings, remove all but one leaf, dip in rooting hormone, and insert in sterile potting soil. Tent with plastic until the cuttings have rooted.

PESTS AND DISEASES: Spider mites may be a problem in very dry locations but can be controlled with regular spraying, particularly the undersides of the leaves, and horticultural oil. Scale may also appear.

RELATED SPECIES: The cultivar 'Variegatus' has variegated foliage. 'Goshiki' (freckle face holly) has gold-flecked leaves.

Propagate by taking 3–5" semihardwood cuttings in early summer.

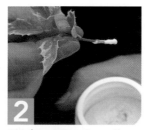

Dip the cuttings in rooting hormone, tapping off the excess powder.

Stick cuttings in holes, tamp gently, water, and cover with plastic.

OXALIS
Oxalis regnellii ocks-AL-iss reg-NEL-ee-eye

Oxalis, also known as purple shamrock, is grown for its clover-shaped leaves as well as its soft pink and white flowers.

SIZE: 12"h × 12"w
TYPE: Bulb
FORM: Mounded
TEXTURE: Fine
GROWTH: Medium
LIGHT: High, indirect

MOISTURE: Evenly moist
SOIL: Potting soil
FEATURES: Velvety leaves
USES: Focal point
FLOWERS: ☐■

SITING: Provide oxalis with bright, indirect light during most of the year. It tolerates full sun in winter if it is actively growing. Daytime temperatures should be 65–75°F and nighttime temperatures around 55–60°F. More warmth than this will cause the plant to go into dormancy faster. Keep oxalis away from drafts and provide average humidity (30–60 percent).

CARE: Keep evenly moist when the plant is actively growing; the soil must be well-drained to prevent waterlogging. The plant may develop brown spots on the leaves if it is overwatered and yellow leaves if underwatered. Feed with half-strength foliage plant food weekly while growing. Remove spent flowers and leaves. If your plant does not bloom, it may be too young; in an older plant, it may need dormancy. Give the plant a shower occasionally to rinse the dust off the leaves. After oxalis finishes blooming, it begins to go into a dormant phase. Gradually reduce water and gently pull off the spent leaves. Once the foliage is gone, store the bulbs in soil in a cool, dark spot for 1–3 months. When green shoots appear, bring the pot back into a sunny window and begin watering and feeding.

PROPAGATION: Small bulbs can be separated when you repot the plant. Simply sever or pull them off and pot them, making sure that they are about ½" below the soil line.

PESTS AND DISEASES: When grown in dry conditions, oxalis may have spider mites. Leaves go off-color long before you see any webbing. Control with frequent showers.

RELATED SPECIES: Triangular leaves and reddish-purple flowers are features of lucky plant *(O. tetraphylla)*. *O. purpurea* is only 4" tall with dark green leaves and pink flowers. Wood sorrel *(O. acetosella)* is dark green with rosy-pink blossoms.

To propagate an oxalis plant, simply lift the plant out of its pot and gently separate the tubers.

Repot the tubers in clean potting soil, making sure they are about ½" below the soil line.

LOLLIPOP PLANT
Pachystachys lutea pak-ee-STAK-iss LOOT-ee-uh

Lollipop plant has long-lasting yellow bracts that reveal sparkling white blossoms.

SIZE: 18"h × 18"w
TYPE: Woody shrub
FORM: Rounded
TEXTURE: Coarse
GROWTH: Medium
LIGHT: High, indirect

MOISTURE: Evenly moist
SOIL: Potting soil
FEATURES: Rich green rugose leaves
USES: Accent
FLOWERS: ■☐☐

SITING: The most striking feature of lollipop plant is its yellow "candles," flower stalks that rise high above the leaves. These stalks are adorned with golden-yellow bracts from which white flowers arise. This plant effectively blooms from spring until fall if given bright, indirect light in summer and full sun in winter. It grows well in temperatures of 60–75°F and not below 55°F at night. It needs high humidity (60 percent and above) to thrive.

CARE: Keep evenly moist during active growth, with watering reduced somewhat during the plant's winter rest. Feed with foliage plant food according to label directions. Repot only when the plant seems to be too packed in the pot to take up water effectively. Prune back the stem tips before blooming to keep the plant compact. Shower occasionally and move the plant outdoors in summer to stimulate growth. Low humidity may cause browning leaf edges and even leaf drop.

PROPAGATION: Propagate by taking stem cuttings in spring or summer. Take 3–5" stem tips, dip in rooting hormone, and insert into sterile potting soil. Provide bottom heat for the best success in rooting.

PESTS AND DISEASES: Treat mealybugs with horticultural oil.

RELATED SPECIES: *P. coccinea* has bright red flowers in green bracts.

Before the plant begins to bloom, pinch back the stem tips to keep the plant shrubby and compact.

Propagate new plants by dipping the stem tips in rooting hormone and sticking them in sterile potting mix.

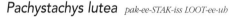

SCREW PINE

Pandanus veitchii *pan-DAN-us VET-chih-eye*

Screw pine is a unique architectural accent for a spot that is hot and in direct sun. It can spend the summer outdoors.

SIZE: 4'h × 4'w
TYPE: Palmlike
FORM: Upright
TEXTURE: Coarse
GROWTH: Medium
LIGHT: High

MOISTURE: Dry
SOIL: Cactus mix
FEATURES: Sword-shape foliage
USES: Architectural accent

SITING: Screw pine has 2–3'-long leaves that are variegated with creamy bands. They are arranged in 3 spiralling ranks, forming a terminal rosette of foliage.

The leaves are slightly serrated and can hurt a passerby, so site the plant away from traffic. A well-grown plant will be tall with an arching crown on an attractive trunk, with many aerial roots alongside it. In its native Polynesia, these aerial rootlets act as prop roots when they come into contact with the soil. It withstands high light, including direct sun during the winter, and tolerates high temperatures, so it is an excellent choice for a hot, sunny site. Provide low humidity (below 30 percent).

CARE: Allow the soil to dry slightly between waterings and reduce watering somewhat during the winter rest time. Feed monthly with a balanced foliage plant food. Repot every 2–3 years. Screw pine sends aerial roots toward the soil as it ages. The roots should not be removed but encouraged to root near the trunk so they can provide support for the increasingly heavy crown. Wash the foliage carefully once a month and remove any damaged or unsightly leaves. Move the plant outdoors for the summer.

PROPAGATION: Propagate by removing basal suckers when they are about 6" long and pot them. Use rooting hormone and bottom heat until they root. Screw pine can also be propagated by seed from a supplier. Soak the seeds for 24 hours before sowing. Screw pine plants are either male or female, and only the female produces fruits and seeds when pollinated by a nearby male. Because the plant is unlikely to bloom indoors, you will probably have to purchase seed from a nursery that specializes in unusual houseplants if you wish to grow plants from seed.

PESTS AND DISEASES: Control scale and spider mites with horticultural oil. Keeping the foliage clean will help eliminate spider mites. You can also keep spider mites at bay by washing the foliage occasionally with a forceful spray of water. Basal stem rot, anthracnose, and leaf spot can occur if screw pine receives excess humidity and moisture.

RELATED SPECIES: *P. utilis* is a green-leaved form with red spines that is similar in all other aspects to *P. veitchii.*

DEVIL'S BACKBONE

Pedilanthus tithymaloides *ped-ill-AN-thus tith-ee-mal-OY-deez*

Devil's backbone resembles a euphorbia with interesting zigzagged succulent stems. This cultivar is 'Variegatus'.

SIZE: 3'h × 1'w
TYPE: Succulent
FORM: Upright
TEXTURE: Medium
GROWTH: Medium
LIGHT: High
MOISTURE: Low

SOIL: Cactus
FEATURES: Zigzag stems
USES: Succulent garden, accent
FLOWERS: ■

SITING: Devil's backbone gets its name from the habit of leaves growing along the stem in zigzag fashion. It will retain the best color with bright, indirect light, although it will tolerate some winter sun. Daytime temperatures are best kept at 70–85°F; nighttime temperatures should be 50–70°F. Provide low humidity (below 30 percent).

CARE: Keep the soil moderately dry, allowing it to dry slightly between soakings. Watch for root rot if the plant is overwatered. If kept very dry, it will have attractive stems and blossoms but no leaves. But if given the right amount of water, it will produce attractive leaves. The plant must have a near-dormant winter rest to initiate its red flowers, which are borne in terminal clusters. Feed only three times in summer with foliage plant food. The plant has a small root system, so repot infrequently. Prune as needed to shape the plant, but beware that the sap is somewhat caustic.

PROPAGATION: Propagate by stem cuttings. Take 3–5" cuttings from the tips or middle of the stems, let sit to dry for 2–3 days, then pot in sterile potting soil. Devil's backbone can also be propagated by seed.

PESTS AND DISEASES: This plant has almost no pests. Powdery mildew and leaf spots are occasional problems.

RELATED SPECIES: The cultivar 'Variegatus' has creamy variegation and pink to red leaf edges. It is the form most commonly available commercially.

Because devil's backbone prefers low humidity, clean leaves by wiping them with a soft cloth rather than washing the foliage.

LEMON-SCENTED GERANIUM
Pelargonium crispum *pel-ar-GOHN-ee-um KRIS-pum*

Lemon-scented geraniums will be graced with soft pink blossoms when grown in a south or west window.

SIZE: 12"h × 12"w
TYPE: Herbaceous
FORM: Mounded
TEXTURE: Medium
GROWTH: Medium
LIGHT: High
MOISTURE: Dry

SOIL: Potting soil
FEATURES: Fuzzy, scented foliage
USES: Focal point, foliage
FLOWERS: ▪

SITING: Scented geraniums are renowned for the delicious scent of the leaves when brushed or crushed. These plants also have attractive enough foliage to stand as a foil for other plants or as a unique potted plant on their own. Scented geraniums are best grown in a south or west window to give them high light to promote blooming. Give them lower light in winter if you want to overwinter them without blooming. Provide cooler temperatures in low light or they will fail.

Provide average warmth (60–75°F) when growing them on a windowsill. Reddening of the leaves indicates that conditions are too cool.

CARE: Overwatering is one of the most common problems with lemon-scented geraniums. Water thoroughly, then allow the soil to dry between waterings. Feed with foliage plant food according to label directions. It is seldom necessary to repot plants. Pinch stem tips often to encourage shrubbiness and remove yellow or brown leaves as they appear.

PROPAGATION: Propagate by stem cuttings. Snip stem tips and middle sections about 3" long, leaving only one leaf. Allow the

cuttings to dry for a day, then insert them in sterile potting mix with a plastic tent. Cuttings should be rooted in 2–3 weeks.

PESTS AND DISEASES: Whiteflies and aphids may be troublesome, particularly when the plant is initially brought indoors in fall. Control both with horticultural oil. You may see blackening of stems during the winter, indicating fungal disease. This is difficult to control, so take cuttings of healthy stems to root and discard the original plant.

RELATED SPECIES: The cultivar 'Peach Cream' has small pink flowers and peach-scented leaves. 'Minor' has tiny leaves. 'Variegatum' has variegated foliage.

1 Propagate by taking stem cuttings any time the plants are in full growth.

2 Snip off all but one or two small leaves on the 3" cuttings.

3 Dip the cuttings in rooting hormone, tapping off the excess powder.

4 Stick cuttings into holes in rooting media, firm in place, and water.

ROSE-SCENTED GERANIUM
Pelargonium graveolens *pel-ar-GOHN-ee-um gray-vee-OH-lenz*

Rose-scented geraniums will fill a room with lovely aroma when given the full sun they love.

SIZE: 3'h × 3'w
TYPE: Herbaceous
FORM: Mounded
TEXTURE: Medium
GROWTH: Medium
LIGHT: High
MOISTURE: Dry

SOIL: Potting soil
FEATURES: Fuzzy, scented foliage
USES: Focal point, foliage
FLOWERS: ▪

SITING: Scented geraniums are renowned for the delicious scent of the leaves when brushed or crushed. These plants also have attractive enough foliage to stand as a foil for other plants or as a unique pot plant on their own. The leaves and blossoms are edible. Scented geraniums are best grown in a south- or west-facing window to give them high light to promote blooming. Give them lower light in winter to overwinter them without blooming. Provide cooler temperatures in low light or they will fail. Provide average warmth (60–75°F) when growing them on a windowsill.

CARE: Water thoroughly, then allow the soil to dry considerably between waterings. Overwatering is one of the most common problems with scented geraniums. Feed with foliage plant food according to label directions. It is seldom necessary to repot plants. Pinch stem tips often to encourage shrubbiness and remove yellow or brown leaves as they develop.

PROPAGATION: Scented geraniums are so easily propagated by stem cuttings that it's possible to give plants to your friends and to use them as bedding plants outdoors in summer. Snip stem tips and middle sections about 3" long, leaving only one leaf. Allow the cuttings to dry for a day, then insert them in sterile potting mix with a plastic tent. Cuttings should be rooted in 2–3 weeks.

PESTS AND DISEASES: Whiteflies and aphids may be troublesome, particularly when the plant is initially brought indoors in fall. Control both with horticultural oil. You may see blackening of stems during the winter, indicating fungal disease. This is difficult to control, so take cuttings of healthy stems to root and discard the original plant. Reddening of the leaves indicates that conditions are too cool.

RELATED SPECIES: The cultivar 'Variegatum' has lightly cream-tinged leaves.

PEPPERMINT-SCENTED GERANIUM

Pelargonium tomentosum *pel-ar-GOHN-ee-um toh-men-TOH-sum*

Peppermint-scented geraniums have fuzzy gray-green hairs that release the bright cleansing scent of peppermint when something brushes against the plant.

SIZE: 2'h × 2'w
TYPE: Herbaceous
FORM: Mounded
TEXTURE: Medium
GROWTH: Medium
LIGHT: High
MOISTURE: Dry

SOIL: Potting soil
FEATURES: Fuzzy, scented foliage
USES: Focal point, foliage
FLOWERS: ■

SITING: Scented geraniums are renowned for the delicious scent of the leaves when brushed or crushed. These plants also have attractive enough foliage to stand as a foil for other plants or as a unique potted plant on their own. The leaves and blossoms are edible. Scented geraniums are best grown in a south- or west-facing window to give them high light to promote blooming. Give them lower light in winter if you want to overwinter them without blooming. Provide cooler temperatures in low light or they will fail. Provide average warmth (60–75°F) when growing them on a windowsill. Reddening of the leaves indicates that conditions are too cool.

CARE: Water thoroughly, then allow the soil to dry considerably between waterings. Overwatering is one of the most common problems with scented geraniums. Feed with foliage plant food according to label directions. It is seldom necessary to repot plants. Pinch stem tips often to encourage shrubbiness, and remove yellow or brown leaves that may appear.

PROPAGATION: Scented geraniums are so easily propagated by stem cuttings that it's possible to give plants to your friends and to use them as bedding plants outdoors in summer. Snip stem tips and middle sections about 3" long, leaving only one leaf. Allow the cuttings to dry for a day, then insert them in sterile potting mix with a plastic tent. Cuttings should be rooted in 2–3 weeks.

PESTS AND DISEASES: Whiteflies and aphids may be troublesome, particularly when the plant is initially brought indoors in fall. Control both with horticultural oil. You may see blackening of stems during the winter, indicating fungal disease. This is difficult to control, so take cuttings of healthy stems to root and discard the original plant.

RELATED SPECIES: The cultivar 'Chocolate Peppermint' has a chocolate-mint scent.

BUTTON FERN

Pellaea rotundifolia *pell-EE-uh roh-tun-dih-FOLE-ee-uh*

Button fern's unique round leaves are borne along glossy brown stems, lending great color to this fine-textured foliage plant.

SIZE: 6"h × 2'w
TYPE: Fern
FORM: Mounded
TEXTURE: Fine
GROWTH: Slow
LIGHT: Medium

MOISTURE: Evenly moist
SOIL: Potting soil
FEATURES: Glossy foliage on black stems
USES: Foliage

SITING: Button fern produces its buttonlike round leaflets best in medium light. Grow in average to cool temperatures (55–75°F) and at least average humidity (30–60 percent). Avoid placing the plant where it receives drying winds or drafts.

CARE: The fronds are somewhat leathery but are not tolerant of drying out. Keep them moist all the time, because drying out even once can cause considerable leaf drop, from which the plant usually doesn't recover. Feed only three times in summer with foliage plant food. Repot annually into a moisture-retentive potting mix; as the pot fills with roots, the plant has a hard time getting adequate moisture. Remove brown fronds, which should be few if the plant is grown well. Shower regularly to keep spider mites at bay.

PROPAGATION: Propagate by dividing the rhizomes or by growing from spores. Spores are borne on the underside edges of the leaflets. When ripe, they turn dark and can be tapped onto a piece of paper. Sprinkle on moist soil mix and cover the container with glass or plastic. Keep moist until small ferns begin to form.

PESTS AND DISEASES: Scale can be a serious pest but can be controlled with horticultural oil.

RELATED SPECIES: Purple-stemmed cliff brake (*P. atropurpurea*) has purple stems. Sickle fern (*P. falcata*) has upright fronds.

Button ferns require average to high humidity, easily obtained when the plant is grown in a terrarium.

WATERMELON PELLIONIA

Pellionia repens pell-ee-OHN-ee-uh REP-enz

Watermelon pellionia will keep its olive-colored foliage in pristine condition with medium light and temperatures.

SIZE: 4"h × 3'w
TYPE: Herbaceous
FORM: Trailing
TEXTURE: Medium
GROWTH: Medium
LIGHT: Medium
MOISTURE: Evenly moist

SOIL: Potting soil
FEATURES: Scalloped, variegated leaves
USES: Hanging basket, terrarium

SITING: The olive and chartreuse leaves look like watermelon rind. The plant is not fussy but must not chill. It thrives in medium light and temperatures of 60–85°F. Provide high humidity; a pot-in-pot system works well in a hanging basket.

Add humidity to watermelon pellionia by using a pot-in-pot system where one pot is placed in another filled with moist sphagnum moss.

A terrarium keeps the humidity high and the plants out of drafts, to which they are unusually sensitive.

CARE: Keep the soil evenly moist but not soggy. For the plant to take in enough moisture, it should be repotted every 2 years. Feed only three times in summer with a general foliage plant food. Remove faded leaves and give the plant regular showers. Pinch the plant occasionally to keep it shrubby.

PROPAGATION: Stem-tip cuttings root easily in 2–3 weeks. Snip off the tips, remove all but one or two leaves, dip in rooting hormone, and insert in sterile potting soil. Tent with plastic to keep the humidity high. Watermelon pellionia can also be propagated by division.

PESTS AND DISEASES: Watch for mealybugs and spider mites, especially when the plant is grown in lower humidity. Control them with horticultural oil.

RELATED SPECIES: Satin pellionia *(P. pulchra)* has dark veins and purple undersides.

WATERMELON PEPEROMIA

Peperomia argyreia (sandersii) pep-per-OH-mee-uh ar-GEYE-ree-uh (san-DER-zee-eye)

Watermelon peperomia, also known as watermelon begonia, is popular for its succulent silver and green foliage.

SIZE: 1'h × 1'w
TYPE: Herbaceous
FORM: Mounded
TEXTURE: Medium
GROWTH: Potting soil
LIGHT: Medium to low

MOISTURE: Dry
SOIL: Potting soil
FEATURES: Succulent foliage
USES: Foliage, accent
FLOWERS: ■

SITING: Peperomias are used for their striking variegated or highly colored foliage, even in low light. They come in enough leaf shapes and sizes that an entire textural garden could be put together with only peperomias. Provide average temperatures (60–75°F) and avoid cold drafts and high-traffic areas; the succulent leaves are easily knocked off or scarred.

CARE: Peperomias are fairly tolerant of drought but perform better if watered as soon as the soil surface begins to dry.

Peperomias are easily propagated by stem tip cuttings. Take a 3-5" cutting and remove all but one or two leaves.

Overwatering can cause rotting, especially if the plants are grown in a cool setting. Feed three times in summer only, and repot as needed when the roots fill the pot. Peperomias tolerate pruning well, so it is easy to keep plants looking attractive and lush. Occasional showers will keep the leaves pristine.

PROPAGATION: Propagate by dividing the root ball or by removing offsets that form at the perimeter of the plant. Most peperomias can also be propagated fairly easily from stem tip cuttings.

PESTS AND DISEASES: Peperomias are so pest free that they seem almost artificial. They may have occasional mealybugs, which can be controlled with a cotton swab dipped in horticultural oil.

RELATED SPECIES: Numerous species of peperomia are available for home culture.

EMERALD RIPPLE PEPEROMIA

Peperomia caperata pep-per-OH-mee-uh cab-per-AH-tuh

Emerald ripple peperomia has dark green puckered foliage and unique flower spikes that stand above the soft mound of leaves.

SIZE: 8–12"h ×
8–12"w
TYPE: Herbaceous
FORM: Mounded
TEXTURE: Medium
GROWTH: Average
LIGHT: Medium
to low

MOISTURE: Dry
SOIL: Potting soil
FEATURES:
Succulent foliage
USES: Foliage,
accent
FLOWERS: ■

SITING: Peperomias are used for their striking variegated or highly colored foliage, even in low light. They come in enough leaf shapes and sizes that an entire textural garden could be put together with only peperomias. Provide average temperatures (60–75°F) and be sure to avoid cold drafts and high-traffic areas; the succulent leaves are easily knocked off or scarred.

CARE: Peperomias are fairly tolerant of drought but perform better if watered as soon as the soil surface begins to dry. Overwatering can cause rotting, especially if the plants are grown in a cool setting. Feed three times in summer only, and repot as needed when the roots fill the pot. Peperomias tolerate pruning well, so it is easy to keep plants looking attractive and lush. Occasional showers will keep the leaves pristine.

PROPAGATION: Propagate by dividing the root ball or by removing offsets that form at the perimeter of the plants. Emerald Ripple pepperomia can be propagated from stem-tip or leaf-petiole cuttings.

PESTS AND DISEASES: Peperomias are so pest free that they seem almost artificial. They may have occasional mealybugs, which can be controlled with a cotton swab dipped in horticultural oil.

RELATED SPECIES: The cultivar 'Little Fantasy' has small, heart-shaped leaves and rattail flowers.

The succulent leaves of emerald ripple peperomia can be easily damaged, so simply pinch them out at the base to keep the plant attractive.

SILVERLEAF PEPEROMIA

Peperomia griseoargentea pep-per-OH-mee-uh grih-zee-oh-are-JEN-tee-uh

SIZE: 1–2'h × 1–2'w
TYPE: Herbaceous
FORM: Mounded
TEXTURE: Medium
GROWTH: Average
LIGHT: Medium
to low

MOISTURE: Dry
SOIL: Potting soil
FEATURES:
Succulent foliage
USES: Foliage,
accent
FLOWERS: ■

Silverleaf peperomia is another striking foliage plant with silver-green round leaves on long petioles.

SITING: Peperomias are used for their striking variegated or highly colored foliage, even in low light. They come in enough leaf shapes and sizes that an entire textural garden could be put together with only peperomias. Provide average temperatures (60–75°F) and be sure to avoid cold drafts and high-traffic areas; the succulent leaves are easily knocked off or scarred.

CARE: Peperomias are fairly tolerant of drought but perform better if watered as soon as the soil surface begins to dry. Overwatering can cause rotting, especially if the plants are grown in cool conditions. Feed three times in summer only, and repot as needed when the roots fill the pot. Peperomias tolerate pruning well, so it is easy to keep the plants looking attractive and lush. Occasional showers will keep the leaves pristine.

PROPAGATION: Propagate by dividing the root ball or by removing offsets that form at the perimeter of the plants. Silverleaf peperomia can also be propagated from stem-tip or leaf-petiole cuttings.

PESTS AND DISEASES: Peperomias are so pest free that they seem almost artificial. They may have occasional mealybugs, which can be controlled with a cotton swab dipped in horticultural oil.

RELATED SPECIES: There are thousands of peperomia species, with many widely available for home culture.

BABY RUBBER PLANT

Peperomia obtusifolia *pep-per-OH-mee-uh ob-too-sih-FOHL-ee-uh*

Baby rubber plant has cupped leaves in dark glossy green, or variegated in shades of cream and olive.

SIZE: 6–8"h × 6–8"w
TYPE: Herbaceous
FORM: Mounded
TEXTURE: Medium
GROWTH: Average
LIGHT: Medium to low

MOISTURE: Dry
SOIL: Potting soil
FEATURES: Succulent foliage
USES: Foliage, accent
FLOWERS: ■

SITING: Peperomias are used for their striking variegated or highly colored foliage, even in low light. There are a myriad of leaf shapes and sizes, enough so that an entire textural garden could be put together with only peperomias.

Provide average temperatures (60–75°F) and be sure to avoid cold drafts and high-traffic areas; the succulent leaves are easily knocked off or scarred.

CARE: Peperomias are fairly tolerant of drought but perform better if watered as soon as the soil surface begins to dry. Overwatering can cause rotting, especially if the plants are grown in cool conditions. Feed three times in summer only, and repot as needed when the roots fill the pot. Peperomias tolerate pruning well, so it is easy to keep plants looking attractive and lush. Occasional showers will keep the leaves pristine.

PROPAGATION: Propagate by dividing the root ball or by removing offsets that form at the perimeter of the plants. Most peperomias can also be propagated fairly easily from stem tip cuttings.

PESTS AND DISEASES: Peperomias are so pest free that they seem almost artificial. They may have occasional mealybugs, which can be controlled with a cotton swab dipped in horticultural oil.

RELATED SPECIES: 'Tricolor' has cream, green, and pink variegation on the leaves; 'Golden Gate' has olive foliage with extensive cream variegation. There are thousands of peperomia species, with many widely available for home culture.

Baby rubber plant leaves are smooth and succulent and can be cleaned easily with a soft cloth.

PRINCESS ASTRID PEPEROMIA

Peperomia orba *pep-per-OH-mee-uh OR-bu*

Princess Astrid peperomia has tiny glossy spoon-shaped leaves that form small soft mounds.

SIZE: 6–12"h × 6–12"w
TYPE: Herbaceous
FORM: Mounded
TEXTURE: Medium
GROWTH: Average
LIGHT: Medium to low

MOISTURE: Dry
SOIL: Potting soil
FEATURES: Succulent foliage
USES: Foliage, accent
FLOWERS: ■

SITING: Peperomias are used for their striking variegated or highly colored foliage, even in low light. There are a myriad of leaf shapes and sizes, enough so that an entire textural garden could be put together with only peperomias. Provide average temperatures (60–75°F) and be sure to avoid cold drafts and high-traffic areas; the succulent leaves are easily knocked off or scarred.

CARE: Peperomias are fairly tolerant of drought but perform better if watered as soon as the surface of the soil begins to dry. Overwatering can cause rotting, especially if the plants are grown in cool conditions. Feed three times in summer only, and repot as needed when the roots fill the pot. Peperomias tolerate pruning, so it is easy to keep the plants looking attractive and lush. Occasional showers will keep the leaves pristine.

PROPAGATION: Propagate by dividing the root ball or by removing offsets that form at the perimeter of the plants. Most peperomias can also be propagated fairly easily from stem tip cuttings.

PESTS AND DISEASES: Peperomias are so pest free that they seem almost artificial. They may have occasional mealybugs, which can be controlled with a cotton swab dipped in horticultural oil.

RELATED SPECIES: 'Pixie' is a dwarf form of the species. There are thousands of peperomia species, with many widely available for home culture.

Princess Astrid's diminutive size makes it the perfect companion for other small plants in a terrarium.

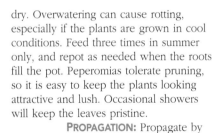

MOTH ORCHID
Phalaenopsis hybrids *fal-in-OP-sis*

Moth orchids are perhaps the easiest of the orchids to grow, highly rewarding for the home gardener.

SIZE: 2'h × 2'w
TYPE: Orchid
FORM: Upright
TEXTURE: Medium
GROWTH: Slow
LIGHT: High

MOISTURE: Moist
SOIL: Epiphyte mix
FEATURES: Long blooming
USES: Accent
FLOWERS: □ ▨ ▨ ■ ■

SITING: Moth orchid produces successive, rounded blossoms for up to 18 months if given the right conditions. It thrives in bright, filtered to medium light with daytime temperatures of 75–85°F. Nighttime temperatures should drop to about 60°F for 3 weeks in autumn to initiate flower bud development. Provide 50–80 percent humidity by using a pebble tray or humidifier. Low humidity can cause the flower buds to drop prematurely. Air movement is essential to prevent fungal leaf diseases.

CARE: Moth orchid is an epiphyte, so it needs evenly moist potting mix. It should not get too moist or sit in water. Rotting from overwatering can kill the plant. Avoid splashing the crown of the plant when watering. Feed with foliage plant food once a month all year. Repot young moth orchids every year with a fine fir bark, and mature plants every 2–3 years after

Moth orchids may need to have their flower spikes supported by bamboo plant stakes or specialized stakes.

blooming. Use a coarse orchid potting mix. Remove the plant from the pot, trim any dead roots, and repot, making sure the roots are surrounded with planting mix. Set the plants in a shady spot for 2–3 days while they recover. Occasionally wipe off the leaves and remove flower spikes just above a node (swollen area where leaves attach to the stem) when blossoming is finished. This will often cause the orchid to produce another flower spike above the node and extend the blooming period.

PROPAGATION: Plantlets, called keikis, sometimes form at the nodes on the flower spike after the plant blossoms. Leave the keikis on the stem until they produce at least two leaves and several roots. Then they can be removed and potted. Cut the keikis from the parent plant, leaving a 2" part of each end of the flower spike. These can be used to anchor the plant in its new pot.

PESTS AND DISEASES: Moth orchid may occasionally have mealybugs, which can be removed with a cotton swab dipped in alcohol.

RELATED SPECIES: Thousands of species and cultivars of moth orchids are available.

TREE PHILODENDRON
Philodendron bipinnatifidum (selloum) *fill-oh-DEN-drun bye-pin-ah-TIF-ih-dum (sub-LOH-uhm)*

Tree philodendron, also known as cut-leaf philodendron is a striking architectural feature with glossy, lobed leaves.

SIZE: 4'h × 4'w
TYPE: Vine
FORM: Vine, upright
TEXTURE: Coarse
GROWTH: Fast
LIGHT: Medium to low

MOISTURE: Dry
SOIL: Average
FEATURES: Leaves
USES: Architectural accent

SITING: Philodendrons are coveted in the home because they take such little care yet have shiny, attractive leaves. If given medium to low light, they will thrive. In very high light it will bleach out. Provide average home temperatures (60–75°F) and average to low humidity (65 percent or lower).

CARE: Allow the soil to dry somewhat between waterings, especially in low light. Cold, wet soil can cause rotting. Feed only

Give these plants plenty of room to spread to their maximum size and beauty and clean the leaves periodically to keep them looking their best.

three times in summer with standard foliage plant food, and repot when the thick roots fill the container or the plant begins to creep out of the pot. To keep the plant smaller, reduce feeding. In nature all types of philodendron are vining and tend to climb. Lacy tree philodendron can grow fairly upright in a container. Wash the leaves regularly to keep spider mites at bay. Remove the occasional faded leaf to keep the plant tidy.

PROPAGATION: Propagate by taking stem cuttings with at least two nodes and inserting them in potting soil. Keep them moist and cover with plastic to keep the humidity high until they root. This philodendron can also be started from seed obtained from a supplier.

PESTS AND DISEASES: Control mealybugs and mites with horticultural oil.

RELATED SPECIES: The cultivar 'Hope' has a dwarf, more compact habit than the species.

RED-LEAF PHILODENDRON
Philodendron erubescens *fill-oh-DEN-drun air-oo-BES-sens*

Red-leaf philodendron will keep its beautiful coppery leaves with medium light and average temperatures.

SIZE: 5'h × 5'w
TYPE: Vine
FORM: Upright
TEXTURE: Coarse
GROWTH: Fast
LIGHT: Medium

MOISTURE: Dry
SOIL: Average
FEATURES: Coppery leaves
USES: Accent, foliage

SITING: Philodendrons are coveted in the home because they take such little care yet have shiny, attractive leaves. The leaves of this philodendron have coppery undersides and edges, making it a striking foliage accent. As long as philodendrons are provided medium light, they will thrive

and maintain their bright leaves. If grown in very high light, the leaves will bleach out; in lower light they will be greener. Provide average home temperatures (60–75°F) and average to low humidity (65 percent or lower).
CARE: Allow the soil to dry somewhat between waterings, especially when the

Philodendrons climb in their natural settings, so they can be trained onto a moss or bark pole by tying the vining stems.

plant is grown in low light. Cold, wet soil can cause rotting. Feed only three times in summer with standard foliage plant food, and repot when the thick roots fill the pot or the plant begins to creep out of the pot. To keep the plant smaller, reduce the feeding. In the home this philodendron can grow fairly upright when trained to a moss pole in a container. Remove the occasional faded leaf.
PROPAGATION: Propagate by taking stem cuttings with at least two nodes and inserting them in potting soil. Keep them moist and cover with plastic to keep the humidity high until they root. These philodendrons can also be started from seed obtained from a supplier.
PESTS AND DISEASES: Control mealybugs and mites with horticultural oil. Wash the leaves regularly to keep spider mites at bay.
RELATED SPECIES: Although the species tends to be vining, several cultivars are shrubby. 'Black Cardinal' has red leaves that mature to almost black. 'Red Empress' has lobed burgundy leaves and is shrubby. 'Burgundy' has glossy reddish leaves, red veins, and red stems.

VELVET-LEAF PHILODENDRON
Philodendron scandens f. *micans* *fill-oh-DEN-drun SKAN-dins MY-kanz*

Velvet-leaf philodendron has velvety heart-shaped leaves that drape gracefully out of a container.

SIZE: 8"h × 6'w
TYPE: Vine
FORM: Trailing
TEXTURE: Medium
GROWTH: Slow
LIGHT: Medium

MOISTURE: Moist
SOIL: Average
FEATURES: Velvety, heart-shaped leaves
USES: Hanging basket, foliage

SITING: Philodendrons are coveted in the home because they take such little care yet have attractive foliage. Velvet-leaf philodendron has soft, velvety dark green to coppery leaves that are arranged along trailing stems. If provided medium light, it will thrive and maintain dense, attractive

foliage. In lower light the plant will survive but may lose some of the velvety appearance. Provide average home temperatures (60–75°F) and average to low humidity (65 percent or lower).

To propagate new plants of velvet-leaf philodendron, pin a stem to damp soil at a leaf node. When rooted, sever from the mother plant and pot up.

CARE: Keep the soil evenly moist but not soggy. Cold, wet soil can cause rotting, and cold drafts can cause leaf drop. Feed only three times in summer with a standard foliage plant food, and repot when the thick roots fill the pot or the plant begins to creep out of the pot. Velvet-leaf philodendron is easily trained to a moss pole to give it an upright form. If the plant begins to get leggy, prune back the stems at different lengths to rejuvenate it.
PROPAGATION: Propagate by taking stem cuttings and inserting them in potting soil or water. Keep them moist and cover with plastic to keep the humidity high until they root. This plant can also be propagated by layering the stems or by starting from seed obtained from a supplier.
PESTS AND DISEASES: Control mealybugs and mites with horticultural oil. Shower the plant regularly to keep spider mites at bay.

HEART-LEAF PHILODENDRON

Philodendron scandens (oxycardium cordatum)

*fill-oh-DEN-drun SKAN-dins
(ahx-ee-KAR-dee-uhm kor-DAH-tum)*

Heart-leaf philodendron, also known as sweetheart plant, looks great in a hanging basket, sitting on a windowsill, or in a dish garden with other plants.

SIZE: 8"h × 6'w
TYPE: Vine
FORM: Trailing
TEXTURE: Medium
GROWTH: Fast
LIGHT: Low to medium

MOISTURE: Dry
SOIL: Potting soil
FEATURES: Heart-shape leaves
USES: Hanging basket, ground cover, dish garden

SITING: Philodendrons are coveted in the home because they take such little care yet have attractive foliage. Heart-leaf philodendron has glossy dark green to coppery leaves that are arranged along trailing stems. The plant thrives if provided medium to low light, making it a superb choice for spots in the home where other plants won't grow well. Provide average home temperatures (60–75°F) and average to low humidity (65 percent or lower).

CARE: Allow the soil to dry slightly between waterings. In low light, reduce

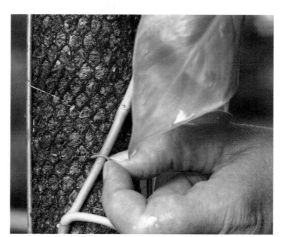

Heart-leaf philodendron has the appeal of growing in very low light. It can be grown on a moss pole for a more upright accent.

watering even more. Cold, wet soil can cause rotting, and cold drafts can cause leaf drop. Feed only three times in summer with a standard foliage plant food, and repot when the thick roots fill the pot or the plant begins to creep out of the pot. Heartleaf philodendron is easily trained to a moss pole to give it an upright form.

If the plant begins to get leggy, prune back the stems at different lengths to rejuvenate it. Remove the occasional faded leaf to keep the plant tidy.

PROPAGATION: Propagate by taking stem cuttings and inserting them in potting soil or water. Keep them moist and cover with plastic to keep the humidity high until they root. The plant can also be propagated by layering the stems or by starting from seed obtained from a supplier.

PESTS AND DISEASES: Control mealybugs and mites with horticultural oil. Shower the plant regularly to keep spider mites at bay.

PYGMY DATE PALM

Phoenix roebelenii FEE-nix roh-buh-LEEN-ee-eye

Pygmy date palms are ideal houseplants because of their tolerance of varying conditions and even some neglect.

SIZE: 6'h × 6'w
TYPE: Palm
FORM: Vase-shaped
TEXTURE: Medium
GROWTH: Slow
LIGHT: High

MOISTURE: Dry
SOIL: Potting soil
FEATURES: Airy fronds
USES: Architectural accent

SITING: Pygmy date palm is an ideal houseplant because it will tolerate some abuse. It performs best in bright, indirect light but tolerates some sun as well as lower light. It does best in a somewhat cool (60–65°F) spot with good air movement. It will tolerate low humidity, but spider mites can be a problem in these conditions. When placing this plant, give it plenty of room so its arching fronds can be

Place pygmy date palms where you can appreciate the arching regal fronds that make a superb architectural statement.

appreciated. Be aware that the lower fronds contain spines that can prick, so place the plant out of traffic areas.

CARE: Pygmy date palm is fairly tolerant of a wide range of moisture, but chronic overwatering will cause leaf tips to blacken. Chronic underwatering will make the fronds droop and become lighter in color. Let the top 1–2" of soil dry out between waterings. Feed monthly during the summer with foliage plant food and not at all in winter. Repot only when the roots fill the pot and the plant is hard to water. The root system is minimal, so repotting will not be frequent. As the lower fronds fade, remove them to reveal the striking trunk.

PROPAGATION: Propagate by seed, usually obtained from a supplier. With plants that have multiple crowns, divide the crown and pot the two parts.

PESTS AND DISEASES: Spider mites occur in low humidity. Treat with monthly showers and horticultural oil.

RELATED SPECIES: Canary Island date palm (*P. canariensis*) is a larger, coarser palm with a spiky appearance and attractive, diamond-shaped markings on its trunk.

ALUMINUM PLANT

Pilea cadierei *pye-LEE-uh kad-ee-AIR-eye*

Aluminum plants have beautifully variegated leaves in shades of silver and deep green. These plants are also appealing because they are so easy to grow.

SIZE: 12"h × 12"w
TYPE: Herbaceous
FORM: Mounded
TEXTURE: Medium
GROWTH: Medium
LIGHT: Medium

MOISTURE: Dry
SOIL: Potting soil
FEATURES: Colorful textured leaves
USES: Foliage, dish garden, terrarium

SITING: Aluminum plant is generally easy to grow. Provide medium light; higher light will burn the leaves. The plant will thrive in a temperature range of 60–70°F; it will tolerate higher temperatures if the humidity is high (60 percent and above). It will not do well when exposed to low humidity.

CARE: Let the soil dry out slightly between waterings, but don't let the soil get so dry that the plant begins to droop. With a small root system, aluminum plant seldom needs to be repotted. Feed with foliage plant food according to label directions during the active growing season. Don't feed at all in winter. Pinch regularly to keep the plant shrubby. When the plant begins to get leggy, start a new plant to replace the old one. Frequent showering will help keep pests at bay. The plant may exhibit brown leaves from low humidity and yellow leaves from too much water.

PROPAGATION: Propagate by stem cuttings or by division.

PESTS AND DISEASES: Spider mites can be a problem in low humidity and will cause the leaf edges to brown. Mealybugs and scale may also appear.

RELATED SPECIES: *P. c. minima* 'Patti's Gold' has yellow flecking that turns cream with maturity. Chinese money plant (*P. peperomioides*) has waxy round leaves on upright stems.

When an aluminum plant starts to stretch and become unappealing, simply cut back the leggy stems to rejuvenate the plant, or take cuttings to start a new plant.

MOON VALLEY FRIENDSHIP PLANT

Pilea involucrata *pye-LEE-uh in-vol-yew-KRAYT-uh*

Moon Valley friendship plant gets its interesting name from the craters in the deeply crinkled green and black leaves.

SIZE: 12"h × 12"w
TYPE: Herbaceous
FORM: Mounded
TEXTURE: Medium
GROWTH: Medium
LIGHT: Medium

MOISTURE: Dry
SOIL: Potting soil
FEATURES: Colorful textured leaves
USES: Foliage, dish garden, terrarium

SITING: Moon Valley friendship plant is generally easy to grow. Its highly textured leaves are reminiscent of the craters and valleys of a moonscape. Provide medium light; higher light will burn the leaves. The plant will thrive in a temperature range of 60–70°F; it will tolerate higher temperatures as long as the humidity is high (60 percent and above). It will not thrive when exposed to drying winds and low humidity.

Friendship plant is easy to share with friends since it is so easily propagated from stem-tip cuttings.

CARE: Let the soil dry out slightly between waterings, but don't let the soil get so dry that the plant begins to droop. With a small root system, friendship plants seldom need to be repotted. Feed with foliage plant food according to label directions during the active growing season. Don't feed at all in winter. Pinch regularly to keep the plant shrubby. When it begins to get leggy, start a new plant to replace the old one. The plant may exhibit brown leaves from low humidity and yellow leaves from too much water.

PROPAGATION: Propagate by stem cuttings or by dividing plants.

PESTS AND DISEASES: Spider mites can be a problem in low humidity and will cause the leaf edges to brown. Mealybugs and scale may also appear. Frequent showering will help keep pests at bay.

RELATED SPECIES: *Pilea repens* grows 4–6" tall with almost black leaves and small white flowers.

ARTILLERY PLANT

Pilea microphylla *pye-LEE-uh mye-kroh-FILL-uh*

Artillery plants are ferny plants that pack a punch by shooting ripe seeds, sometimes across the room.

SIZE: 12"h × 12"w
TYPE: Herbaceous
FORM: Mounded
TEXTURE: Medium
GROWTH: Medium
LIGHT: Medium

MOISTURE: Dry
SOIL: Potting soil
FEATURES: Colorful, textured leaves
USES: Foliage, dish garden, terrarium

SITING: Artillery plant is unique in that it shoots its seeds when they ripen, sometimes several feet. This plant often becomes a nuisance in a greenhouse, and in the home you may have small plants appear in other plant pots. Provide medium light; higher light will burn the leaves. The plant will thrive in a temperature range of 60–70°F; it will tolerate higher temperatures as long as the humidity is high (60 percent and above). It doesn't thrive when exposed to drying winds and low humidity.

CARE: Let the soil dry out slightly between waterings, but don't let it get so dry that the plant begins to droop. With a small root system, artillery plant seldom needs to be repotted. Feed with foliage plant food according to label directions during the active growing season. Don't feed at all in winter. Pinch regularly to keep the plant shrubby. When it begins to get leggy, start a new plant to replace the old one. The plant may exhibit brown leaves from low humidity and yellow leaves from too much water.

1 Keep artillery plants shrubby and attractive by pinching out the stem tips periodically.

PROPAGATION: Propagate by stem cuttings or by dividing plants. Artillery plant produces many seeds, so if you can catch them, you can easily start new plants. Otherwise you will find seedlings starting themselves in the pot.
PESTS AND DISEASES: Spider mites can be a problem in low humidity and will cause the leaf edges to brown. Mealybugs and scale may also appear. Frequent showering will help keep pests at bay.
RELATED SPECIES: The cultivar 'Variegata' has white new leaves. *Pilea depressa* is a small-leaved creeping form.

2 Start new plants by dipping the pinched tips in rooting hormone and sticking into sterile potting soil.

JAPANESE PITTOSPORUM

Pittosporum tobira *pit-oh-SPOR-um toh-BYE-ruh*

Japanese pittosporums are beautiful backdrops for other blooming plants. The plants will occasionally produce orange-scented flowers.

SIZE: 3'h × 3'w
TYPE: Woody shrub
FORM: Rounded
TEXTURE: Medium
GROWTH: Slow
LIGHT: High

MOISTURE: Dry
SOIL: Potting soil
FEATURES: Glossy foliage
USES: Foliage accent, fragrance

SITING: Japanese pittosporum is fairly carefree in the home environment as long as it is given bright light. In the right light conditions, its glossy foliage is a foil for other blooming plants. In bright light it will occasionally bloom with orange-blossom-scented flowers, a characteristic that leads to an alternate common name, Japanese mock orange. Provide it with temperatures of 50–70°F and average humidity (30–65 percent).
CARE: Allow the plant to dry slightly between waterings. Feed once a month with foliage plant food during the active growing season; cease feeding during the winter when it is semidormant. Repot only when the plant outgrows its container. Using a small pot will help keep the plant in bounds. (It can grow to 10'.) Prune Japanese pittosporum regularly to shape it. This plant is often used for bonsai.

PROPAGATION: Propagate by taking softwood cuttings in spring and inserting them in sterile potting mix. Cover cuttings with a plastic tent to keep in humidity. Provide bottom heat to speed rooting.
PESTS AND DISEASES: Spider mites may be a problem in low humidity, and scale can be a frequent visitor on Japanese pittosporum. Treat either with horticultural oil. A monthly shower keeps pests at bay.
RELATED SPECIES: The cultivar 'Variegata' has white leaf margins. It is more commonly available than the green-leaved species. Pittosporums are used for outdoor plants in southern climates, so you may find the greatest selection from a southern nursery source. 'Compactum' is a dwarf variety and may be preferable for the home environment because is will not grow as quickly as other varieties.

STAGHORN FERN

Platycerium bifurcatum plat-ee-SEER-ee-um bye-fur-KAY-tum

Staghorn ferns offer a unique look in the interior landscape. Give plants bright light and good air circulation.

SIZE: 3'h × 3'w
TYPE: Fern
FORM: Abstract
TEXTURE: Coarse
GROWTH: Slow

LIGHT: High
MOISTURE: Dry
SOIL: Moss
FEATURES: Fronds
USES: Focal point

SITING: Whether grown on a slab or in a hanging basket, staghorn fern should be located high up where the drooping fronds will not be in the way of passersby. Although the sterile frond that is attached to the slab lies flat, the fertile fronds, from which the plant gets its name, hang down. Provide bright but indirect light and average home temperatures (60–80°F). The plant will tolerate average (30–60 percent) humidity but must have good air circulation. A humidifier is a good way to provide both.

CARE: Staghorn fern is an epiphyte, so it can take moisture from the air. However, in the home this is seldom possible, so when growing this plant on a slab in high light, soak the slab in the sink for about 15 minutes every couple of days. During

A favorite way to display staghorn ferns is to fix them to a wooden slab which is then hung on the wall.

winter rest, give the plant only enough water to keep it from drying out completely. To grow in a hanging basket, pot the fern in equal parts peat moss and sphagnum moss. Or mount young plants on a slab, to which they will eventually root. Place the same potting mix for a hanging basket between the flat frond and the slab, cover the fern and potting mix with chicken wire, and staple it to the slab. Replace the potting mix once a year. Feed newly potted staghorn ferns weekly with half-strength foliage plant food. Once the fern is established, feed it once a month with full-strength food. Dust the fronds occasionally.

PROPAGATION: Staghorn fern produces plantlets on its roots. Propagate by separating these plantlets and potting them. A healthy mature fern can be divided. Make sure to get adequate roots with each part of the division; seldom should you divide the fern into more than two pieces.

PESTS AND DISEASES: Scale insects are common. Treat by dabbing them with horticultural oil.

RELATED SPECIES: *P. grande* has wedge-shaped fertile fronds 4–6' long.

CUBAN OREGANO

Plectranthus amboinicus plek-TRAN-thus am-boh-IN-ih-kus

Cuban oregano, with gray-green leaves, is a carefree plant that thrives outdoors in summer as well as indoors. It is also known as Mexican mint.

SIZE: 12–18"h × 3'w
TYPE: Herbaceous
FORM: Trailing
TEXTURE: Medium
GROWTH: Fast
LIGHT: Medium
MOISTURE: Moist

SOIL: Potting soil
FEATURES: Fuzzy foliage
USES: Hanging basket, culinary
FLOWERS: ☐

SITING: This easy-to-grow plant is favored by gardeners because it looks good even when neglected. It has velvety gray-green leaves edged in white. Given the right conditions, it will produce starry white flowers on stalks held above the foliage. The leaves are used in Cuban and Indonesian cooking to flavor meats. It thrives in medium light and average temperatures (60–75°F) but will tolerate cooler temperatures. Provide average humidity (30–60 percent). This plant can easily be grown outdoors, and many gardeners use cuttings from their indoor plant to provide outdoor vining plants for hanging baskets.

CARE: Keep the soil evenly moist but not soggy. Feed only three times in summer. Repot occasionally. Once the plants start looking drab and leggy, take cuttings to start new plants. Pinch stem tips to keep the plant shrubby and full, but be aware that the sap may turn your fingers orange.

PROPAGATION: Propagate from stem cuttings rooted in water or soil. The crown can also be divided easily. Cut the plant back when you divide it in order to rejuvenate it as well as to make it easier to separate shorter vines.

PESTS AND DISEASES: Treat mealybugs and whiteflies with horticultural oil or insecticidal soap.

RELATED SPECIES: The cultivar 'Variegatus' has thin white margins. 'Ochre Flame' has varying shades of green and cream.

Cuban oregano is at its best in a hanging basket where the tips should be periodically pinched to keep it shrubby and attractive.

SWEDISH IVY
Plectranthus australis *plek-TRAN-thus aus-TRALL-iss*

Swedish ivy, with glossy foliage and scalloped edges, is an easy-to-grow plant that will tolerate most temperatures and light levels. This is a variegated form.

SIZE: 12–18"h × 3'w
TYPE: Herbaceous
FORM: Trailing
TEXTURE: Medium
GROWTH: Fast
LIGHT: Medium
MOISTURE: Moist
SOIL: Potting soil
FEATURES: Foliage
USES: Hanging basket
FLOWERS: □

SITING: This easy-to-grow plant is favored by gardeners because it looks good even when neglected. The species has medium green scalloped leaves. Given the right conditions, it will produce starry white flowers on stalks held above the foliage. It thrives in medium light and average temperatures (60–75°F) but will also tolerate cooler temperatures. Provide average humidity (30–60 percent). This plant can easily be grown outdoors, and many gardeners use cuttings from their indoor plant to provide outdoor vining plants for hanging baskets.

CARE: Keep the soil evenly moist but not soggy. Feed only three times in summer. Repot occasionally. Once the plant starts looking drab and leggy, take cuttings to start new plants. Pinch off stem tips to keep the plant shrubby and full, but be aware that the sap may turn your fingers orange.

PROPAGATION: Propagate from stem cuttings rooted in water or soil. The crown can also be divided easily. Cut the plant back when you divide it in order to rejuvenate it as well as to make it easier to separate shorter vines.

PESTS AND DISEASES: Treat mealybugs and whiteflies with horticultural oil or insecticidal soap.

RELATED SPECIES: The cultivar 'Variegata' has white marked leaves. Other selections are variegated with green centers and gold leaf margins. *P. prostratus* has tiny green leaves and forms a solid mat.

Regularly pinching out the tips of Swedish ivy keeps the plant shrubby and attractive.

SPURFLOWER
Plectranthus forsteri (coleoides) 'Marginatus' *plek-TRAN-thus FOR-stir-eye (koh-lee-OY-deez)*

Spurflower has deep green foliage edged in white and makes a beautiful hanging basket. In medium light it will occasionally bloom with white, starry blossoms.

SIZE: 18"h × 10"w
TYPE: Herbaceous
FORM: Trailing
TEXTURE: Medium
GROWTH: Fast
LIGHT: Medium
MOISTURE: Moist
SOIL: Potting soil
FEATURES: Foliage
USES: Hanging basket
FLOWERS: □

SITING: This easy-to-grow plant is favored by gardeners because it looks good even when neglected. Its large, succulent leaves are fuzzy and variegated white and green with occasional pink streaks. Spurflower thrives in medium light and average temperatures (60–75°F) but tolerates cooler temperatures. Provide average humidity (30–60 percent). This plant can easily be grown outdoors, and many gardeners use cuttings from their indoor plant to provide outdoor vining plants for hanging baskets.

CARE: Keep the soil evenly moist but not soggy. This *Plectranthus* is more drought tolerant than the other species. Feed only three times in summer. Repot more often than its relatives because everything about it is larger, including the roots. Once a year cut the plant back and repot into clean soil. If the plant starts looking drab and leggy, take cuttings to start new plants. Pinch off stem tips to keep the plant shrubby and full, but be aware that the sap may turn your fingers orange.

PROPAGATION: Propagate from stem cuttings rooted in water or soil. The crown can also be divided easily. Cut the plant back when you divide it in order to rejuvenate it as well as to make it easier to separate shorter vines.

PESTS AND DISEASES: Treat mealybugs and whiteflies with horticultural oil or insecticidal soap.

RELATED SPECIES: The cultivar 'Green on Green' has gray-green leaves edged with chartreuse. Silver spurflower, *P. argentatus,* grows upright with strong stems and large gray leaves.

PURPLE-LEAVED SWEDISH IVY
Plectranthus purpuratus plek-TRAN-thus pur-pur-AY-tus

Purple-leaved Swedish ivy has velvety dark purple-green leaves with dark purple undersides and purple stems.

SIZE: 12–18"h × 3'w
TYPE: Herbaceous
FORM: Trailing
TEXTURE: Medium
GROWTH: Fast
LIGHT: Medium
MOISTURE: Moist

SOIL: Potting soil
FEATURES: Purple foliage
USES: Hanging basket
FLOWERS: ■

SITING: This easy-to-grow plant is favored by gardeners because it looks good even when neglected. It has velvety dark purple-green leaves with dark purple undersides and purple stems. Given the right conditions, it will produce lavender flowers on stalks held above the foliage. The plant thrives in medium light and average temperatures (60–75°F) but tolerates cooler temperatures. Provide average humidity (30–60 percent). This plant can easily be grown outdoors, and many gardeners use cuttings from their indoor plant to provide outdoor vining plants for hanging baskets.

CARE: Keep the soil evenly moist but not soggy. Feed only three times in summer. Repot occasionally. Once the plants look leggy, take cuttings to start new plants. Pinch out stem tips to keep the plant shrubby and full.

PROPAGATION: Propagate from stem cuttings rooted in water or soil. The crown can also be divided easily. Cut the plant back when you divide it in order to rejuvenate it as well as to make it easier to separate shorter vines.

PESTS AND DISEASES: Treat mealybugs and whiteflies with horticultural oil or insecticidal soap.

RELATED SPECIES: *Plectranthus* 'Mona Lavender' has magenta flowers and glossy deep purple leaves on purple stems.

You can easily start new plants of purple-leaved Swedish ivy by rooting cuttings in water.

BUDDHIST PINE
Podocarpus macrophyllus poh-doh-KAR-pus mak-roh-FILL-us

Buddhist pines, dark green to almost black in color, are beautiful architectural accents in cool spots such as entryways and foyers.

SIZE: 8'h × 3'w
TYPE: Woody evergreen
FORM: Upright
TEXTURE: Fine
GROWTH: Slow
LIGHT: Medium to high

MOISTURE: Moist
SOIL: Potting soil
FEATURES: Foliage, tree form
USES: Architectural accent

SITING: Buddhist pine is an excellent candidate for a cool space with bright light, such as a foyer. The dark green, almost black foliage contrasts well with the cinnamon-colored bark. This plant is fairly carefree and will maintain its attractive foliage if given medium to high light and average to cool temperatures (50–75°F). It tolerates low humidity (below 30 percent) but may be prone to spider mites.

CARE: Keep the soil evenly moist during the growing season and allow to dry between waterings during dormancy in winter. Feed three times in summer with foliage plant food, or only once a year if the plant is as large as you want it. Repot only when the plant would look better in a larger pot. It grows so slowly that roots will seldom overtake the pot. This plant seldom needs pruning except to shape it gently. It has a natural tendency to lose its inner leaves regularly, so remove them as part of regular grooming. It may need the support of a stake as it gets tall. Find a stake that looks as natural as possible and insert it close to the trunk. Tie the trunk to the stake with soft dark brown jute. Give the plant monthly showers.

PROPAGATION: Buddhist pine can be propagated by stem cuttings, but not easily. Take semihardwood cuttings in late spring; use rooting powder and bottom heat.

PESTS AND DISEASES: Control scale, mealybugs, and spider mites with horticultural oil.

RELATED SPECIES: The cultivar 'Maki' has white new foliage.

These plants respond well to pruning and can be kept attractive by attending to this task when necessary.

MING ARALIA
Polyscias fruticosa *pah-lih-SKEE-us froo-tih-KOH-suh*

Ming aralias with their ferny graceful foliage can be grown in the home as long as the right conditions are provided.

SIZE: 5'h × 2'w
TYPE: Woody tree
FORM: Upright
TEXTURE: Fine
GROWTH: Slow
LIGHT: Medium

MOISTURE: Dry
SOIL: Potting soil
FEATURES: Foliage
USES: Architectural accent, Asian theme

SITING: Ming aralia has a reputation for being difficult to grow in the average home. This delicate, Asian-looking plant can be successful once the right environmental conditions have been provided, but it is not one to neglect. It responds by dropping all its leaves. Provide medium to bright light, average to high temperatures (60–85°F), and, most important, high humidity (above 65 percent). Putting the plant on a bed of moist pebbles works well, as does a humidifier, as long as the air does not circulate too much. Cool drafts are deadly for Ming aralia.

CARE: Even though Ming aralia needs high humidity, it does not need constantly moist

Since Ming aralias need high humidity to keep them healthy, place pots on trays of moist pebbles to raise the ambient humidity around the plant.

soil. It can be prone to root rot from overwatering. Allow it to dry slightly between soakings. Feed three times in summer with foliage plant food, or according to label directions during active growth. This plant grows so slowly that it needs repotting infrequently, only when the plant is no longer able to take up water. Ming aralia can be pruned to keep it looking good, but it seldom needs drastic pruning.

PROPAGATION: Propagating Ming aralia is difficult at best, but stem cuttings taken in late spring and rooted with hormone powder and bottom heat may be successful. The plant can be air-layered with some success as well.

PESTS AND DISEASES: Scale and spider mites can be controlled with high humidity, regular showering, and horticultural oil.

RELATED SPECIES: The cultivar 'Elegans' has contorted, curled leaves. Parsley-leaf aralia (*P. filicifolia*) has slightly larger leaves and denser foliage. *P. guilfoylei* 'Victoriae' has small, deeply cut leaves edged with white teeth.

BALFOUR ARALIA
Polyscias scutellaria (balfouriana) *pah-lih-SEE-us skoo-tuh-LAR-ee-uh (bal-foor-ee-AY-nuh)*

Balfour aralias are unique Asian-looking plants that need average temperature, medium light, and high humidity to thrive.

SIZE: 6'h × 3'w
TYPE: Woody tree
FORM: Upright
TEXTURE: Fine
GROWTH: Slow
LIGHT: Medium

MOISTURE: Dry
SOIL: Potting soil
FEATURES: Foliage, tan bark
USES: Architectural accent, Asian theme

SITING: Balfour aralia has a reputation for being hard to grow in the average home.

This Asian-looking plant can be quite successful once the right environmental conditions have been provided, but it is not a plant to neglect. It responds by dropping all its leaves. Provide medium light, average to high temperatures (60–85°F), and, most important, high humidity (above 65 percent). Putting the plant on a bed of moist pebbles works well, as does a humidifier, as long as the air does not circulate too much. Cool drafts are deadly for Balfour aralia.

CARE: Even though Balfour aralia needs high humidity, it does not need constantly moist soil. It is more prone to root rot from overwatering than the other species. Overwatering will show up first as shiny dark spots on the backs of leaves, which will then yellow and fall. Allow the plant to dry slightly between soakings. Feed three times in summer with foliage plant food, or according to label directions during active growth. This plant grows

so slowly that it needs repotting only when it isn't able to take up water any longer. Balfour aralia can be pruned to keep it looking good, but it seldom needs drastic pruning.

PROPAGATION: Propagating Balfour aralia is difficult at best, but stem cuttings taken in late spring and rooted with hormone powder and bottom heat may be successful. The plants can be air-layered with some success as well.

PESTS AND DISEASES: Balfour aralia may have scale and spider mites. Both can be controlled with high humidity, regular showering, and horticultural oil.

RELATED SPECIES: The cultivar 'Pennockii' has vertically held leaves that are mottled gray and green. (This cultivar is reputed to be hard to grow.) 'Marginata' leaves are delicately and irregularly edged in white. Chicken gizzard aralia 'Ruffles' (*P. crispata*) has lime green foliage and is more compact than other aralias.

PRIMROSE
Primula spp. *PRIM-yoo-luh*

In cool regions primroses can be planted into the outdoor garden as perennials after you have enjoyed their bloom indoors.

SIZE: 4–6"h × 6–8"w
TYPE: Herbaceous
FORM: Mounded
TEXTURE: Medium
GROWTH: Medium
LIGHT: Medium to high
MOISTURE: Evenly moist

SOIL: Potting soil
FEATURES: Fragrant blossoms
USES: Blooming accent
FLOWERS: ▨ ■ ■ ■ □

SITING: Indoors, primroses need only medium light to keep them attractive while blooming, although they will tolerate bright, indirect light as long as they are kept cool. They tolerate medium temperatures (65–75°F), but cool temperatures (55–65°F) will keep them blooming much longer. Average humidity (30–60 percent), easily achieved with a pebble tray, keeps the leaves looking their best.

CARE: Keep primroses evenly moist for their entire blooming time or the buds may shrivel. However, do not let the plants sit in water. Feed with half-strength plant food at every watering while in bud and in flower. Repotting is seldom needed; put

Primrose flowers come in a broad array of cheery spring colors.

the plants outdoors into the garden after the blossoms fade. Regularly remove faded blossoms to keep the buds coming.

PROPAGATION: Propagate by crown division or by seed. Start seeds indoors and move the plants outdoors as seedlings. The plants are perennials and usually need 2 years to come into bloom outdoors.

PESTS AND DISEASES: Primroses may have occasional problems with mealybugs and spider mites. Control mealybugs with a cotton swab dipped in alcohol, and spider mites with a strong spray of water on the undersides of the leaves.

RELATED SPECIES: Common primrose (*P. vulgaris*) is most often sold as a blooming houseplant. The dark, crinkly leaves surround bouquets of flowers held close to the center of the plant. The blossoms are usually sweet scented. Fairy primrose (*P. malacoides*) has tall flower spikes of white, pink, red, and lavender. These plants are not hardy outdoors so are best treated as annuals and discarded after blooming. *P. obconica* is also sold as a blooming plant with large, showy flowers. Be aware that leaf contact can cause dermatitis in some people.

TABLE FERN
Pteris cretica *TAIR-iss KREH-tih-kuh*

'Albo-linata' table fern brightens the home with its white-banded fronds that look best viewed from above.

SIZE: 12–24"h × 12–24"w
TYPE: Fern
FORM: Mounded
TEXTURE: Medium
GROWTH: Medium
LIGHT: Medium to high

MOISTURE: Evenly moist
SOIL: Potting soil
FEATURES: Fronds
USES: Foliage, accent, terrarium

SITING: Table fern does not drape like other ferns, so it is more suited to a table than to a hanging basket. Provide medium to bright, indirect light for the best growth. It prefers cool to medium temperatures (55–75°F). It needs high humidity, as do most ferns, but will survive at even 40 percent humidity.

CARE: Keep the soil evenly moist but not soggy. It requires more water than it would seem for its size, so work to find the right balance. It may take twice-a-week watering. Leaves will brown on the edges and then curl if the plant is in low humidity or gets too little water. Feed three times in summer with foliage plant food. Because of its vigorous nature, it needs to

Table fern is also known as brake fern or Cretan brake. The species has solid green branching fronds.

be repotted annually. Use a rich, moisture-retentive planting mix and move up one pot size larger each time.

PROPAGATION: Table fern can be propagated by careful division. It is easier to propagate by spores. Spores form in lines along the edges of the frond leaflets and, when ripe, can be tapped out of the spore cases and scattered on fresh potting soil.

PESTS AND DISEASES: Table fern may have occasional scale and mealybugs; both are controlled with a cotton swab dipped in horticultural oil or alcohol. Do not spray the entire plant with oil, however, or the fronds will be damaged. The plant benefits from monthly showering to keep the fronds clean and free of spider mites.

RELATED SPECIES: The cultivar 'Albo-linata' has a broad white central band on the fronds. Other cultivars have various types of cresting and lobing on the fronds. Silver brake (*P. argyraea*) has dark green fronds with a broad silver stripe in the center. Australian brake (*P. tremula*) is a vigorous plant with ferny fronds. Painted brake (*P. tricolor*) has reddish fronds when young.

CHINA DOLL
Radermachera sinica *ray-der-MAK-er-uh SIN-ih-kuh*

China doll is grown in bright, indirect light, it will grow quickly but remain attractive. In lower light it becomes leggy. A south- or east-facing window with a gauze curtain is ideal. This plant is tolerant of average temperatures (60–75°F) and low humidity (below 30 percent). It performs well in a heated home in winter, unlike many other foliage plants.

CARE: Keep the soil evenly moist. Leaves will yellow if the plant is too dry or turn brown on the edges and fall if the plant is too wet. Reduce watering somewhat in winter. Repot annually in spring into a pot one size larger. When the desired size is reached, continue repotting annually, but root-prune to put it back in the same pot. Feed three times in summer with foliage plant food. Let the plant rest in winter. To keep the plant shrubby and compact, pinch the stem tips often. Remove faded leaflets and give it a shower once a month.

PROPAGATION: Propagate by stem-tip cuttings taken in summer. Use rooting hormone and bottom heat as well as a plastic tent. Do not expect a high rate of success.

PESTS AND DISEASES: Spider mites can become a problem when the plant is grown in low humidity. Monthly showering should help keep them in check. Mealybugs may also appear but are easily controlled with horticultural oil.

RELATED SPECIES: The cultivar 'Crystal Doll' has golden-edged leaves.

China doll, as its name implies, is a delicately elegant plant with glossy leaves and an attractive upright shape.

SIZE: 3–4'h × 2'w
TYPE: Herbaceous
FORM: Upright
TEXTURE: Medium
GROWTH: Medium
LIGHT: High
MOISTURE: Moist
SOIL: Potting soil
FEATURES: Glossy leaves
USES: Foliage

SITING: China doll has been around for many years as a beautiful foliage plant, but it didn't become popular in the United States until the 1980s. Its lovely glossy compound leaves make an appealing statement in a foliage plant collection or as a backdrop for a blooming plant. When

China dolls grow best in bright indirect light, achieved easily in a west or south window that is draped with a gauzy curtain to block direct sunlight.

LADY PALM
Rhapis excelsa *RAY-pis ek-SELL-suh*

Lady palm, one of the most elegant of the palms, has short leaflets on stiff fronds and thrives in low light.

SIZE: 5–6'h × 4–5'w
TYPE: Palm
FORM: Upright
TEXTURE: Coarse
GROWTH: Slow
LIGHT: Low to medium
MOISTURE: Moist
SOIL: Potting soil
FEATURES: Glossy leaves
USES: Architectural accent

SITING: Lady palm performs best in low to medium light. It thrives in average temperatures (60–75°F) but will tolerate low temperatures (below 60°F) for short periods. Lady palm needs high humidity (60 percent or higher), which can be accomplished by the pot-in-pot method, a tray of wet pebbles, or a room humidifier.

CARE: Keep the soil evenly moist, but allow it to dry somewhat between waterings in winter. Feed only three times in summer with a foliage plant food. Repot when considerable new growth forms around the edge of the pot. Remove the occasional faded leaf. If leaf edges and tips brown from low humidity, trim them or remove the leaflet.

PROPAGATION: Propagate by dividing the rhizomes or by sowing seeds obtained from a supplier.

PESTS AND DISEASES: This plant is fairly carefree but may have occasional bouts with spider mites, scale, and mealybugs. All can be controlled fairly easily with horticultural oil. Shower the plant regularly to keep spider mite populations under control and retain the glossy, clean look of the foliage.

RELATED SPECIES: The cultivar 'Zuikonishiki' is variegated. 'Tenzan' has curling leaves. Several dwarf varieties are popular for bonsai.

Give lady palm plenty of room to enjoy its full size and shape as an architectural accent.

EASTER CACTUS
Rhipsalidopsis spp. (*Hatiora gaertneri*) *rip-sal-ih-DOP-sis (hah-tee-OR-uh GART-nur-eye)*

Easter cactus blooms with its exquisite pink, red, or white flowers in April and May after being given a cool resting period from September through March.

SIZE: 12–18"h ×
12–18"w
TYPE: Forest cactus
FORM: Upright,
trailing
TEXTURE: Medium
GROWTH: Slow
LIGHT: High

MOISTURE: Dry
SOIL: Potting soil
FEATURES:
Scalloped leaves,
showy flowers
USES: Blooming
accent
FLOWERS: ■■□

SITING: Easter cactus does best in medium light during active growth and bright, indirect light in winter. Ideal temperatures during active growth and blooming are 70–80°F, no less than 60°F during bloom time. It is tolerant of low humidity (less than 30 percent).

CARE: Easter cactus is magnificent in bloom, but it takes a specific regimen to get it to bloom. If it does not get a cool resting time with short daylength, it will not form flower buds. It may drop flower buds if the growing conditions are changed once buds are set. The plant blooms in spring, during which time it should be watered regularly. Allow the

Easter cactus performs best if taken outdoors to spend the summer months and then brought back indoors in mid-September.

potting soil to dry slightly between waterings. In summer move it outdoors to a shady spot. Around mid-September, bring it indoors into a cool spot (around 55°F) and reduce watering for its resting phase. Keep the soil only slightly moist. Continue to keep it somewhat dry and cool as it forms flower buds. At the end of March, bring it into warmth and begin watering. It should begin flowering again in April.

PROPAGATION: Propagate from leaf cuttings. Pinch off leaf segments and allow them to dry for a couple of days before inserting into sterile soil mix. When propagating by seed, allow the fruits to ripen, then extract the seeds. Clean the seeds and dry them for a few days, then sow on sterile soil mix.

PESTS AND DISEASES: Spider mites, scale, and aphids may affect Easter cactus. Dab scale with alcohol and wash off spider mites and aphids. The plant may develop root rot if overwatered.

RELATED SPECIES: *R. gaertneri* is the standard Easter cactus, with fuchsia to dark red flowers. *R. sirius* is white flowered, and *R. rosea* has tiny pink flowers and is smaller overall.

AZALEA
Rhododendron spp. *roh-doh-DEN-drun*

Azaleas are favorite plants to share for all occasions, and with a little perseverance, can be brought back into bloom.

SIZE: 30"h × 30"w
TYPE: Woody shrub
FORM: Rounded
TEXTURE: Medium
GROWTH: Slow
LIGHT: Medium to
high

MOISTURE: Evenly
moist
SOIL: Potting soil
FEATURES: Blossoms
USES: Blooming
focal point, foliage
FLOWERS: ■■□■

SITING: During blooming time, medium light is the best for azaleas. When blossoming is over, move the plant into bright light to bring it back into bloom. The key to bud set is a distinct difference between summer and fall/winter temperatures. In summer it will tolerate warm temperatures (75–90°F). In fall and winter the temperature needs to drop to 40–50°F and be held there until buds set. Average humidity (30–60 percent) is preferred, although the plant will tolerate lower humidity.

CARE: Allowing soil to dry out at all will damage the plant and cause the flower buds to abort. Feed with acid plant food

Azaleas must be kept evenly moist throughout their blooming time, and drying out even one time may cause the flower buds to abort.

according to label directions during active growth. Stop feeding in fall and don't resume until after flower buds are set in February or March. If you intend to keep your azalea, repot it into a larger pot after blooming. Prune immediately after blooming to rejuvenate and shape the plant. Azalea benefits from spending the summer outdoors, but be sure to place it in shade. Bring it indoors before danger of frost and keep it in a cool spot with low humidity until flower buds are set. In late February or March, bring it into warmth and raise the humidity. Azalea can have chlorosis from soil that is not acidic enough. Remedy with acid fertilizer.

PROPAGATION: Propagate by stem cuttings soon after blooming. Take semihardwood cuttings in late spring, dip in rooting hormone, and insert in sterile potting mix. Cover with a tent and provide bottom heat.

PESTS AND DISEASES: Watch for spider mites in dry conditions. Wash them off with a forceful spray of water.

RELATED SPECIES: There are thousands of species and cultivars of *Rhododendron*. The most commonly grown houseplants are *R. indica* and *R. simsii*.

MONKEY PLANT

Ruellia makoyana roo-EL-ee-uh mak-oy-AH-nuh

Monkey plant, also known as trailing velvet plant, has attractive foliage and bright pink blossoms that resemble petunias.

SIZE: 6–12"h × 12–18"w
TYPE: Herbaceous
FORM: Trailing
TEXTURE: Medium
GROWTH: Medium
LIGHT: High
MOISTURE: Moist

SOIL: Potting soil
FEATURES: Olive-colored leaves with silver veins
USES: Hanging basket, blooming focal point
FLOWERS: ▨

SITING: Monkey plant will keep its attractive velvety foliage and will bear attractive petunia-like pink flowers during almost all of its growing season if given bright, indirect light in summer and some direct sun in winter. Provide average home temperatures (65–75°F), not below 55°F. High humidity (above 60 percent) is best and easily accomplished by using a pebble tray or room humidifier.

CARE: Although monkey plant is fairly tolerant of neglect, it's best to keep the soil evenly moist when the plant is blooming. Reduce the water somewhat in winter, allowing the plant to dry slightly between waterings. Feed three times in summer with blooming plant food at full strength. Repot as necessary, usually every couple of years. Pinch the growing tips regularly to keep the plant shrubby. Remove faded blossoms to keep the plant attractive.

PROPAGATION: Propagate by stem-tip cuttings taken in summer. Provide rooting hormone and bottom heat for the best success. Monkey plant is also started easily from seed. When the green pods open, extract the black seeds and sow on sterile potting mix. Keep moist until the seeds germinate.

PESTS AND DISEASES: Spider mites can be a problem if the humidity is not kept high. Shower the plant with a forceful spray of water to control them. Also, poor air circulation can encourage mildew to grow on the leaves.

RELATED SPECIES: *R. macrantha* is a larger plant with darker flowers and solid green leaves. *R. brittoniana* 'Katie' is a dwarf form with lance-shaped solid green leaves and blue flowers. *R.* 'Strawberries and Cream' has purple flowers and speckled foliage.

AFRICAN VIOLET

Saintpaulia ionantha saynt PAWL ee uh eye oh NAN thuh

African violets have long been favorites because of the multitude of colors and forms available and their ability to thrive under artificial lights.

SIZE: 2–6"h × 4–8"w
TYPE: Herbaceous
FORM: Mounded
TEXTURE: Medium
GROWTH: Medium
LIGHT: Bright
MOISTURE: Moist

SOIL: Potting soil
FEATURES: Attractive foliage, constant bloom
USES: Blooming focal point
FLOWERS: ■▨□■

SITING: African violets do well in bright, indirect light or under artificial lights placed about 12" from the plant and left on for 13 hours a day. The plants will be injured if kept too cool; 60°F at night and 75–80°F during the day are adequate. African violets perform better in low humidity (below 30 percent).

CARE: Keep the soil evenly moist. Avoid getting cold water on the leaves; it may cause spotting. Many gardeners water from the bottom instead of the top. Feed with blooming plant food according to label directions. Repot annually or when the leafless portion of the stem is about 1½" long. Remove faded blossoms and leaves. To remove dust, use a soft feather duster or pressurized air. Avoid washing or rubbing the leaves.

PROPAGATION: Propagate by leaf cuttings. Cut off a leaf and insert the petiole and bottom of the leaf into sterile potting mix or vermiculite. In 2–6 months, small plants will form at the soil level.

PESTS AND DISEASES: African violets are generally carefree but may become infested with cyclamen mites, thrips, mealybugs, or aphids.

RELATED SPECIES: Cultivars have single or double flowers in many colors and many bicolors. There are varieties with crinkly, scalloped, or variegated leaves and trailing, upright, or miniature forms.

African violet leaves can be harmed if they get wet, but watering from the bottom can prevent this.

1 Propagate African violet by snipping off a leaf and its petiole.

2 Dip the petiole into rooting hormone and insert it in potting soil.

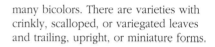

SNAKE PLANT

Sansevieria trifasciata san-seb-VEER-ee-ub trye-fas-ee-AH-tub

Snake plant, also known as mother-in-law's tongue, makes a beautiful upright accent plant and thrives on neglect.

SIZE: 6–48"h × 10–36"w
TYPE: Succulent
FORM: Upright
TEXTURE: Coarse
GROWTH: Slow
LIGHT: Low to medium

MOISTURE: Dry
SOIL: Potting soil
FEATURES: Variegated foliage
USES: Low light, foliage accent
FLOWERS: ☐

SITING: Snake plant grows well in medium light but tolerates extremely low light. It thrives in average home temperatures but tolerates hot conditions as well. It does best in average humidity (30–60 percent) and tolerates dry but not high humidity.

CARE: Let the soil dry out between waterings; snake plant will quickly rot if overwatered. When planted in low-light situations where it takes up little water, allowing it to stand in a saucer of water can be deadly. The leaves will fall over at the soil line, accompanied by a foul-smelling ooze. Feed only once a year with foliage plant food and repot only when the plant fills the pot. It has a minimal root system, so the leaves will fill the pot before the roots do. Remove damaged leaves. Wipe the leaves regularly to keep them looking good.

PROPAGATION: Propagate by leaf cuttings or by separating the rhizomes. Leaf cuttings with yellow bands at the margins produce solid green-leaved plants. Cut leaves into 3" sections and place in sterile potting mix or vermiculite. New plants will arise at the soil level and can be potted.

PESTS AND DISEASES: Few insects bother snake plant.

RELATED SPECIES: Bird's nest snake plant (*S. t.* 'Hahnii') is small and has dark green rosettes striped with lighter green. 'Golden Hahnii' has gold and olive green striped leaves and grows to about 6" high. 'Laurentii' (pictured at left) is a tall cultivar with light and dark green variegation and wide yellow leaf margins.

1 **Propagate from leaf cuttings several inches long. Notch the top side so you don't insert a cutting upside down.**

2 **Dip the bottom end in rooting hormone and insert in sterile potting soil. Cover with plastic until the cuttings take root.**

STRAWBERRY BEGONIA

Saxifraga stolonifera saks-ib-FRAY-gub stob-lub-NIH-fer-ub

Strawberry begonia, also known as strawberry geranium, makes a superb accent with its scalloped leaves and multitudes of plantlets.

SIZE: 3"h × 12"w
TYPE: Herbaceous
FORM: Mounded, trailing
TEXTURE: Fine
GROWTH: Medium
LIGHT: Medium

MOISTURE: Moist
SOIL: Potting soil
FEATURES: Leaves with silver veins
USES: Hanging basket, ground cover
FLOWERS: ☐

SITING: Strawberry begonia is irresistible with its delicate foliage in shades of red and maroon with silver veins and its tiny plantlets that seem to leap over the sides

To start new plants, simply peg the plantlets down on moist soil with hairpins. They will root quickly and can then be cut from the main plant.

of the plant like spiders on silk. This plant thrives in medium light and average home temperatures (60–75°F). It needs average humidity (30–60 percent), easily provided with a pebble tray or pot-in-pot system.

CARE: Keep the soil evenly moist during active growth, but water less in winter when it is resting. Too much water will quickly rot the plant. Feed three times in summer with foliage plant food and repot annually, or when the pot fills with small plants and the stolons hanging over the sides become a thick mat. Remove faded leaves. Remove the stolons if you don't care for that look. Give it an occasional shower. Move the plant outdoors for the summer.

PROPAGATION: Strawberry begonia almost propagates itself with its tiny plants hung on delicate pink stolons. Give these plants moist soil on which to rest and they will readily root. You can also propagate the plants by dividing the root ball.

PESTS AND DISEASES: Treat mealybugs and aphids with a strong spray of water or alcohol-dipped cotton swabs.

RELATED SPECIES: The cultivar 'Cuscutiformis' is a dwarf form with tiny leaves and plantlets. 'Tricolor' is variegated green, white, and rose. 'Rubra' has dark reddish leaves.

UMBRELLA TREE
Schefflera actinophylla (Brassaia) <small>*schef-LAIR-uh ak-tin-oh-FYE-luh (brass-AY-ee-uh)*</small>

Umbrella tree, also known as schefflera, is a carefree houseplant that gives a tropical impression to the indoor landscape.

SIZE: 8'h × 4'w
TYPE: Herbaceous
FORM: Upright
TEXTURE: Coarse
GROWTH: Fast
LIGHT: Medium

MOISTURE: Moist
SOIL: Potting soil
FEATURES: Glossy foliage
USES: Architectural accent

SITING: Umbrella tree has been the standard for large houseplants for many years, appreciated for its ease of maintenance and its tropical, glossy foliage. It does well in medium light and average home temperatures (60–75°F), although it tolerates high light and high temperatures.

It drops leaves if it gets too cold. Umbrella tree needs only average humidity (30–60 percent). When siting it, place it out of the way of drying winds and cold drafts. Keep umbrella tree out of high-traffic areas because it takes up so much room.

Occasionally wipe the leaves of schefflera with a soft cloth to avoid pest problems.

CARE: Keep the soil evenly moist during active growth; reduce moisture in winter. These plants will rot if overwatered, so make sure the potting mix is well drained. Feed three times in summer with foliage plant food, and repot when the rootball completely fills the pot. These plants are fast growing, so if you fertilize regularly, you may need to repot annually. Scheffleras tolerate pruning well, so you can shape them to a smaller size. A plant that gets top-heavy should be pruned back to a better shape. Remove any wayward branches or faded leaves. If the stems become spindly, move the plant into higher light and cut it back to 12" to produce new growth at ground level. Scheffleras benefit from spending the summer outdoors if they are gradually exposed to the elements.

PROPAGATION: Propagate by stem cuttings or air-layering.

PESTS AND DISEASES: Control mealybugs, scale, and spider mites with horticultural oil. Shower the plant occasionally to deter spider mites.

RELATED SPECIES: The cultivar 'Amate' stays compact even in lower light.

SCHEFFLERA
Schefflera arboricola (Heptapleurum, Brassaia) <small>*schef-LAIR-uh ar-bor-ih-KOH-luh (hep-tuh-PLUR-um, brass-AY-ee-uh)*</small>

Arboricola, a miniature version of the standard schefflera, has more diminutive umbrella foliage in medium and dark green.

SIZE: 2–3'h × 2–3'w
TYPE: Herbaceous
FORM: Upright
TEXTURE: Coarse
GROWTH: Fast
LIGHT: Medium

MOISTURE: Moist
SOIL: Potting soil
FEATURES: Foliage
USES: Architectural accent

SITING: Scheffleras do well in medium light and average home temperatures (60–75°F), although they are tolerant of high temperatures. They will drop leaves if they get too cold. They need only average humidity (30-60 percent). Place them out of the way of drying winds and cold drafts.

Keep them out of high-traffic areas because they take up so much room.

CARE: Keep the soil evenly moist while the plant is actively growing; reduce moisture somewhat in winter. These plants will rot if overwatered, so make sure the potting mix is well drained. Feed only three times in summer with foliage plant food and repot when the rootball completely fills the pot. These plants are fast growing, so if you feed regularly, you may need to repot annually. Scheffleras tolerate pruning well, so you can shape them to a smaller size. A plant that gets top-heavy should be pruned to a better shape. Remove any wayward branches or faded leaves. If the stems become spindly, move the plant into higher light and cut it back to 12" to produce new growth at ground level. Scheffleras can spend the summer outdoors if they are gradually exposed to the elements.

PROPAGATION: Propagate by stem cuttings and air-layering.

PESTS AND DISEASES: Control mealybugs, scale, and spider mites with horticultural oil. Shower the plant occasionally to deter spider mites.

RELATED SPECIES: The cultivar 'Green Gold' has golden-flecked leaves. 'Pittman's Pride' is a compact form.

Scheffleras may get leggy, but are easy to contain by cutting back. They will take severe pruning if necessary to get them back to an attractive shape.

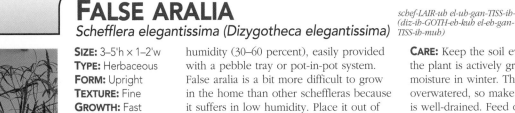

FALSE ARALIA
Schefflera elegantissima (Dizygotheca elegantissima)

*schef-LAIR-uh el-uh-gan-TISS-ih-muh
(diz-ih-GOTH-eh-kuh el-eh-gan-
TISS-ih-muh)*

SIZE: 3–5'h × 1–2'w
TYPE: Herbaceous
FORM: Upright
TEXTURE: Fine
GROWTH: Fast
LIGHT: Medium
MOISTURE: Moist
SOIL: Potting soil
FEATURES: Linear leaves
USES: Architectural accent, foliage

False aralia, also known as finger aralia, has deep green linear foliage that looks almost black. The foliage stands at a 90-degree angle from the black stems.

SITING: False aralias do well in medium light and average home temperatures (60–75°F), although they are tolerant of high temperatures. They will drop leaves if they get too cold. They need only average humidity (30–60 percent), easily provided with a pebble tray or pot-in-pot system. False aralia is a bit more difficult to grow in the home than other scheffleras because it suffers in low humidity. Place it out of the way of drying winds and cold drafts. Keep it out of high-traffic areas, because it takes up so much room.

False aralias need average humidity, and in a dry home, this can be accomplished by placing the plant pot on a tray of moist pebbles.

CARE: Keep the soil evenly moist while the plant is actively growing, but reduce moisture in winter. The plant will rot if overwatered, so make sure the potting mix is well-drained. Feed only three times in summer with foliage plant food, and repot when the rootball completely fills the pot. This plant is fast growing, so if you feed it regularly, you may need to repot annually. False aralias tolerate pruning well, so you can shape them to a smaller size. Remove any wayward branches or faded leaves. If the stems get spindly, move the plant into higher light and cut it back to 12" to produce new growth at ground level. False aralias can spend the summer outdoors as long as they are hardened off before being exposed to the elements.
PROPAGATION: Propagate from stem cuttings or by air-layering.
PESTS AND DISEASES: Control mealybugs, scale, and spider mites with horticultural oil. Shower the plant occasionally to deter spider mites.
RELATED SPECIES: 'Pink Rim' has pink-edged leaves.

CHRISTMAS CACTUS
Schlumbergera xbuckleyi *shlum-BER-ger-uh BUK-lee-eye*

Christmas cactus blooms in shades of red, pink, and white. It needs slightly moist soil, medium light, and warm temperatures when blooming.

SIZE: 8–12"h × 12–18"w
TYPE: Forest cactus
FORM: Upright, trailing
TEXTURE: Medium
GROWTH: Slow
LIGHT: High
MOISTURE: Dry
SOIL: Potting soil
FEATURES: Scalloped leaves, showy flowers
USES: Blooming accent
FLOWERS: ■■□□

SITING: Christmas cactus does best in medium light during active growth and bright, indirect light in winter. Ideal temperatures during active growth and blooming are 70–80°F. Give it no less than 60°F during bloom time. It is tolerant of low humidity (less than 30 percent).
CARE: Christmas cactus is magnificent in bloom, but it takes a specific regimen to get it to bloom. It needs a cool resting time with short daylengths to form flower buds. In summer put it outdoors in a shady spot. Around mid-September or after the outdoor temperatures have fallen to 45°F

Place Christmas cactus outdoors in summer where they will receive good light. Leave outdoors until temperatures fall to 45°F in order to set flower buds.

at night, bring it indoors into a cool spot (around 55°F) and reduce watering for its resting phase. Keep the soil only slightly moist. The plant may develop root rot if overwatered. Continue to keep the plant somewhat dry and cool as it forms flower buds. It may drop flower buds if the growing conditions are changed once buds are set. Fertilize monthly with half-strength blooming plant food starting in April and continuing until the plant comes indoors in fall. Repot only every 3 years, because it does better if somewhat pot-bound. The potting mix must be well drained but not as coarse as regular cactus mix.
PROPAGATION: Propagate from leaf cuttings. Pinch off leaf segments and allow them to dry for a couple of days before inserting into sterile soil mix. When propagating by seed, allow the fruits to ripen, then extract the seeds. Clean the seeds and dry them for a few days, then sow on sterile soil mix.
PESTS AND DISEASES: Treat scale with a cotton swab dipped in alcohol. Wash off spider mites and aphids.
RELATED SPECIES: There are hundreds of cultivars of Christmas cactus, with all colors of flowers, bicolors, and doubles.

THANKSGIVING CACTUS

Schlumbergera truncata *shlum-BER-ger-uh trun-KAY-tuh*

Thanksgiving cactus is a magnificent fall bloomer with blossoms in shades of red, salmon, and white. Give it a cool period outdoors in fall to set flower buds.

SIZE: 8–12"h × 12–18"w
TYPE: Forest cactus
FORM: Upright, trailing
TEXTURE: Medium
GROWTH: Slow
LIGHT: High

MOISTURE: Dry
SOIL: Potting soil
FEATURES: Scalloped leaves, showy flowers
USES: Blooming accent
FLOWERS: ■ ▨ □

SITING:. When siting Thanksgiving cactus, consider a spot that is not visible when it is resting, then bring it onto center stage when in bloom. It does best in medium light during active growth and bright, indirect light in winter. Ideal temperatures during active growth and blooming are 70–80°F. Give it no less than 60°F during bloom time. It is tolerant of low humidity (less than 30 percent).

CARE: Thanksgiving cactus is magnificent in bloom, but it needs a cool resting time and long nights to form flower buds. This plant usually blooms in November, during which time it should be watered regularly. Allow it to dry slightly between waterings. The plant may develop root rot if overwatered. In June, July, and August, put it outdoors in a shady spot protected from pests. Around mid-September, or after outdoor temperatures have fallen to 45°F at night, bring it indoors into a cool spot (around 55°F) and reduce watering for its resting phase. Keep the soil only slightly moist. Continue to keep the plant somewhat dry and cool as it forms flower buds. It may drop its buds if the growing conditions are changed once buds are set. Around the beginning of November, bring it into warmth and begin watering.

Commercial growers give Thanksgiving cactus 20–25 days of short days to ensure prolific bud set and bloom in time for late November bloom. Fertilize monthly with half-strength blooming plant food starting in April and continuing until the plant comes indoors in fall. Repot only every 3 years; the plant does better if pot-bound. Potting mix must be well drained but not as coarse as regular cactus mix; this cactus grows in moist conditions in the wild.

PROPAGATION: Propagate from leaf cuttings. Pinch off leaf segments and allow them to dry for a couple of days before inserting into sterile soil mix. When propagating by seed, allow the fruits to ripen, then extract the seeds. Clean the seeds and dry them for a few days, then sow on sterile soil mix.

PESTS AND DISEASES: Treat scale with a cotton swab dipped in alcohol; wash off spider mites and aphids.

RELATED SPECIES: There are hundreds of cultivars of Thanksgiving cactus, with all colors of flowers, bicolors, and doubles.

BURRO'S TAIL

Sedum morganianum *SEE-dum mor-gan-ee-AY-num*

Place burro's tail, also known as donkey's tail, out of traffic because the succulent leaves break off easily when touched.

SIZE: 4–6"h × 3'w
TYPE: Succulent
FORM: Trailing
TEXTURE: Medium
GROWTH: Medium
LIGHT: High
MOISTURE: Dry

SOIL: Cactus mix
FEATURES: Silver-blue foliage
USES: Hanging basket, succulent garden

SITING: Burro's tail is a delightful, unique plant. Provide it with bright light, either filtered or direct sun, for the best growth. It will tolerate medium light but tends to become leggy. Burro's tail thrives in average to hot temperatures (60–85°F) and low humidity (below 30 percent). Be sure to site the plant away from traffic because the "tails" are easily damaged and will drop leaves.

CARE: Let it dry out fairly well between waterings, then soak. Make sure the pot drains well; overwatering will cause crown

Even though the leaves break off easily, you can take advantage of the situation by sticking the leaves in potting soil to start new plants.

rot. In winter allow the plant to dry out completely between waterings, giving only enough water to keep the leaves from shriveling. A plant that is underwatered will experience leaf drop. Repot only if the plant becomes top-heavy. It performs best in a terra-cotta pot, which allows the soil to dry out easily. Be sure the rim of the pot is rounded or it will cut the stems and leaves of the heavy tails. Feed only once a year, in summer, with foliage plant food. Remove any damaged leaves and shorten the tails if they become too heavy.

PROPAGATION: Propagate by leaf or stem cuttings. Pinch off a leaf or a stem tip, let it dry for a couple of days, and then set it on moist soil.

PESTS AND DISEASES: Burro's tail has no pest problems except for occasional mealybugs.

RELATED SPECIES: *S. sieboldii* 'Mediovariegatum' has flat leaves with a creamy center and blue-green edges.

CINERARIA

Senecio xhybridus (Pericallis xhybrida) seb-NEE-shee-oh HYE-brid-us (pair-ib-KAL-iss HI-brid-uh)

Cineraria, lovely blooming plants in all shades of purples, pinks, and blues, are showy additions to a blooming display.

SIZE: 6–8"h × 8–12"w
TYPE: Herbaceous
FORM: Rounded
TEXTURE: Medium
GROWTH: Medium
LIGHT: Medium

MOISTURE: Moist
SOIL: Potting soil
FEATURES: Flowers
USES: Blooming accent
FLOWERS: ■ ■ ■ ■ ■ □

SITING: Provide cineraria with medium or indirect, bright light. This plant is enjoyed for its intense blossoms, so site it in a cool spot to prolong the display. Temperatures above 65°F will make the flowers open and fade quickly, so provide temperatures of 55–65°F during the day. If kept cool, cineraria will bloom for 4–6 weeks. It is not particular about humidity.
CARE: The key to keeping cineraria blooming as long as possible is to keep the soil evenly moist throughout its bloom cycle. The plant wilts easily if not provided plenty of moisture, and once it wilts, cineraria seldom recovers. At time of purchase, the plant is usually pot-bound so it will take up little water and may need watering every other day. Discard these plants after blooming rather than attempting to grow them for rebloom. Cineraria is forced into bloom by a rigorous schedule in the greenhouse. After blooming, plants begin to look ragged and unkempt in spite of ideal care.

PROPAGATION: Propagate by seed, but be aware that greenhouse conditions are needed to get the plants to bloom unless raised outdoors as a bedding plant.
PESTS AND DISEASES: Shower the plant regularly to remove aphids. Other pests include spider mites and whiteflies. Check the undersides of the leaves for pests before you purchase a plant. If you start with a blooming pest-free plant, control measures will likely be unnecessary.

Pay close attention to watering of cinerarias. Once they wilt, they seldom recover.

STRING-OF-BEADS

Senecio rowleyanus seb-NEE-shee-oh rob-lee-ANN-us

String-of-beads is an unusual-looking plant with gray-green foliage that forms small balls of leaves strung on green thread. High light and average temperatures are best.

SIZE: 2"h × 2'w
TYPE: Herbaceous
FORM: Trailing
TEXTURE: Fine
GROWTH: Medium
LIGHT: High

MOISTURE: Dry
SOIL: Potting soil
FEATURES: Ball-like foliage
USES: Hanging basket, focal point

SITING: String-of-beads seems to catch everyone's fancy, especially that of children. This plant will keep its unique shape and form a dense mat of "beads" on the surface of the soil when given high light filtered by a gauzy curtain during active growth. In winter the plant can tolerate a couple of hours of direct sun every day. Average home temperatures (60–75°F) are fine during the growing season, but reduce the temperature to 50–55°F in winter.
CARE: Allow the soil to dry between waterings during active growth. In winter when the plant is semidormant, provide only enough water to keep the beads from shriveling. Feed string-of-beads every 2 weeks with half-strength foliage plant food when it is actively growing. Repot about every 2 years or when the plant begins to look ragged. Cut it back severely to keep the plant compact. Use trimmings as cuttings to start new, fresh plants.
PROPAGATION: String-of-beads propagates easily by stem cuttings or leaf cuttings. Simply place some of the beads on the soil, where they will root. Or pin a stem to moist soil at a leaf node; roots will quickly form.
PESTS AND DISEASES: Keep aphids at bay by washing the plant periodically. Remove mealybugs with a cotton swab dipped in alcohol or horticultural oil. Keep the plant somewhat dry to prevent root rot.
RELATED SPECIES: The genus *Senecio* includes a large array of species, but few others adapt well to indoor environments. German ivy (*S. mikanioides*) is a succulent vine sometimes grown as a houseplant. Dusty miller (*S. cineraria*) is well known in the flower garden for its velvety, deeply lobed silver foliage.

GLOXINIA

Sinningia speciosa sin-NIN-gee-uh spee-see-OH-sah

Gloxinias are lovely velvet-flowered plants with coarse, deep green foliage that is reddish on the undersides. Keep the plants cool while blooming.

SIZE: 12"h × 12"w
TYPE: Herbaceous, tuberous
FORM: Mounded
TEXTURE: Coarse
GROWTH: Medium
LIGHT: High
MOISTURE: Moist

SOIL: Potting soil
FEATURES: Velvety leaves, large blossoms
USES: Blooming accent
FLOWERS: ■□■ ■■

SITING: Gloxinia's large, tubular flowers are set off by velvety foliage that is reddish on the undersides. It needs bright, filtered light to keep it blooming for a long period.

It thrives in average home temperatures (60–75°F) but needs high humidity.
CARE: Keep the soil evenly moist but not soggy while in active growth. Avoid getting water on the leaves, because they will spot. The leaves will curl when the air is too dry, and the plant may rot if kept too cool and moist. Direct sun will scorch the leaves. Gloxinia doesn't need fertilization when blooming. After blooming reduce the watering and fertilize every 2 weeks. To bring into bloom, stop watering when the

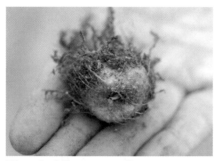

When the foliage turns yellow, stop watering to let the leaves dry. Remove the foliage and store the tuber in a cool, dry spot. Repot in spring and begin watering.

foliage turns yellow. Remove the foliage and store the tuber in a cool, dry spot in its pot until spring. Then repot the tuber, placing it at soil level to prevent rotting. Bring it into a warm spot and begin watering sparingly. When foliage appears, keep the soil evenly moist and provide high humidity.
PROPAGATION: Propagate by leaf cuttings or stem cuttings. Use bottom heat and insert the cuttings in vermiculite or sand for rooting. This plant can also be grown fairly easily from seed.
PESTS AND DISEASES: Mealybugs, spider mites, and whiteflies may cause problems. Check the undersides of the leaves carefully for pests before bringing a plant home. Use a strong spray of water to dislodge spider mites and whiteflies. Treat mealybugs with a cotton swab dipped in alcohol.
RELATED SPECIES: Cultivars are classified into two groups: The Fyfiana group has upright flowers, and the Maxima group has nodding flowers. *S. canescens* has dull green leaves and pink flowers. *S. cardinalis* has scalloped leaves with upright red blossoms.

BABY'S TEARS

Soleirolia soleirolii sol-eh-ROH-lee-uh sol-eh-ROH-lee-eye

Baby's tears has the look of a delicate mossy cascading plant, but it is a tenacious plant that thrives in bright or medium light and cool to medium temperature.

SIZE: 2"h × 9–12"w
TYPE: Herbaceous
FORM: Trailing
TEXTURE: Fine
GROWTH: Fast
LIGHT: Medium
MOISTURE: Moist

SOIL: Potting soil
FEATURES: Tiny leaves
USES: Hanging basket, terrarium, ground cover

SITING: Baby's tears is a delicate, sweet plant that makes a lovely hanging basket or a soft ground cover for larger plants. Site it carefully because it grows quickly and can overwhelm other plants. It does

best in bright, indirect light but will tolerate medium light. Provide cool to medium temperatures (55–75°F) and average humidity (30–60 percent).
CARE: Baby's tears should not dry out or the succulent stems and leaves will collapse and die. The plant can rot fairly easily if kept soggy. Feed every second or

Baby's tears makes a superb groundcover plant in the container of a larger plant. Be careful not to use it with a small plant as it will quickly overcome the other plant.

third week with half-strength foliage plant food. Stop fertilizing when the plant stops active growth in winter. It can be repotted annually, but older plants look ragged after a while. Start new plants every year from cuttings; they grow quickly. Remove faded leaves occasionally.
PROPAGATION: Propagate by stem cuttings, which root readily at the leaf nodes. Because the stems are so fine, remove a chunk of the plant and lay it on moist potting soil. It will soon take root. You can also divide the root ball when repotting.
PESTS AND DISEASES: Baby's tears may have occasional whiteflies and aphids. The plant is very hard to treat because of the tiny leaves and succulent, breakable stems, so cut it back severely or simply discard an affected plant.
RELATED SPECIES: The cultivar 'Aurea' has bright green foliage with a golden cast. 'Variegata' has silver-edged leaves.

COLEUS
Solenostemon scutellarioides sob-len-AH-steb-mun skoo-tub-lair-ee-OY-deez

Coleus's variegated foliage makes a great indoor plant. Bright light and high humidity indoors keeps it colorful.

SIZE: 6–12"h ×
6–12"w
TYPE: Herbaceous
FORM: Mounded
TEXTURE: Medium
GROWTH: Fast
LIGHT: High

MOISTURE: Moist
SOIL: Potting soil
FEATURES: Colored foliage
USES: Foliage accent
FLOWERS: ■

SITING: Because coleus is grown for its bright foliage, give it ideal conditions. A poorly grown coleus is not appealing. Coleus provides wonderful colors as long as it receives bright, filtered light and fairly high humidity (above 60 percent). In low

light the plant will get leggy and the leaf colors will fade. Full sun will also fade the leaves. Average home temperatures (60–75°F) are fine.
CARE: Keep the soil evenly moist during the growing season. Leaves will drop if the plant dries out. Keep it barely moist in winter when the plant is resting. Feed every 2 weeks with half-strength foliage plant food during active growth. Repot annually by cutting the plant back

substantially and repotting into new organic soil. This plant will flower in the house. Some gardeners feel that the flowers detract from the foliage; simply pinch the flower stems if you don't like the look. Pinch the leaf tips regularly to keep it shrubby and full. It will send out new shoots quickly at leaf nodes.
PROPAGATION: Grow from seed and from stem cuttings. Start stem cuttings in water or soil; they will produce roots in a week or so.
PESTS AND DISEASES: Spider mites may be a problem if the humidity is low and temperatures are warm.
RELATED SPECIES: There are hundreds of cultivars with all types of wildly variegated leaves that are ruffled, deeply incised, and scalloped.

1 Coleus readily roots from cuttings of any size and from anywhere along the stem.

2 Coleus roots as well in water as it does in soil. Roots form quickly.

PEACE LILY
Spathiphyllum wallisii spath-ib-FYE-lum wall-EE-see-eye

Peace lily is a superb foliage plant that tolerates neglect. Its foliage looks good when grown in low light, and it will thrive in low humidity.

SIZE: 18–24"h ×
12–18"w
TYPE: Herbaceous
FORM: Vase-shaped
TEXTURE: Coarse
GROWTH: Medium
LIGHT: High to low

MOISTURE: Dry
SOIL: Potting soil
FEATURES: Glossy foliage, attractive blossoms
USES: Foliage, low light conditions
FLOWERS: □

SITING: Peace lily tolerates neglect and is the plant of choice for offices, because the glossy foliage and attractive white spadix and spathe flowers do well in bright,

filtered light as well as medium, and even artificial light. Light that is too intense will yellow the leaves. The plant performs well in average to warm temperatures (60–85°F) and will thrive even in low humidity (below 30 percent). It may suffer chilling injury if the temperature drops below 60°F.
CARE: If growing peace lily in high light, keep the soil somewhat moist. The lower the light, the drier the soil should be kept. If the plant is allowed to dry to the point of wilting, the leaf edges will turn yellow,

then brown. Peace lily does well in a self-watering container. Feed only three times in summer with foliage plant food. Overfeeding will prevent flowering and cause brown spots on the leaves. Repot only when shoots begin to crowd the original plant. Dust or shower the leaves once a month. Plants begin blooming when they are more than a year old.
PROPAGATION: Propagate by dividing the root ball. Lift the plant from its pot, cut through the root ball, and pot the divisions separately.
PESTS AND DISEASES: Control mealybugs with horticultural oil.
RELATED SPECIES: The cultivar 'Mauna Loa' is larger and more robust. 'Lynise' has matte-finish leaves and is one of the most floriferous peace lilies available.

1 To repot the plant, pull it from its pot and slice cleanly through the root ball.

2 Replant the two portions of the root ball in clean potting soil in separate pots.

CAPE PRIMROSE

Streptocarpus ×*hybridus* strep-toh-KAR-pus HYE-brid-us

Cape primrose is a favorite blooming houseplant with its attractive foliage and pink, white, purple, or blue flowers.

SIZE: 6–12"h ×
6–12"w
TYPE: Herbaceous
FORM: Mounded
TEXTURE: Medium
GROWTH: Medium
LIGHT: High
MOISTURE: Moist

SOIL: Potting soil
FEATURES:
Blossoms, fuzzy
foliage
USES: Blooming
accent
FLOWERS: ■■□■

SITING: Cape primrose will bloom continuously if given the right conditions and not moved around. It does best in bright, indirect light and temperatures of 60°F at night and 75–85°F during the day.

Higher temperatures may cause plants to rot; cool temperatures cause leaf injury. Cape primrose performs best in medium to high humidity (30 percent and higher).
CARE: Keep the soil evenly moist. Avoid wetting the leaves; it may cause spotting. Many gardeners water from the bottom instead of the top. Feed with blooming plant food according to label directions. Repot only when the plant seems to be languishing. Remove faded leaves; remove

False African violet has fuzzy gray-green leaves and blue-purple flowers that seem to dance on long wiry petioles.

False African violets perform best in medium to high humidity. Place the pots on trays of moist pebbles.

faded flowers quickly unless you want seeds for propagation. Preventing seed production will promote longer blooming.
PROPAGATION: Propagate by leaf cuttings. Break off a leaf and insert the petiole and bottom half of the leaf into sterile potting mix or vermiculite. In 2–6 months, small plants will form at the soil level.
PESTS AND DISEASES: Cape primrose is generally carefree but may become infested with mites, thrips, mealybugs, or aphids. Wash off most insects with a strong spray of lukewarm water. Heavy infestations may call for a pesticide; choose appropriately so the plant will not be harmed, or discard the plant.
RELATED SPECIES: False African violet (*S. saxorum*) has gray-green leaves and abundant light lilac blossoms.

ARROWHEAD VINE

Syngonium podophyllum (Nephthytis) sin-GOH-nee-um poh-doh-FIL-lum (nef-THIGH-tiss)

Arrowhead vines are well loved for their variegated silvery-green arrowhead-shaped leaves. These plants thrive in average to low light and average temperatures.

SIZE: 1–3'h × 6'w
TYPE: Herbaceous
FORM: Trailing,
upright
TEXTURE: Medium
GROWTH: Fast
LIGHT: Medium to
low

MOISTURE: Dry
SOIL: Potting soil
FEATURES: Arrow-
shaped foliage
USES: Hanging
basket, foliage
accent

SITING: Arrowhead vine is a lush foliage plant that is an old favorite because of its fairly carefree nature. Leaves retain their variegation in medium and low light.

It does well in the artificial light of an office but is more compact and shrubby in higher light. Low light makes the plant leggy. It performs well in average home temperatures (60–75°F) and humidity above 30 percent, easily provided with a pebble tray or room humidifier.

Arrowhead vine can be trained to an upright form by pinning the vining stems onto a moss pole.

CARE: In low light allow the soil to dry slightly between waterings; in medium light keep the soil somewhat moist. Avoid soggy soil or the plant will rot. Repotting is seldom needed. Feed with foliage plant food three times in summer. Because the plant is naturally vining, pinching it often will help keep it compact and shrubby. To train it to a moss pole, pin the aerial roots to the pole and keep the pole moist. Remove the occasional faded leaf.
PROPAGATION: Propagate easily by stem tip cuttings or by division.
PESTS AND DISEASES: Arrowhead vine may have scale, mealybugs, and spider mites. Give monthly showers to control spider mites.
RELATED SPECIES: Arrowhead vine has many cultivars with gold, light green, cream, and white markings. Several cultivars have pinkish variegation on the leaves, which lose their blush in lower light. New cultivars are less vining and more compact.

PINK QUILL

Tillandsia cyanea till-AND-zee-uh sye-ANN-ee-uh

Pink quill is an easy-care bromeliad with stunning pink bracts from which emerge bright blue flowers.

SIZE: 1–2'h × 1'w
TYPE: Bromeliad
FORM: Upright, vase-shaped
TEXTURE: Coarse
GROWTH: Medium
LIGHT: High

MOISTURE: Moist
SOIL: Epiphyte mix
FEATURES: Flower spike, grassy foliage
USES: Blooming accent
FLOWERS: ■ ■

SITING: Pink quill's rewarding flowers begin with a bright, fan-shaped flower head that emerges from the grassy foliage. Then brilliant blue flowers emerge one or two at a time from between the pink bracts. To get this plant to produce its flower, provide bright, indirect light, such as from a south window with a gauzy curtain. It performs best in daytime temperatures of 68°F and above and nighttime temperatures of 50–65°F.

CARE: Although this plant is an air plant that can be grown on a slab, it performs better and blooms better when grown in an epiphyte potting mix. Keep the mix evenly moist. Feed with a foliage plant food according to label directions. Avoid handling the plant, which will rub off the small scales on the leaves that help absorb moisture. Repot when the potting mix breaks down. Occasionally wash off the leaves and remove spent flowers.

PROPAGATION: Propagate by dividing the root ball, starting from seed, or removing offsets. "Pups" will form at the base of the parent plant and can be removed and rooted.

RELATED SPECIES: *T. c.* var. *tricolor* has blue flowers with white throats. *T. caput-medusae* has curled silvery leaves and a red flower stalk. *T. utriculata* var. *pringleyi* has a branched orange or red flower stalk.

1 Propagate pink quill by carefully removing offsets produced at the base of the plant.

2 Plant the "pups" in loose potting mix and place in a protected spot until roots form.

PIGGYBACK PLANT

Tolmiea menziesii TOLL-mee-uh men-ZEE-see-eye

Piggyback plant, also known as mother-of-thousands, has the unique feature of producing plantlets right on the leaves.

SIZE: 6–12"h × 12–18"w
TYPE: Herbaceous
FORM: Mounded, trailing
TEXTURE: Medium
GROWTH: Fast
LIGHT: High to medium, indirect

MOISTURE: Dry
SOIL: Potting soil
FEATURES: Scalloped foliage with plantlets
USES: Hanging basket, unique focal point

SITING: Piggyback plant thrives in average home conditions. The plantlets that grow on top of the leaves are abundant and fun to see. Give piggyback plant indirect, bright to medium light. It will be more compact in higher light but will not tolerate direct sun. Provide cool to average temperatures (55–75°F) and average humidity (30–60 percent). Low humidity will cause the leaf margins to brown.

CARE: Allow the soil to dry out between waterings when grown in medium light; keep more moist in higher light. Letting the plant dry out to the point of wilting will cause the leaf margins to brown. Repot only when roots fill the container. This plant looks best when several are planted in one pot. Feed with foliage plant food three times in summer only. Pinch frequently to keep it shrubby and compact.

PROPAGATION: Start from seed or take leaf cuttings. Remove a leaf with a plantlet and a short piece of the petiole attached. Insert the petiole into the soil so the leaf lies on the soil surface. Pin the leaf to the soil with a hairpin to keep it in contact with moisture. The plantlet will soon produce roots, and the old leaf can be cut away.

PESTS AND DISEASES: Treat spider mites, aphids, and mealybugs with horticultural oil and raise the humidity somewhat.

RELATED SPECIES: The cultivar 'Taff's Gold' has golden-variegated leaves. 'Aurea' has leaves with a golden tinge.

1 To quickly produce a new plant, clip off a leaf with a sturdy plantlet intact.

2 Set the leaf and plantlet on moist potting mix and pin it to the soil to keep it in place.

STRIPED INCH PLANT

Tradescantia fluminensis *trad-es-KANT-ee-uh floo-min-EN-sis*

Striped inch plant is a carefree vining plant that makes a stunning hanging basket with brightly variegated foliage.

SIZE: 4–6"h × 12–18"w
TYPE: Herbaceous
FORM: Trailing
TEXTURE: Medium
GROWTH: Fast
LIGHT: High

MOISTURE: Dry
SOIL: Potting soil
FEATURES: Variegated foliage
USES: Hanging basket
FLOWERS: ■

SITING: Striped inch plant is a rewarding foliage plant that offers bright variegation with little care. Its foliage brightens up a foliage display almost as effectively as do flowers. Although it tolerates medium light, provide bright, indirect light to keep the

variegation strong. It bleaches out in full sun. Cool to average home temperatures (55–75°F) keep it compact; give it 30 percent or higher humidity to prevent the leaf edges from browning.

When striped inch plant begin to get leggy, prune it back substantially to produce compact new growth.

CARE: Allow the soil to dry between waterings; give a bit more water in bright light. Feed only three times in summer with foliage plant food. Repot as soon as roots fill the container. Pinch regularly to keep them shrubby. If they get leggy, prune them back severely to promote new, compact growth. Shower them occasionally, because it is impossible to wipe off the leaves. Start new plants regularly; older ones may begin to look ragged.

PROPAGATION: Propagate by stem cuttings in soil or water.

PESTS AND DISEASES: Control mealybugs with horticultural oil.

RELATED SPECIES: The cultivar 'Albovitatta' has light green leaves with white stripes. 'Aurea' has golden stripes. 'Variegata' has white, purple, and cream leaves.

PURPLE HEART

Tradescantia pallida (Setcreasea purpurea) *trad-es-KANT-ee-uh PAL-id-uh (set-KREE-zee-uh pur-pur-EE-uh)*

Purple heart has deep purple leaves that add a rich element to any display. In bright, indirect light it will bloom with delicate three-petaled blossoms.

SIZE: 4–6"h × 12–18"w
TYPE: Herbaceous
FORM: Trailing
TEXTURE: Medium
GROWTH: Fast
LIGHT: High, indirect

MOISTURE: Dry
SOIL: Potting soil
FEATURES: Purplish foliage
USES: Hanging basket, ground cover
FLOWERS: ■

SITING: Purple heart offers bright foliage with little care. Its foliage brightens a display almost as effectively as flowers. Although it tolerates medium light, provide bright, indirect light to keep the color

strong. Cool to average home temperatures (55–75°F) will keep it compact. Give it 30 percent or higher humidity to keep the leaf edges from browning.

CARE: Allow the soil to dry between waterings; give a bit more water in bright light. Feed only three times in summer with foliage plant food. Repot as soon as roots fill the container. Pinch regularly to keep plants shrubby. If stems become

leggy, prune severely to promote new, compact growth. Shower them occasionally, because it is impossible to wipe off the individual leaves.

PROPAGATION: Propagate by stem cuttings in soil or water.

PESTS AND DISEASES: Control mealybugs with horticultural oil.

RELATED SPECIES: The cultivar 'Purpurea' has dark purple foliage and pink flowers.

1 Tip cuttings of purple heart root easily to produce new plants.

2 Dip tip cuttings in rooting hormone and stick in sterile potting soil mix. Keep away from high light until the cuttings take root.

BOAT LILY

Tradescantia spathacea *trad-es-KANT-ee-uh spath-ay-SEE-uh*

Boat lily is also known as Moses-in-the-cradle or oyster plant. Bracts and flowers are cradled in leaf axils, giving rise to the common names.

SIZE: 6–12"h ×
12–18"w
TYPE: Herbaceous
FORM: Trailing
TEXTURE: Medium
GROWTH: Fast
LIGHT: High, indirect

MOISTURE: Dry
SOIL: Potting soil
FEATURES: Deep
purple foliage
USES: Hanging
basket
FLOWERS: ☐

SITING: Boat lily is a rewarding foliage plant that offers bright color with little care. Its foliage livens up a display almost as flowers would. Provide bright, indirect light to keep the color strong. It bleaches out in full sun. Cool to average home temperatures (55–75°F) will keep it compact. Give boat lily 30 percent or higher humidity to keep the leaf edges from browning.

Boat lily spreads enough that it makes an effective ground cover when planted in a container with a larger plant.

CARE: Allow the soil to dry between waterings; give a bit more water in bright light. Feed only three times in summer with foliage plant food. Repot as soon as roots fill the container. Pinch regularly to keep them shrubby. If they become leggy, prune severely to promote new, compact growth. Shower them occasionally, because it is impossible to wipe off the leaves. Start new plants regularly; the older ones begin to look ragged.

PROPAGATION: Propagate by stem cuttings in soil or water.

PESTS AND DISEASES: Control mealybugs with rubbing alcohol or horticultural oil.

RELATED SPECIES: The cultivar 'Variegata' has red and yellow-green striped leaves. 'Vitatta' has longitudinal yellow stripes.

WANDERING JEW

Tradescantia zebrina (Zebrina pendula) *trad-es-KANT-ee-uh zeb-BRIGH-nuh (zeb-BRIGH-nuh PEN-dyew-luh)*

Wandering Jew is a traditional easy-care favorite with variegated olive and cream foliage with purple undersides.

SIZE: 4–6"h ×
12–18"w
TYPE: Herbaceous
FORM: Trailing
TEXTURE: Medium
GROWTH: Fast
LIGHT: High

MOISTURE: Dry
SOIL: Potting soil
FEATURES:
Variegated foliage
USES: Hanging
basket
FLOWERS: ☐

SITING: Although these plants tolerate medium light, provide bright, indirect light to keep the variegation strong. They bleach out in full sun. Cool to average home temperatures (55–75°F) will keep them compact. Give them 30 percent or higher humidity to keep the leaf edges from browning.

CARE: Allow the soil to dry between waterings; give a bit more water in bright light. Feed only three times in summer with foliage plant food. Repot as soon as roots fill the container. Pinch regularly to keep them shrubby. If they become leggy, prune severely to promote new, compact growth. Shower them occasionally, because it is impossible to wipe off the leaves. Start new plants regularly; the older ones begin to look ragged.

PROPAGATION: Propagate by stem cuttings in soil or water.

PESTS AND DISEASES: Control mealybugs with horticultural oil.

RELATED SPECIES: The cultivar 'Quadricolor' has more intense variegation. 'Purpusii' has bronze-green leaves.

1 Wandering Jew gets leggy over time if not pinched regularly. The tips that are pruned out can be easily used to start new plants.

2 Dip tip cuttings in rooting powder, tap off the excess, and stick in sterile potting soil. These tips can also be rooted in water.

FLAMING SWORD
Vriesea splendens VREE-see-uh SPLEN-dens

Flaming sword, also known as painted feather, is often grown for its striking foliage, but it also sends up a tall flower spike with bright red bracts.

SIZE: 1–3'h × 1–3'w
TYPE: Bromeliad
FORM: Vase-shaped
TEXTURE: Medium
GROWTH: Slow
LIGHT: High to medium
MOISTURE: Dry

SOIL: Epiphyte mix
FEATURES: Variegated leaves, colorful blooms
USES: Focal point, blooming
FLOWERS: ■■

SITING: Flaming sword shows its best leaf color in bright, filtered light. In the right conditions, it will send up a tall red flower spike, but often the plants are grown only for their attractive foliage. They will not tolerate direct sun but do well in medium light. Provide average to hot temperatures (60°F and above) to keep the plant from rotting. High humidity (above 65 percent) is crucial to prevent leaf spots.

CARE: Let the soil dry out almost completely between waterings and keep the "vase" full of water. Every couple of months, empty and refill the vase to keep the water somewhat fresh. Feed with

Flaming sword is a bromeliad, so the soil should be kept somewhat dry and the plant watered by filling the cup, formed by the leaves, with water.

blooming plant food applied to the potting soil three times in summer or add half-strength formula to the vase every month. Flaming sword has a minuscule root system that seldom outgrows a pot. Repot only when the potting mix begins to break down and no longer has recognizable chunks of bark. This bromeliad can be grown on a wood slab or pole if high humidity is provided.

PROPAGATION: Propagate by removing the offsets or side shoots when the parent plant has died. Take the plant out of the pot and gently pull off each offset, making sure it has some roots. Pot up the offsets and keep them in a warm, bright spot until they establish themselves. Water daily. A plant started this way should bloom in 1–2 years.

PESTS AND DISEASES: Treat scale and spider mites with insecticidal soap.

RELATED SPECIES: 'Vulcana' has an all-red flower head. *V. hieroglyphica* is grown for its light and dark green mottled foliage. *V. carinata* has a yellow and red flower head. *Vriesea* 'Red Chestnut' has white flecks and bands on the leaves and a yellow flower head.

SPINELESS YUCCA
Yucca elephantipes YUK-uh ell-uh-fan-TYP-eez

Spineless yucca is a coarse-textured architectural plant for a spot out of the way of traffic. Although called spineless, the tips are sharp and pointed.

SIZE: 3–5'h × 2–3'w
TYPE: Woody tree
FORM: Upright
TEXTURE: Coarse
GROWTH: Slow
LIGHT: High

MOISTURE: Dry
SOIL: Potting soil
FEATURES: Spiky foliage
USES: Architectural accent

SITING: Spineless yucca is an ideal plant for a neglectful situation as long as its light requirements are met. When grown in full sun, it stays compact and sturdy. If grown in lower light, it stretches and loses its attractive shape. It tolerates low humidity (below 30 percent) and all temperatures except freezing. Choose a site carefully, because the leaf edges and spines on the tips are sharp.

CARE: In the active growing season, water the plant when the top 2" of soil dry out. During winter rest, water only enough to keep the foliage from wilting. Overwatering will result in brown tips; underwatering shows as shrunken trunks and solidly brown or yellow lower leaves. Feed with foliage plant food twice a year. Repot every 2 years in spring. Cut back severely if the plant becomes too tall; new heads will grow. Spineless yucca benefits from a summer outdoors and a cool, bright spot in winter.

PROPAGATION: Propagate by separating and potting the offsets that form at the base of the plant. Propagating by root cuttings is more difficult.

PESTS AND DISEASES: None are serious.

RELATED SPECIES: The cultivar 'Variegata' has cream-edged leaves.

Spineless yucca looks its best when grown in full sun, so move it outdoors in summer if possible to give it a good dose of sunlight.

ZEEZEE PLANT

Zamioculcas zamiifolia   *zam-ee-oh-KULL-kus zam-ee-ih-FOH-lee-uh*

Zeezee plant is a glossy foliage plant that will tolerate neglect and low light, yet continue to look attractive.

SIZE: 3'h × 3'w
TYPE: Herbaceous
FORM: Upright
TEXTURE: Medium
GROWTH: Slow
LIGHT: High to low
MOISTURE: Dry
SOIL: Potting soil
FEATURES: Glossy attractive leaves
USES: Foliage accent

SITING: Zeezee plant is popular because it tolerates neglect yet keeps its attractive foliage. Choose a site where the plant can make its natural spread and not be crowded. Zeezee plant can take very low light but also does well in bright, filtered light. Direct sun may burn the leaves. This

plant prefers temperatures above 40°F and low humidity (below 30 percent). Colder temperatures will cause rotting.

CARE: Keep the plant slightly more moist in high light; let it dry between waterings in lower light. Overwatering will result in yellow leaves. Repot when suckers fill the container. Feed three times in summer. Remove faded leaves. Give occasional

showers to keep the foliage shiny and clean. Move it outdoors in summer to a shaded site.

PROPAGATION: Propagate from leaf cuttings. Remove a leaf and insert it in sterile potting mix. Water lightly and provide a tent for humidity. Rooting takes a long time.

PESTS AND DISEASES: None are serious.

1 Propagate zeezee plant from leaf cuttings. Simply remove a leaf, dip in rooting hormone, and insert it in potting soil.

2 It may take several months to form roots, but the plant will send up new shoots from the soil at the base of the leaf.

CALLA LILY

Zantedeschia aethiopica   *zan-teh-DES-kee-uh ee-thee-OH-pik-uh*

Calla lily has long been a favorite for its striking spadix and spathe blossoms in shades of pink, white, and yellow.

SIZE: 1–3'h × 1'w
TYPE: Bulb
FORM: Upright
TEXTURE: Coarse
GROWTH: Medium
LIGHT: High, indirect
MOISTURE: Moist
SOIL: Potting soil
FEATURES: Glossy foliage, flowers
USES: Blooming accent
FLOWERS: □ ■ ■

SITING: Calla lily is a striking plant that needs perfect conditions to grow indoors. It requires bright, indirect light to produce blossoms. It tolerates average home temperatures (60–75°F) but needs high humidity (above 60 percent) to thrive.

CARE: Keep the soil evenly moist while in active growth. Feed with half-strength foliage plant food from February to November. Stop watering in November and allow the foliage to die. Remove the tubers and store them in vermiculite or peat moss at around 40°F. In February, repot, bring into warmth and light, and begin watering. Foliage should appear quickly. Remove

faded flowers as they develop. Give it an occasional shower to remove dust.

PROPAGATION: Divide the rhizomes before potting in February. The small offsets that form take 18 months to bloom.

RELATED SPECIES: The cultivar 'Red Desire' has a pink spadix. 'White Giant' has white-speckled leaves and 7' flower stalks. 'Pink Mist' has soft pink-blushed spathes.

1 To coax calla lily back into bloom, stop watering it in November and allow the foliage to die.

2 Trim off dead foliage and remove the tubers from their soil, brushing off as much soil as possible.

3 Store tubers until midwinter. Then pot up, water, and bring into warmth to renew growth.

INDEX

*Note: Page references in bold type refer to Encyclopedia entries. Page references in italic type refer to additional photographs, illustrations, and information in captions. Plants are listed under their common names.

RESOURCES FOR PLANTS & SUPPLIES

Please call nurseries and greenhouses before planning a visit; some are open by appointment only and many are not open to the public every day of the week. Note: Canadian nurseries cannot ship plants to the United States.

PLANTS

Alannah's Greenhouses
Box 1342
Grand Forks, BC V0H 1H0 Canada
250/442-2552
www.alannahs.com
African violets, gesneriads, specialty geraniums, and assorted flowering tropical houseplants

Davidson-Wilson Greenhouses
3147 E. Ladoga Rd.
Crawfordsville, IN 47933
877/723-6834
www.davidson-wilson.com
Unusual houseplants; specialty geraniums

Glasshouse Works
Church St.
P.O. Box 97
Stewart, OH 45778
740/662-2142
Orders: 800/837-2142
www.glasshouseworks.com
Tropical and rare plants

Harborcrest Gardens
1581-H Hillside Ave., Suite 230
Victoria, BC V8T 2C1 Canada
250/642-7309
www.harborcrestgardens.com
Tropical flowering and foliage plants and African violets

Kartuz Greenhouses,
Sunset Island Exotics
1408 Sunset Dr.
Vista, CA 92085
760/941-3613
www.kartuz.com
Gesneriads, begonias, flowering tropicals, subtropicals, vines

Logee's Greenhouses
141 North St.
Danielson, CT 06239
888/330-8038
www.logees.com
Tropicals and subtropicals

Lyndon Lyon Greenhouses
14 Mutchler St.
P.O. Box 249
Dolgeville, NY 13329
315/429-8291
www.lyndonlyon.com
African violets and orchids

Northridge Gardens
9821 White Oak Ave.
Northridge, CA 91325
818/349-9798
Succulents, hard-to-find items

Oak Hill Gardens
37W 550 Binnie Rd.
P.O. Box 25
Dundee, IL 60118
847/428-8500
www.oakhillgardens.com
Specialty plants, orchids, and supplies

Packer Nursery
P.O. Box 4056
Kailua-Kona, HI 96745
888/345-5566
www.alohapalms.com
Palms and tropicals

Rhapis Gardens
P.O. Box 287
Gregory, TX 78359
361/643-2061
www.rhapisgardens.com
Lady and sago palms, grape ivy, ming aralias

Stokes Tropicals
4806 W. Old Spanish Trail
Jeanerette, LA 70544
337/365-6998
Orders: 800/624-9706
www.stokestropicals.com
Exotic tropical plants

SUPPLIES

Eco Enterprises
1240 N.E. 175th St., Suite B
Shoreline, WA 98155
800/426-6937
www.ecogrow.com
Growing supplies, lighting

Charley's Greenhouse & Garden
17979 State Route 536
Mount Vernon, WA 98273
800/322-4707
www.charleysgreenhouse.com
Growing supplies, ornaments, greenhouses, lighting

Gardener's Supply Co.
128 Intervale Rd.
Burlington, VT 05401
800/955-3370
www.gardeners.com
Seed-starting supplies, organic fertilizers and pest controls, hand tools, and watering systems

Hydro-Farm
755 Southpoint Blvd.
Petaluma, CA 94954
707/765-9990
www.hydrofarm.com
High-intensity lighting and indoor growing supplies

The Scotts Company
800/225-2883
www.scotts.com
www.ortho.com
www.miracle-gro.com
Fertilizers, mulches, and pest controls

Worms Way
7850 N. State Road 37
Bloomington, IN 47404
800/274-9676
www.wormsway.com
Indoor gardening equipment; hydroponic supplies.

Miracle-Gro® www.miracle-gro.com

For more information on how to garden successfully, go to www.miracle-gro.com where you'll find:

■ **Miracle-Gro Garden Helpline:** 800/645-8166
■ **Email Reminder Service:** Free gardening tips and reminders sent to you via email.
■ **Miracle-Gro Product Consumer Guide:** The latest information on all Miracle-Gro products, including plant foods, soil mixes, plants, and exciting new product lines from Miracle-Gro.
■ **Garden Problem Solver:** Link into a comprehensive library of diagnostic tools and solutions for insect, disease, and weed problems.
■ **Streaming How-to Videos:** Click into a library of more tham 50 quick gardening and lawn care video clips.

USDA PLANT HARDINESS ZONE MAP

This map of climate zones helps you select plants for your garden that will survive a typical winter in your region. The United States Department of Agriculture (USDA) developed the map, basing the zones on the lowest recorded temperatures across North America. Zone 1 is the coldest area and Zone 11 is the warmest area.

Plants are classified by the coldest temperature and zone they can endure. For example, plants hardy to Zone 6 survive where winter temperatures drop to –10°F. Those hardy to Zone 8 die long before it's that cold. These plants may grow in colder regions but must be replaced each year. Plants rated for a range of hardiness zones can usually survive winter in the coldest region as well as tolerate the summer heat of the warmest one.

To find your hardiness zone, note the approximate location of your community on the map, then match the color band marking that area to the key.

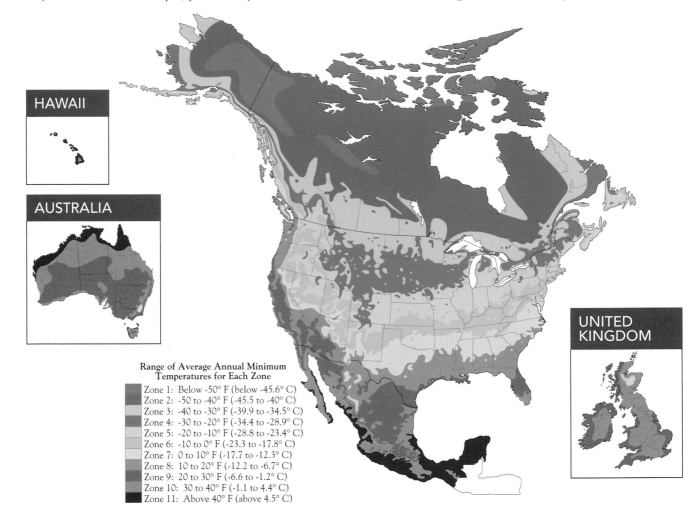

HAWAII

AUSTRALIA

UNITED KINGDOM

Range of Average Annual Minimum Temperatures for Each Zone

Zone 1: Below -50° F (below -45.6° C)
Zone 2: -50 to -40° F (-45.5 to -40° C)
Zone 3: -40 to -30° F (-39.9 to -34.5° C)
Zone 4: -30 to -20° F (-34.4 to -28.9° C)
Zone 5: -20 to -10° F (-28.8 to -23.4° C)
Zone 6: -10 to 0° F (-23.3 to -17.8° C)
Zone 7: 0 to 10° F (-17.7 to -12.3° C)
Zone 8: 10 to 20° F (-12.2 to -6.7° C)
Zone 9: 20 to 30° F (-6.6 to -1.2° C)
Zone 10: 30 to 40° F (-1.1 to 4.4° C)
Zone 11: Above 40° F (above 4.5° C)

METRIC CONVERSIONS

U.S. Units to Metric Equivalents			Metric Units to U.S. Equivalents		
To Convert From	Multiply By	To Get	To Convert From	Multiply By	To Get
Inches	25.4	Millimeters	Millimeters	0.0394	Inches
Inches	2.54	Centimeters	Centimeters	0.3937	Inches
Feet	30.48	Centimeters	Centimeters	0.0328	Feet
Feet	0.3048	Meters	Meters	3.2808	Feet
Yards	0.9144	Meters	Meters	1.0936	Yards

To convert from degrees Fahrenheit (F) to degrees Celsius (C), first subtract 32, then multiply by ⁵⁄₉.

To convert from degrees Celsius to degrees Fahrenheit, multiply by ⁹⁄₅, then add 32.